HIGHER EDUCATION IN TEXAS

ITS BEGINNINGS TO 1970

Charles R. Matthews

University of North Texas Press

Denton, Texas

10 9 8 7 6 5 4 3 2 1

Permissions:
University of North Texas Press
1155 Union Circle #311336
Denton, TX 76203-5017

The paper used in this book meets the minimum requirements of the
American National Standard for Permanence of Paper for Printed Library
Materials, z39.48.1984. Binding materials have been chosen for durability.

Library of Congress Cataloging-in-Publication Data
Matthews, Charles R., 1939- author.
Higher education in Texas : its beginnings to 1970 / Charles R. Matthews.
pages cm
Includes index.
ISBN 978-1-57441-716-6 (cloth : alk. paper) — ISBN 978-1-57441-724-1 (ebook)
1. Education, Higher—Texas—History. 2. Universities and colleges—Texas—History.
LA370.5.M37   2018
378.764—dc23
2017044552

The electronic edition of this book was made possible by the support
of the Vick Family Foundation. Typeset by vPrompt eServices.

CONTENTS

Part IV: Structure

Historical Photographs

PREFACE

Before I served as Chancellor of the Texas State University System I attended the University of Texas at Austin late in life to obtain a doctorate in Higher Education Administration. I enjoyed those five years, but as I reflected later on my coursework, I realized that my university offered no course on the history of higher education in Texas. This was particularly important to me as chancellor of the oldest university system in Texas. When I inquired as to why there was no such course, I was told the lack of a current text on the subject was one important reason.

During my five years as chancellor there were many times when I worked through a difficult decision with the president of one of the system's colleges. In those situations I often felt that a clearer understanding of the history and culture of the institution would have allowed me to make a better decision. Texas has a complex history of people and politics and a unique public land situation, all of which have affected the development of many of the state's institutions and infrastructure, including higher education. Understanding something about how we got where we are can only help the administrative decision-making process.

I loved the opportunity I had to work with others in higher education helping students realize their dreams. When I retired I was encouraged by my colleagues to write this book, the book I hope will be used to teach that very course I wish I could have taken. Here I hope to provide some insight into the history of higher education in this great state and help those who follow to make better decisions for the institution under their purview. In addition, I believe the history of higher education in Texas is of interest and importance to many others in and outside of academia. I hope this book will also prove useful to those readers.

ACKNOWLEDGMENTS

There are so many people who have helped in this long effort. I appreciate my wife providing her support and understanding while I worked on the research.

The members of the Board of Regents of the Texas State University System announced at my retirement that they had arranged support for this effort from Texas State University. To Dr. Denise Trauth, President of Texas State University, and her staff I owe an immense debt of gratitude.

In addition I received support from Sam Houston State University and Lamar University and the Sam Houston Memorial Museum. For their assistance I give them my thanks.

I was able to use the libraries at Baylor University and I appreciate all of the help I received from the library staff, in particular Amie Oliver, Geoff Hunt, and the staff at the Texas Collection Library. Also the librarians at the University of North Texas were of great assistance, particularly Tara Carlisle.

Dr. Susan Walters Schmid, owner of Teton Editorial Services, was very helpful to me in organizing my research, and she guided me through the writing process. I have appreciated her good work.

Finally, I would like to thank the outstanding staff of the Texas State System for all of their support as I worked my way through this manuscript.

INTRODUCTION

There is a common notion that those who do not know or understand history are bound to repeat the mistakes of the past. The history of how we got to a certain point in running any large institution is often far more important than we first realize.

This book is not intended to be "a complete history of higher education in Texas"—no single book could possibly examine all the events, participants, and controversies adequately. My goal here is to provide a broad view of defining events and critical participants in the development of higher education in Texas from approximately 1838 to 1970. I chose the opening date because one can easily argue that President Mirabeau Lamar's 1838 speech to the Second Congress of the Republic of Texas asking for approval of two colleges of the first order began the formal discussion of public higher education in Texas. The choice of 1970 as an approximate end date reflects the time by which most of the critical civil rights case law had been decided on higher education issues affecting both African Americans and Hispanics. It is not, however, meant to suggest some formal end or resolution to all problems at that date; it is rather an acknowledgment that this is a complex story that can sometimes be better understood in segments.

Although this is not a history book per se because the history of each institution is so vast, it is a book about a complex of historical events and the importance of the context of those events. While writing this book, at the back of my mind always were the graduate students in all the colleges and universities in Texas who are planning as their life's work to be part of higher education administration. I hope to raise awareness and understanding, suggest some important considerations for professional application, and highlight issues worthy of further investigation depending on where those readers find themselves in their professional practice. At the same time, there are many other readers I hope to serve as well. Students and educators in other programs and fields will find useful information here, as will the many general readers I have come to realize are interested in developing a more nuanced understanding of the many important decisions made in the past on behalf of our schools and how those decisions will continue to affect the management of Texas's colleges and universities.

* * * * *

In many ways, the story of Texas and its colleges and universities—public and private—is a wondrous story of land, oil, people, cultures, and education. But, as with any history, the pathway to today's success is strewn with challenges and mistakes; I have attempted to tell the good with the bad.

At the founding of the Texas Republic in 1836 the primary asset of the Republic was the vast quantity of land available to be used for the benefit of its citizens. The exemplary leadership of the second president of the Republic, Mirabeau B. Lamar, led the Second Congress of the Republic to pledge a great deal of that land to be used for two universities of the "first order."

When Texas became part of the United States, the effort of the State to support education through gifts of land continued; while the land was of little agricultural value at the time, everything changed with the discovery of the Santa Rita well—named in honor of the saint of the impossible. Its gusher and the wells still being drilled on Permanent University lands have provided billions of dollars to the benefit of education. This was only possible because the early leaders of Texas negotiated with the United States Congress for Texas to be allowed to retain most of its public lands—the only state in the union to have that right.

Before the government of Texas could organize the first of the public colleges, many religious denominations began to fund and support the very first efforts to provide higher education to the citizens of the state. Theirs is an important story of communities giving money that had been difficult to obtain to support colleges in their towns. Many of these early efforts were driven by the desire to have a well-educated clergy and a well-educated community.

As Texas grew, it began to provide educational opportunities for women; the path was long and the struggle difficult before political leaders began to understand that women were entirely capable of outstanding scholarship. Much of this first effort to provide higher education for women occurred on the campus of Sam Houston State College.

After the Civil War and the Emancipation Proclamation, former slaves were hungry to acquire basic skills of reading, writing, and mathematics, as well as many other new skills. They had been prohibited from education by laws throughout the South. The various religious denominations provided classes after Sunday services and during the week, and those efforts bore fruit that eventually became colleges. Most of the funding came from donations by newly freed slaves, supported by contributions from some northern philanthropists.

Perhaps, the path to a college degree was most difficult for the state's Hispanic citizens. Ironically, because the state constitution was silent on their legal status, it took even longer for their rights to be properly recognized so they could also enjoy the benefits of a good education.

All these threads of the story are examined here, along with the efforts of educational and political leaders to put the organizations in place that today make the enterprise we call higher education perform successfully and efficiently. By necessity, some topics are considered separately that clearly do not function independently in real life. For example, one can examine the experience of women and higher education, but it is important to keep in mind that in any given situation, being African American or Hispanic might be a critical factor in that experience as well. Or, the student experience in a religious school might have been different from that in a secular school and might further be affected by whether or not the student was female or was a person of color. During the period covered here, 1838 to 1970, many critical social and political events occurred that affected opinions and actions in local, state, and national arenas. Several major wars, the movement for women's suffrage, and the civil rights movement all affected how citizens perceived and interacted with institutions of higher education. Wherever possible I have tried to point out connections between different threads of the story, but it will be incumbent on readers to keep these in mind as well.

The story is as big as Texas; I hope you enjoy it and find it enlightening.

TEXAS: SPAIN, MEXICO, REPUBLIC, STATE

One of Texas's main stories has always been about land—how big it is, what it contains, and the uniquely generous land policy put in place by the Spanish, continued by the Mexicans, and later followed when Texas was a republic and finally a state. These farsighted policies were the main reason that Texas grew so rapidly. Having all that land proved to be critical to how Texans envisioned providing for education, which would sometimes be in ways different from what any other state did. It is worthwhile to understand how it came to be this way and how it affected people's thinking.

★ ★ ★ ★ ★

Modern-day Texas is large in land mass, yet appears small when compared with the immensity of sixteenth-century Spanish land holdings. Spain's New World empire stretched from the southern tip of South America across the entire western half of the continent, as far north as a territory not yet called Oregon. It ranged from the Pacific shore east to the Mississippi River and along the Gulf Coast to today's Florida peninsula. Its lands made up almost one third of what would later become the United States.[1] Most of the early wealth that came from the new empire came from Mexico and the lands farther south where the Spanish found the gold and silver that soon began to fill the ships making their way back to Spain. The compliant natives in the southern part of the empire provided cheap labor for Spain's economic enterprises, and made it a very rich country.[2]

Spain began to explore the area that came to be known as Texas— from a Hasinai Indian word—with the hope of discovering more economic opportunities.[3] The first European to explore the region was most likely Alonso Alvarez de Pineda who came by boat from Jamaica to explore the Gulf of Mexico in 1519. The second expedition, in 1528, was led by Álvar Núñez Cabeza de Vaca, and was shipwrecked off the coast of present-day Galveston. There were four survivors—including Cabeza de Vaca—who spent eight years traveling Texas, were enslaved by the Indians, and endured many hardships before returning to "civilization." When Cabeza de Vaca returned to Mexico he wrote about all that he had seen and experienced, making his writings among the first about Texas.[4]

Then, in 1541, from the west came Francisco Vazquez de Coronado who was searching for Quivira and the Seven Cities of Cíbola. The Indians had learned that the Spanish were interested in gold so they told them stories about the fabulous wealth in these cities, which increased the desire of the Spanish to explore the region and made them more willing to dispense gifts. The natives told them that in the Kingdom of Gran Quivira "everyone had their ordinary dishes made of wrought plate and the jugs and bowls were of gold." And, about the Seven Hills, for which Cabeza de Vaca had searched, they said: "the natives not knowing any of the other metals, make of it everything they need, such as vessels and the tips of their arrows and lances." While Coronado's journey was unsuccessful in discovering gold, it did add a considerable amount of land to the Spanish empire.[5]

For more than 160 years, the Spanish viceroys in Mexico who governed the land that included Texas made no attempt to develop the area.[6] This was in large measure because it was difficult to recruit men from Mexico who were willing to live in such a wild and undeveloped place. Other than a few Mexicans, the only people willing to go to Texas were Anglo-Americans, and the Spanish considered them to be unreliable subjects. Even after a hundred years the Spanish had produced only three small Texas settlements with a total population of about 3,000.[7]

During Spanish ownership of Texas and in spite of Spanish claims of conquest, the land was really controlled by the various Indian tribes. They viewed the Spanish not as conquerors or rulers of the land, but merely as people who lived in a small part of it. The Indians had many fighting men while the Spanish had but a few. In fact, a Franciscan missionary explained in a 1750 report to the Spanish king that the missions in the Spanish towns of San Antonio de Bexar and La Bahia lay outside of the "Province of Texas." In other words, Texas was the province in which resided Tejas Indians and it must be understood that Spain did not control any of that land. In 1778 Fray Juan Agustin Morfi said, "though we still call ourselves masters, we do not exercise dominion over a foot of land beyond San Antonio."[8] The Indians knew that they were the rulers of the land, and outside of the settlements the Spanish were of little consequence to them. True development of Texas would have to wait.[9]

When Mexico declared its independence from Spain in 1821, the Mexican government faced a twofold problem concerning Texas. First, it feared the United States, which had publicly discussed taking the undeveloped Texas land. Second, it had to deal with the difficult Indian tribes that were continually raiding and burning Mexican towns, killing citizens, and stealing both cattle and horses. It became Mexican policy to find a way to attract settlers who would both provide a buffer between the United States and Mexico and provide some defense against the Indians.[10]

The first effort involved Moses Austin—and after his death, his son Stephen F. Austin—and the use of empresario grants. Under these grants an empresario was given a large tract of land contingent on its being settled by a specified minimum number of families. The empresario became an agent of the Mexican government and was accountable for the selection of colonists, allocation of land, and enforcement of various regulations required by the Mexican government. The Austin colony was a large block of land that covered much of the lower Brazos and Colorado river basins.[11] To receive individual allotments of land, settlers were required to sign an oath like this one found in Spanish records:

> In the name of God, Amen. In the town of Nacogdoches before me, Don Jose Maria Guadiana, appeared Don Samuel Davenport and Don William Barr, residents of this place, and took a solemn oath of fidelity to our Sovereign, and to reside forever in his Royal Dominions: and to manifest this more fully, put their right hands upon the Cross of our Lord Jesus Christ, to be faithful vassals of His Most Catholic Majesty, to act in obedience to all laws of Spain and the Indies, henceforth adjuring all other allegiance to any other Prince or Potentate, and to hold no correspondence with any other foreign power without permission from a lawful magistrate, and to inform against such as may do so, or use seditious language unbecoming a good subject of Spain.[12]

Copies of these oaths were preserved in Spanish records, and one can see that the form changed over time to meet the needs of the Mexican government. In return for signing the oath, each settler received title to land at terms unheard of in the United States, and it was good land—broad bottomlands with a mixture of both prairie and woodlands, good grass, and abundant water. The Mexican Congress passed the Imperial Colonization Act of 1823, which granted a league (4,428 acres) of grazing land plus a *labor* (177 acres) of farming land to each family brought to Texas by an empresario. Single men received one-third the acreage assigned to a family. In 1825, the state of Coahuila y Texas passed the colonization measure that operated until the Texas Revolution. It specified that a league of land would be granted to a family man who became a naturalized Mexican citizen and adopted the Roman Catholic religion, and one quarter of a league would go to a single man who met the same requirements.[13]

The new settlers came quickly, mostly from Louisiana, Arkansas, Alabama, Tennessee, Kentucky, and Missouri. In many cases they brought cattle and hogs, and in some cases they brought slaves.

These settlers were, in the main, the grandchildren of men who had fought in the American Revolution and they were aware of their heritage. They embodied a strong doctrine of self-help and were very resentful of any authority they perceived to be arbitrary. They had a hunger for land, a disdain for brown-skinned people, and a contempt for Spanish authority and culture.[14]

Because the opportunity that Austin offered was so great and the amount of land so large, he was able to pick the settlers he wanted from a sizeable group of applicants. He tried to pick men who were industrious—the "better classes" he called them—and the Old Three Hundred, as these settlers were known, were perhaps unique on the frontier because they were better off financially then most settlers. They were people of substance, and nearly 25 percent had slaves—one individual actually owned ninety. Many of these settlers had a background in cotton farming and the land in the lush river valleys was excellent for that enterprise. From their perspective, growing cotton at a profit required slaves. All but four of this group of three hundred could read and write, an extremely large percentage for frontier times.[15]

There were other empresarios, and in total about thirty-five hundred land titles were issued. Thus, by the end of the Mexican era in 1836, the population of Texas was about 25,000, including slaves. This was an historic achievement by the Mexican government in light of the very long period that Texas had been under Spanish control with a population of only about 3,000.[16]

Not all of the settlements contained families of means. An early description by a young man recruited by Sterling C. Robertson, who had obtained a grant for a colony from the Mexican government in 1826, tells what it was like when he arrived in 1827. He noted that the colonists—at the time twelve families—had built their houses close together as security against the Indians. The houses were rough log cabins with no windows and dirt floors. While the men were excited about their future prospects, the women were sad about the homes and friends they had left behind. Their lives left a lot to be desired. There was not a proper house to keep and their food was so meager as to require little time to prepare a meal. They had left their spinning wheels and looms behind because there was nothing to spin. There was no poultry, no dairy, no garden, no books, and no local papers to read. The lack of schools and churches meant that there was little to break the monotony of their lives. One woman said, "Texas was a heaven for men and dogs, but a hell for women and oxen."[17]

Frontier historians who have studied these early settlers note that the mood among them was mainly one of discontent. Many had come from the United States driven out by debt, and they held a distaste for religious and social restraints, overcrowding, high land prices, oppressive taxation, and unrepresentative government. This created a class of people that in retrospect can be seen to embody a perfect storm of causes for a revolution. The ruling Mexican government was far away, and Texas had no representatives in that government and little influence.[18]

Among cotton farmers there was also a fear that Mexico would make the use of slaves unlawful. During the 1820s and 1830s Mexican leaders had made many unsuccessful attempts to pass antislavery laws, but the big cotton farmers considered slaves an absolute necessity for running a profitable business. Ultimately, it was the large, successful cotton growers who provided much of the support for the Texas Revolution, because they needed to continue to use slaves to economically produce their cotton.[19]

Had the Mexican government been more attuned to the settlers they were attracting with their land policies, they might very well have discontinued their immigration practices. The long-simmering discontent among the settlers finally boiled over and support for a Texas free of Mexican control took hold with the majority of families. Even Stephen Austin, who had tried for a long time to make the relationship between Texans and the Mexican government work, finally realized that Texans were no longer willing to be ruled by a far-away government that seemed not to have their interests at heart.

Austin and other Texas leaders felt it was time to make Texas its own republic.[20]

War broke out in October 1835 when Mexican soldiers demanded that the citizens of the town of Gonzales hand over the one small cannon they possessed. A quickly assembled group of volunteer soldiers told the Mexicans to "Come and Take It." During the attack that followed, the Texans repulsed the Mexican army and the Texas Revolution had begun. It ended eight months later with the capture of the Mexican general Santa Anna who was forced to order his remaining troops to return to Mexico. On May 14, 1836, the Treaty of Velasco was signed, ending the revolution and beginning the Republic of Texas.[21]

As the new leaders of Texas began to review the republic's prospects, they understood that the survival of their new country would depend upon increasing its population as quickly as possible. The principle asset for achieving that growth was a vast amount of land: Texas possessed 216,314,560 acres of unappropriated public lands. To further its goals, the government began offering 4,605.5 acres of land to all new families, and 1,476.1 acres to single men over the age of seventeen. This forward-looking policy not only rapidly increased the population, but it began to create wealth and taxable property that allowed the new government to start developing its society and improving the lives of its citizens.[22]

The Republic of Texas lasted for ten years, during which time many Texans hoped Texas would become part of the United States. After years of debate that centered upon whether or not Texas would be admitted as a slave state, the U.S. Congress, by a very close vote—120 to 98 in the House of Representatives and 27 to 25 in the Senate—allowed Texas to join the Union. On December 29, 1845, the United States formally annexed Texas.[23]

When the resolution that had passed the Congress arrived, it contained conditions for acceptance into the Union. Texas could join the United States and write its own constitution in regard to slavery. In addition, the state would remain liable for the massive debt of the Republic. The federal government would take custody of all public buildings and forts, but the state would retain ownership of its public lands, which were extensive. This offer was acceptable to the Anglo-Americans in Texas as the only way they could continue to be successful and increase business in their slave-based agriculture.[24]

A war with Mexico soon followed, and from 1846 to 1848 the United States fought the Mexicans. When the United States won the war, Mexico signed the Treaty of Guadalupe Hidalgo in which the boundary between Texas and Mexico was firmly established at the Rio Grande. With three Texas boundaries settled by rivers—the Red, the Sabine and the Rio Grande—only the northwest boundary remained unsettled. Texas had long claimed lands in New Mexico, Oklahoma, Kansas, Colorado, and Wyoming. As part of the original state admission settlement, Congress had authorized the purchase of these long-claimed lands, giving Texas its present boundaries.

When Texas was annexed to the United States it was allowed to keep its public lands. In 1850, it ceded 67,000,000 acres to the United States to settle a boundary dispute, which left it with 168,732,160 acres of land, including 149,314,560 acres not owned by anyone that the state had complete freedom to dispose of as it wished.[25]

All along, Texas's advantages of low-priced, abundant land and economic potential meant people wanted to move there. It has been estimated that by 1835, 1,000 people per month were entering Texas by way of the Brazos River. Population estimates in 1836 pegged the total population at 50,000, with 30,000 Anglo-Americans, 5,000 African Americans, 3,470 Mexicans, and an Indian population of 11,000. The population ratio of Anglos to Tejanos was already ten to one. Ten years later when the republic ended and Texas became part of the United States, the population had reached 125,000. The first U.S. census in 1850 showed that Texas had grown to 154,034 whites, 58,161 slaves, and 397 free blacks. By 1900 the census listed Texas as the sixth most populous state in the Union with a total population of 3,048,710.[26]

* * * * *

Texas had land and people, but what it did not have was sufficient economic resources to properly develop and improve the quality of life for its citizens. Eventually, policies would need to be put in place to help the state discover what resources the land held and what their potential for development might be. As a new state, Texas attracted people who were as anxious as the settlers who had come before them to build a great place. For that greatness to occur there would have to be a system of education so Texans could obtain the knowledge and training needed to develop their abundant resources and take advantage of other economic opportunities being created. The early settlers had been strong-willed men and women who came to a land with little in the way of infrastructure; it needed everything. It was the land that had brought most of them, and they believed that land could endow an education system.

NOTES

1. William Davis, *Lone Star Rising* (New York: Free Press, 2004), 9.

2. William Davis, *Lone Star Rising*, 10.

3. Phillip L. Fry, "TEXAS, ORIGIN OF NAME," Handbook of Texas Online (http://www.tshaonline.org/handbook/online/articles/pft04), accessed May 06, 2014. Uploaded on June 15, 2010. Published by the Texas State Historical Association.

4. Donald E. Chipman, *Spanish Texas: 1519–1821* (Austin: University of Texas Press, 1992), 30.

5. Chipman, *Spanish Texas*, 36–39.

6. Eula Phares Mohle, *Texas, Its Land, History and Government* (New York: Oxford Book Co., 1958), 30.

7. Donald W. Meinig, *Imperial Texas* (Austin: Steck Co., 1969), 28.

8. Juliana Barr, *Peace Came in the Form of a Woman: Indians and Spaniards in The Texas Borderlands* (Chapel Hill: University of North Carolina Press, 2007), 3.

9. Ibid., 2.

10. Davis, *Lone Star Rising*, 59.

11. T. R. Fehrenbach, *Lone Star: A History of Texas and the Texans* (Boulder, CO: Da Capo Press, 2000), 137.

12. Fehrenbach, *Lone Star*, 138.

13. Mark E. Nackman, "Anglo-American Migrants to the West: Men of Broken Fortunes? The Case of Texas 1821–1846," *Western Historical Quarterly* 5, no. 4 (1974): 441–55.

14. Davis, *Lone Star Rising*, 60.

15. Davis, *Lone Star Rising,* 60; Andrew J. Torget, *Seeds of Empire: Cotton, Slavery and the Transformation of the Texas Borderlands, 1800–1850* (Chapel Hill: University of North Carolina Press), 13.

16. Meinig, *Imperial Texas,* 31–32.

17. Quoted in Noah Smithwick, *Recollections of Old Texas Days* (Austin: University of Texas Press, 1983), 5.

18. Nackman, "Anglo-American Migrants to the West," 443.

19. Torget, *Seeds of Empire,* 14.

20. Nackman, "Anglo-American Migrants to the West," 443. For an in-depth look at Stephen Austin's life and his efforts as empresario see Gregg Cantrell, *Stephen F. Austin: Empresario of Texas* (New Haven, CT: Yale University Press, 1999).

21. Davis, *Lone Star Rising,* 137–38.

22. Davis, *Lone Star Rising,* 282; Dudley G. Wooten, *A Comprehensive History of Texas: 1685 to 1897* (Dallas: William G. Scharff, 1898), 681.

23. Thomas Lloyd Miller, *The Public Lands of Texas 1519–1970* (Norman: University of Oklahoma Press, 1971), 61.

24. Torget, *Seeds of Empire,* 253–54.

25. Davis, *Lone Star Rising,* 282.

26. "CENSUS AND CENSUS RECORDS," *Handbook of Texas Online* (http://www.tshaonline. org/handbook/online/articles/ulc01), accessed May 24, 2014. Uploaded on June 12, 2010. Published by the Texas State Historical Association.

BIBLIOGRAPHY

Barr, Juliana. *Peace Came in the Form of a Woman: Indians and Spaniards in the Texas Borderlands.* Chapel Hill: University of North Carolina Press, 2007.

Bolton, Herbert Eugene. *Texas in the Middle Eighteenth Century.* Austin: University of Texas Press, 1915.

———. "The Spanish Occupation of Texas, 1519–1690." *Southwestern Historical Association* 16, no. 1 (1912): 1–26.

Cantrell, Gregg. *Stephen F. Austin: Empresario of Texas.* New Haven, CT: Yale University Press, 1999.

"Census and Census Records." *Handbook of Texas Online* (http://www.tshaonline.org/handbook/online/articles/ulc01), accessed May 24, 2014, Uploaded on June 12, 2010. Published by the Texas Historical Association.

Chipman, Donald E. *Spanish Texas, 1519–1821.* Austin: University of Texas Press, 1992.

Davis, William C. *Lone Star Rising.* New York: Free Press, 2004.

De Leon, Arnoldo. *The Tejano Community: 1836–1900.* Albuquerque: University of New Mexico Press, 1945.

Evans, C. E. *The Story of Texas Schools.* Austin: Steck Co., 1955.

Fehrenbach, T. R. *Lone Star: A History of Texas and the Texans.* Boulder, CO: Da Capo Press, 2000.

———. *Seven Keys to Texas.* El Paso: Texas Western Press, 2009.

Glasscock, Sallie. *Dreams of Empire.* San Antonio: Naylor Company, 1951.

Hatcher, Mattie Austin. "Conditions in Texas Affecting the Colonization Problem, 1795–1801." *Southwestern Historical Quarterly* 25 (2): 81–97.

Hesseltine, William B. *A Syllabus of United States History.* Madison: University of Wisconsin Press, 1955.

Jenkins, John Holmes. *Recollections of Early Texas.* Austin: University of Texas Press, 1958.

Meinig, Donald W. *Imperial Texas.* Austin: Steck Co., 1969.

Miller, Thomas Lloyd. *The Public Lands of Texas 1519–1970*. Norman: University of Oklahoma Press, 1971.

Mir, Andrew Forest. *Texas in 1837*. Austin: University of Texas Press, 1958.

Mohle, Eula Phares. *Texas, Its Land, History and Government*. New York: Oxford Book Co., 1958.

Morfi, Juan Agustin. *History of Texas 1673–1779*, Translated, with biographical introduction and annotations by Carlos Eduardo Castaneda. Albuquerque, NM: Quivira Society, 1935.

Nackman, Mark E. "Anglo-American Migrants to the West: Men of Broken Fortunes? The Case of Texas 1821–1846." *Western Historical Quarterly* 5, no. 4 (1974): 441–55.

Sheppard, Lorna Geer. *An Editor's View of Early Texas*. Austin: Eakin Press, 1998.

Smithwick, Noah. *Recollections of Old Texas Days*. Austin: University of Texas Press, 1983.

Teja, Jesus F. de la. *San Antonio de Bexar: A Community on New Spain's Northern Frontier*. Albuquerque: University of New Mexico Press, 1995.

Torget, Andrew J. *Seeds of Empire: Cotton, Slavery, and the Transformation of the Texas Borderlands, 1800–1850*. Chapel Hill: University of North Carolina Press, 2015.

Wooten, Dudley G. *A Comprehensive History of Texas: 1685 to 1897*. Dallas: William G. Scharff, 1898.

2

EARLY ATTEMPTS AT EDUCATION: THE LEADERSHIP OF MIRABEAU B. LAMAR AND OTHERS

During the early 1800s, many Americans viewed the population of Texas as composed of either fugitives from the law or wild and uncultured adventurers. There is some truth to those perceptions, but Texas was also able to attract well-educated men from the United States who provided excellent and farsighted leadership for the new republic. These men had the intellectual strength to build early Texas from a rough-and-tumble place on the frontier to a new country brimming with promise, and they understood the importance of education in building that new country. Most of them had been active in both the Texas Revolution and the establishment of the Republic of Texas. Several held government positions under the republic and some served in the U.S. Congress after annexation. Aside from statesman or soldier, the most common occupation held by these founders was lawyer or physician.[1]

THE PHILOSOPHICAL SOCIETY OF TEXAS

Many of these men were charter members of the Philosophical Society of Texas, which was founded in 1837 along the lines of the American Philosophical Society, which had been founded in 1769. The Texas society's purpose was "the collection and diffusion of correct information regarding the moral and social education of our country; its finances, statistics and political and military history;

its climate, soil and productions . . . animals . . . aboriginal tribes . . . natural curiosities . . . mines . . . and the thousand other topics of interest which our new and rising republic unfolds to the philosopher, our scholars and men of science."[2] The members of the society met from time to time to discuss issues affecting Texas, among them how to go about establishing an education system. The group drew up a resolution petitioning the Congress of the Republic to establish a system of public education. Eventually the group began to wane and it had stopped meeting altogether by 1845, but in the early years it offered an opportunity for discussions about how to make Texas a better place. The men of the society played a role in forming ideas that Mirabeau Lamar proposed when he became president of the Republic. A brief review of the backgrounds and accomplishments of the first officers of the Philosophical Society of Texas gives an appreciation of their personal qualities.[3]

The first president of the society was Mirabeau B. Lamar (1789–1859), who at the time was vice president of the Republic. Lamar was born August 16, 1789, on his father's plantation in Georgia not far from Louisville, Kentucky. Of French descent, his family had been in the United States for five generations. His father was a strong believer in education who pushed his children to pursue higher education, but as a young man Lamar was an indifferent student and he never went to college. However, he did attend several academies and was an avid reader; as a result he was largely self-taught. In Georgia he was secretary to a governor and was elected to the Georgia State Senate. Within two years of coming to Texas he was elected vice president and later president of the republic.[4]

The Philosophical Society of Texas's first elected vice president was Ashbel Smith (1805–1886), who had earned AB and AM degrees from Yale University by the time he was nineteen years old. After teaching at a private school in North Carolina for a year, he returned to Yale to earn his medical degree. Awarded a Phi Beta Kappa key in 1824, he wore it proudly for the rest of his life. After moving to Texas he was instrumental in the formation of the Texas Medical Society.[5]

He was devoted to education and advocated that the state under-
write education for every child in Texas. He also supported public
education for African Americans and women. Governor Richard
Coke appointed him to the commission charged with establishing
an "Agricultural and Mechanical College of Texas, for the benefit of
the Colored Youths," which is now Prairie View A&M University.
He is known both as the "Father of Texas Medicine" and the "Father
of the University of Texas" where he served as the first president of
its board of regents.[6]

The society's second elected vice president (it had eight) was
Stephen F. Austin (1793–1836). His father, Moses, enrolled him in
the Bacon Academy in Colchester, Connecticut, which was known
for its well-rounded education that included classes in English
grammar and writing, rhetoric, logic, mathematics, geometry, natural
philosophy, astronomy, moral philosophy, geography, Latin, and
Greek. After attending the school for three years, Austin enrolled in
Transylvania University in Lexington, Kentucky, where he studied
mathematics, geography, astronomy, natural philosophy, moral
philosophy, and history. After he started his colony in Texas he made
many efforts to establish schools for the children of the area.[7]

Anson Jones (1798–1858), who was elected third vice president
of the society, was also a medical doctor and a congressman of the
Republic of Texas. He studied medicine in Oneida, New York, and
received his medical license in 1820. When his medical practice was
unsuccessful he opened a drug store. In 1827 he earned a medical
degree from Philadelphia's Jefferson Medical College, and he moved
to Texas in 1833 where he opened a medical practice. He served as the
last president of the republic and helped establish the first Masonic
lodge in Texas. During his time in the Congress of the Republic he
advocated for legislation to establish a uniform education system and
an endowment for a university.[8]

Another vice president was David S. Kaufman (1813–1851),
a lawyer and politician from Pennsylvania who had studied law after
graduating from Princeton with honors in 1830. He moved to Texas

in 1838 where he practiced law and later served in several political positions in the Republic of Texas and the U.S. government.[9]

William Fairfax Gray (1787–1841), who served as a secretary of the society, was a lawyer and author from Virginia who settled in Texas in 1837. He served in various government positions including as a district attorney and a clerk of the Texas Supreme Court.[10]

There were, of course, other members in the society, but this select list reflects the depth of interest these men had in education, not only for themselves but for others. They made up the core group of the best thinkers and were among the most able citizens of the new republic. Their discussions at society gatherings must have helped form the ideas for education that Lamar expressed so well in his December 1838 presidential speech, which is examined below.[11]

EDUCATION AND THE REPUBLIC OF TEXAS

The new constitution of the Republic of Texas (1836) made it the duty of the congress, as soon as circumstances permitted, to provide by law a general system of education. The increase in population helped spur efforts to form schools and academies, and other educational institutions also sought charters from the government. As early as June 5, 1837, President Sam Houston approved an act to incorporate the Trustees of Independence Academy and the University of San Augustine, separate institutions but included in the same act passed by the Congress. On the same day, President Houston signed a separate act that incorporated the Trustees of Washington College in Washington County. These first acts and others that followed all stated that the educational institutions must provide access to all students regardless of religion or political opinions. This, of course, occurred before slaves were emancipated, so it only included whites, and it should be noted that people of Mexican descent were considered white.[12]

By December 1837, there was a movement by members of the Texas senate to persuade Lamar to put his name forward as a candidate for president of the republic since Houston had announced his intention to retire from office. Lamar was elected president on September 3, 1838.

It is his presidential message to the Second Congress of the Republic, given on December 21, 1838, for which he is most famous. In it, all of his skills come together—knowledge of what the republic needed to achieve greatness, the ability to speak well in public, and the skill to inspire others and call the congress and citizens to action.[13] The speech was long and touched upon many subjects, but it is important here to consider the section on education:

> Education is a subject in which every citizen, and especially every parent, feels a deep and lively concern. It is one in which no jarring interests are involved, and acrimonious political feelings excited; for its benefits are so universal that all parties can cordially unite in advancing it. It is admitted by all, that a cultivated mind is the guardian genius of democracy, and while guided and controlled by virtue, it is the noblest attribute of man. It is the only dictator that freemen acknowledge, and the only security that freemen desire. The influence of education in the moral world is like light in the physical, rendering luminous what was before obscure. It opens a wide field for the exercise and improvement of all the faculties of man, and imparts a vigor and clearness to those important truths in the science of government, as well as mortals, which would otherwise be lost in the darkness of ignorance. . . . The present is a propitious moment to lay the foundations of a great moral and intellectual edifice, which will in after ages be hailed as the chief ornament and blessing of Texas. A suitable appropriation of lands to the purpose of general education, can be made at this time without inconvenience to the Government or the people; but defer it until the public domain shall have passed from our hands, and the uneducated youths of Texas will constitute the living monuments of our neglect and remissness . . . and the establishment of a University where the highest branches of science may be taught, can now be effected without the expenditure of a single state dollar. Postpone it a few years and millions will be necessary to accomplish the great design.[14]

Lamar's speech must have been the outgrowth of a much larger discussion with his friends in the Philosophical Society of Texas, and in his speech are the ideas the society addressed in the preamble to its statement of purpose. In addition to the ideas provided by the society, there was a general feeling in Texas that some of the very large amount of public land the state held could be made available for the purpose of educating young Texans. This soon became evident when the Congress of the Republic began passing legislation providing for land to be used in service to education.[15]

At the time Lamar made his recommendations on higher education, the estimated population of Texas was 60,000.[16] Lamar, who had never attended college, proposed not one but two colleges to a congress that contained a majority of members who also had never attended college. That this happened at a time when there was no established primary or secondary school system is astonishing. Lamar believed in the future greatness of the Republic of Texas, but he was aware that developing its potential would depend on having a well-educated citizenry.[17]

Lamar's speech motivated the congress, and on June 20, 1839, it passed a bill setting aside fifty leagues of land (221,400 acres) to meet the educational needs of Texans by providing for the creation of institutions of primary, secondary, and higher education. Section 4 of the act directed the republic's president to "appoint a surveyor and have surveyed from any vacant lands of the Republic, fifty leagues of land, which is to be set apart and is hereby appropriated for the establishment and endowment of two colleges or universities, hereafter to be created."[18] This legislation also called for the establishment of the University Fund, set up for the purpose of holding funds and lands to benefit higher education. The legislature then began passing bills that put into place the policies needed to fund education.[19]

On January 20, 1840, the congress took another action that would have important consequences for the future of public education when it passed a bill that adopted English common law as the legal standard for Texas. As part of that legislation, all mineral rights on Texas lands were specifically reserved to the republic.

Ownership of these lands would later provide tremendous wealth for the University of Texas and Texas A&M College.[20]

Despite land being set aside by the congress in 1839, there were still challenges. For example, there were numerous problems with the sale of the first gift of fifty leagues of land—land that was to be sold to raise the money needed to begin to put the education systems into place. Most of the difficulty lay with the republic's General Land Office. Beginning in 1839 and going until 1850—five years after the end of the republic—many parcels of public land were privately surveyed and the resulting surveys and requests to purchase land were filed with the Commissioner of the General Land Office. The commissioner, unaware of the existence of an earlier survey that had established the boundaries of the fifty leagues of land intended for the University Fund, was collecting money and conveying title to tracts of land to anyone who applied to buy them. Because the commissioner and his office were unaware that the land had been reserved for the University Fund, some of the land was sold off without the money going to the fund. When the mistake was discovered, a review of the records showed that the surveyor who had been hired to perform the original survey had indeed done the work; however, he had neglected to file his work with the General Land Office. Ultimately, in order to correct this problem, the third state legislature in 1850 passed a joint resolution that canceled the survey on the University Fund land and validated all of the good faith purchases. As only three leagues of land had been sold from the original fifty, the joint resolution further instructed the General Land Office to employ a surveyor to survey an additional three leagues of land to replace the land that had been sold.[21]

EDUCATION AND THE STATE OF TEXAS

It is interesting to note that when Texas joined the United States of America, the new state Constitution of 1845 did not mention either higher education or the fifty leagues of land. This lack would have reflected the majority sentiment in the legislature at that moment in time. As shall be seen later, not all elected officeholders felt as strongly about higher education as did Lamar and his friends in the Philosophical Society of Texas. This situation was finally fully corrected by the state Constitution of 1876, under which Texas still operates.[22]

In the meantime, the legislature continued to be interested in the sale of the fifty leagues, and in an effort to make it easier for small buyers to purchase property, a bill was passed on August 30, 1856, directing that the remaining forty-seven of the original fifty leagues be surveyed into 160-acre tracts.[23] A companion bill directed the governor, rather than the land commissioner, to "cause to be surveyed as soon as possible, on any vacant or unappropriated lands belonging to the State, two hundred and twenty-two thousand, two hundred and fifty acres of land, or unallocated balance donated and set apart by the late Republic of Texas for endowment and establishment of the two universities."[24] The governor was further instructed to "cause each alternate section of 640 acres to be sold in lots of 160 acres each, at public auction to the highest bidder, at the county seat of the county in which the same may be situated."[25] The minimum price was set at $3.00 per acre. Tracts were to be sold with 5 percent down and the balance financed on a twenty-year note at 8 percent interest.[26]

On November 2, 1857, Governor Elisha M. Pease addressed the joint session of the seventh legislature:

> On former occasions, I have called the attention to [sic] the
> Legislature, to the importance of establishing a State University,
> where all the facilities can be furnished for obtaining a thorough
> education, that are to be found in other states. . . . The necessity for
> such an institution is felt and acknowledged by everyone; and I trust
> that you will not let this Session pass, without adopting measures for
> its establishment at an early date.[27]

The state's Senate Committee on State Affairs on January 21, 1858, passed "a Bill to Establish the University of Texas." The model for the university, as envisioned by the committee, was the University of Virginia. The legislature approved the bill on February 8 and the governor signed it into law on February 11.[28] It provided for establishment of an institution of learning to be called the University of Texas, and granted the university $100,000 in U.S. bonds held by the state treasury as well as the money from the original fifty leagues of land. In addition, the bill gave the university land reserved for the state under the Texas Railroad Grant Act of 1854—public lands originally given to the railroads as an incentive to encourage them to build tracks across Texas. Section 3 of the bill placed the control, management, and supervision of the university and its property under a ten-member board of administrators consisting of the governor, the chief justice of the state supreme court, and eight persons appointed by the governor with the consent of the senate.[29]

All did not go well for the University Fund during these early years. A reversal came when Sam Houston was elected governor of the state in late 1859. Houston was not as supportive of higher education as his predecessor. The state had financial difficulties because of the impending Civil War, and in a message to the legislature on January 13, 1860, Houston asked that it approve use of the fund (consisting of the previous $100,000 appropriation plus interest earned from the bonds that had been purchased with the appropriation) for frontier defense in an effort to avoid increasing taxes.[30] He said:

> The establishment of a University is, in my opinion, a matter alone for the future. At this time it is neither expedient, not is it good policy to provide for the sale of those lands set apart for the University fund. If, at some future period it should be deemed expedient, or in keeping with a more enlarged policy, to devote our entire energies to a more general diffusion of knowledge that a University would afford, or even if the voice of the State should demand the establishment of one, these lands will provide the means for advancing the cause of education. When that period arrives, their value will be greatly increased. If sold now, but little will be realized from them, and before the expiration of twenty years—the time upon

which over fifty thousand acres have already been sold—the land will be worth more than three-fold the amount they would bring now, with accumulated interest.[31]

So far as the one hundred thousand dollars of bonds, and their interest, taken from the general fund and applied to the University fund, by the last Legislature are concerned, I believe the condition of the treasury and our immediate necessities demand that the act be repealed, and the money again placed subject to appropriation. We need money for the protection of our frontier, and to save us from taxation, more than a fund which promises no immediate benefit. Our common school fund already provided for the education contemplated by the Constitution, and if this amount, thus unnecessarily withdrawn for the general fund, will reduce the burden of taxation, the people will be able, in the future, to bear taxation to support a University, if one should be necessary.[32]

Houston believed frontier defense was needed to protect settlers in the western part of Texas from Indian attacks. Because that need was pressing and the university had not yet been established, it seemed to him more logical to use the money for the immediate need. He made a valid point about the sale of the land. He believed that waiting until later years to sell the lands would be the correct business decision and, in fact, the price of land did rise over time. The political benefit of raiding the fund was that he did not have to raise taxes to pay for frontier defense, and at the time of his speech he had already ordered troops to begin taking up positions in the west. The legislature, on January 31, 1860, approved a bill that directed the fund to "be used at any time during the next two years to meet any appropriation made by law for frontier defense."[33]

It is clear from Houston's speech that he was not particularly supportive of the idea of a university, at least not at the time he gave his speech. Historians, and many others, have speculated that he was opposed to the idea because it had been primarily promoted by his archrival, Lamar. The feud between the two men was well known, and it had been most evident at the time Houston stepped down as president of the republic in 1837. Many senators had wanted Lamar to run for president to follow Houston who went to extraordinary lengths to find a candidate to run against Lamar.[34]

After the Civil War, a new state constitution, written in 1866 at the direction of the federal government, provided for the maintenance of the University Fund and directed the legislature to make provisions for the organization and operation of a university.[35] The legislature passed a bill establishing the Agricultural and Mechanical College of Texas and declared that it should be constituted, controlled, managed, and supervised as a branch of the University of Texas. This act also specified that the college should own at least 1,280 acres of good land and that the legislature would provide $75,000 from the "school fund" to build the college. The "school fund" had been created in January 1854, when a bill was passed that caused $2,000,000 to be placed into a fund for public schools and thus created the first public school system in Texas.[36] The Constitution of 1876 cemented the direction that Texas would take on education.

Early Texans believed that they could provide for public education endowed by the vast amount of public land held by the state. That is easy to understand; after all, most immigrants came to Texas because of the opportunity to obtain land as explained by the following quote:

> Fabulously rich in unoccupied land but lacking in coin, the great-hearted Texans proposed to found a school system, from the primary grades through the university, entirely on the bounty of the state. The boundless resources dedicated to the education of oncoming generations would, they believed, make the imposition of fees or taxes forever unnecessary. What a glorious prospect! Only gradually did these empire-builders awaken to the sad fact that schools cannot subsist on land alone, especially when land brings ten cents or less per acre.[37]

Without the public interest evidenced by the actions of the Congress of the Republic and later the activities of the Texas legislature, there would not have been a University Fund. The legislature's wisdom was also evident in the reservation of mineral interests on state land, which greatly benefited the state for years to come. However, it must be said that the difficulties in drawing legislative attention to getting the university open sooner was a major problem during the time covered in this chapter. President Sam Houston was not helpful when he took back the $100,000 previously given to the University Fund and stating that if the citizens of Texas wanted a university in the future then they could appropriate the funds. As has been pointed out he considered protection from the Indian tribes to be more important than a university. Houston was correct in pointing out that the university lands would be more valuable in the future, but no one could have known how true that would turn out to be.

NOTES

1. C. E. Evans, *The Story of Texas Schools* (Austin: Steck Company, 1955), 40.

2. Herbert Gambrell, *Mirabeau Buonaparte Lamar* (Dallas: Southwest Press, 1934), 209–11.

3. Frederick Eby, *The Development of Education in Texas* (New York: Macmillan Co., 1928), 81.

4. Stanley Siegel, *The Poet President of Texas* (Austin: Jenkins Publishing Company, The Pemberton Press, 1977), 7–8.

5. Elizabeth Silverthorne, *Ashbel Smith of Texas: Pioneer, Patriot, Statesman, 1805–1886* (College Station: Texas A&M University Press, 1982), 8.

6. Ibid., 194.

7. Thomas A. Fain, Jr., "The Contributions of Ashbel Smith to Education in Texas" (PhD diss., Texas A&M University-Commerce, 2008), 36.

8. Herbert Gambrell, "JONES, ANSON," *Handbook of Texas Online* (http://www.tsaonline.org/handbook/online/aricles/fjo42), accessed April 18, 2011.

9. Natalie Ornish, "KAUFMAN, DAVID SPANGLER," *Handbook of Texas Online* (http://www.tshaonline.org/handbook/online/articles/fka12) accessed April 18, 2011. Uploaded on June 15, 2010. Published by the Texas State Historical Association.

10. Andrew Forest Muir, "GRAY, WILLIAM FAIRFAX," *Handbook of Texas Online* (http://www.tshaonline.org/handbook/online/articles/fgr27), accessed on April 18, 2011.

11. A. K. Christian, "Mirabeau Buonaparte Lamar," *Southwestern Historical Quarterly* 24, no. 3 (Jan 1921): 232.

12. Constitution of the Republic of Texas (1836). Retrieved May 23, 2005, from http://tarlton.law.utexas.edu/constitutions/texas1836.

13. Gambrell, *Mirabeau Buonaparte Lamar*, 218.

14. Mirabeau Buonaparte Lamar, *The Papers of Mirabeau Buonaparte Lamar*, ed. Charles Adams Gulick, Jr., with the assistance of Katherine Elliott, vol. 2 (Austin: A. C. Baldwin & Sons, 1922), 346–69.

15. Eby, *The Development of Education in Texas*, 81–87.

16. Charles R. Matthews, "The Early Years of the Permanent University Fund" (Ed.D. thesis, University of Texas, Austin, 2006), 11.

17. Matthews, "The Early Years of the Permanent University Fund," 11.

18. Christian, "Mirabeau Buonaparte Lamar," 234.

19. Christian, "Mirabeau Buonaparte Lamar," 235.

20. Matthews, "The Early Years of the Permanent University Fund," 12–13.

21. Berte R. Haigh, *Land, Oil and Education* (El Paso: Texas Western Press, 1986), 6–7.

22. Evans, *The Story of Texas Schools*, 92.

23. Governor Pease signed O.B. 119.

24. O.B. 119, Chapter 144, Acts of the Sixth Legislature, Adjourned Session [1856], pp. 489–92. The companion bill was H.B. 27.

25. Ibid., 490.

26. O.B. 119, Chapter 144, Acts of the Sixth Legislature, Adjourned Session (1856), pp. 489–492.

27. Journal of the Senate (Texas), 7th Legislature, 1857, Part 1, p. 20, http://www.lrl.state.tx.us/collections/journals/journalsSenate7.cfm.

28. O.B. 102.

29. "A Bill to Establish the University of Texas," Journal of the Senate (Texas), 7th Legislature, 1857, Part 1, page 78, http://www.lrl.state.tx.us/collections/journals/journalsSenate7.cfm.

30. Matthews, "The Early Years of the Permanent University Fund," 15–16.

31. Journal of the House of Representatives (Texas), 8th Legislature, 1860, Part 4, p. 396, http://www.lrl.state.tx.us/collections/journals/journalsHouse8.cfm.

32. Journal of the House of Representatives (Texas), 8th Legislature, 1860, Part 4, p. 396, http://www.lrl.state.tx.us/collections/journals/journalsHouse8.cfm.

33. Tex. Special Laws, 1859, p. 29.

34. Jack Ramsey, Jr., *Thunder Beyond the Brazos* (Austin: Eakin Press, 1985), 61–62.

35. Texas General Laws, 1866, p. 30.

36. Charles W. Funkhouser John N. Bruscemi, *Perspectives on Schooling for Texas Educators* (Dubuque, IA: Kendall Hunt Publishing Co., 1981), 158.

37. Ibid., 123.

BIBLIOGRAPHY

Benham, Pricilla Myers. "RUSK, THOMAS JEFFERSON," *Handbook of Texas Online,* (http://www.tshaonline.org/handbook.online/articles/fru16), accessed January 02, 2014. Published by the Texas Historical Association.

Breitenkamp, Edward C. "BIRDSALL, JOHN," *Handbook of Texas Online,* (http://www.tshaonline.org/handbook/online/articles/fbi18), accessed January 02, 2014. Published by the Texas Historical Association.

Cantrell, Gregg. *Stephen F. Austin: Empresario of Texas.* New Haven, CT: Yale University Press, 1999.

Christian, A. K. "Mirabeau Buonaparte Lamar." *Southwestern Historical Quarterly* 24, no.1 (Jul 1920): 39–80; no. 2 (Oct 1920): 87–139; no. 3 (Jan 1921): 195–234; no. 4 (Apr 1921): 317–24.

Cutrer, Thomas W. "INGRAM, IRA," *Handbook of Texas Online* (http://www.tshaonline.org/handbook/online/articles/fin03), accessed January 02, 2014. Published by the Texas State Historical Association.

Eby, Frederick. *The Development of Education in Texas.* New York: Macmillan Co., 1928.

Evans, C. E. *The Story of Texas Schools.* Austin, TX: Steck Company, 1955.

——— "MCLEOD, HUGH," *Handbook of Texas Online,* (http://www.tshaonline.org/handbook/online/articles/fmc90), accessed January 02, 2014. Published by the Texas State Historical Association.

Fain, Thomas A., Jr. "The Contributions of Ashbel Smith to Education in Texas." PhD diss., Texas A&M University-Commerce, 2008.

Funkhouser, Charles W., and John N. Bruscemi. *Perspectives on Schooling for Texas Educators.* Dubuque, IA: Kendall Hunt Publishing Co., 1981.

Gambrell, Herbert. "JONES, ANSON," *Handbook of Texas Online*, (http://www.tshaonline.org/handbook/online/articles/fjo42), accessed January 02, 2014. Published by the Texas State Historical Association.

———. *Mirabeau Buonaparte Lamar*. Dallas: Southwest Press, 1934.

Haigh, Berte R. *Land, Oil and Education*. El Paso: Texas Western Press, 1986.

Henson, Margaret Swett. "BURNET, DAVID GOUVERNEUR," *Handbook of Texas Online*, (http://www.tshaonline.org/handbook/online/articles/fbu46), accessed January 02, 2014. Published by the Texas State Historical Association.

———. "CHAMBERS, THOMAS JEFFERSON (1802–1865)," *Handbook of Texas Online*, (http://www.tshaonline.org/handbook/online/articles/fch08), accessed on January 03, 2014. Published by the Texas State Historical Association.

Hudson, Linda Sybert, "IRION, ROBERT ANDERSON," *Handbook of Texas Online*, (http://www.tshaonline.org/handbook/onlline/articles/fir04), accessed January 02, 2014. Published by the Texas State Historical Association.

Jorgenson, Lloyd P. "Materials on the History in State Historical Journals: Part I, The South." *History of Education Quarterly* 7, no. 2 (Summer 1967): 234–54.

Kreneck, Thomas H., "HOUSTON, SAMUEL," *Handbook of Texas Online*, (http://www.tshaonline.org/handbook/online/articles/fho73), accessed on January 02, 2014. Published by the Texas State Historical Association.

Lamar, Mirabeau Buonaparte. *The Papers of Mirabeau Buonaparte Lamar*. Edited by Charles Adams Gulick, Jr., with the assistance of Katherine Elliott, Archivist, Texas State Library. Vol. 2. Austin: A. C. Baldwin & Sons, 1922.

Lang, Aldon S., and Cristopher Long, "LAND GRANTS," *Handbook of Texas Online*, (http://www.tshaonline.org/handbook/online/articles/mp101), accessed August 17, 2011. Published by the Texas State Historical Association.

Matthews, Charles R. "The Early Years of the Permanent University Fund." Ed.D. thesis, University of Texas, Austin, 2006.

Muir, Andrew Forest, "GRAY, WILLIAM FAIRFAX," *Handbook of Texas Online*, (http://www.tshaonline.org/handbook/online/articles/fgr27), accessed January 02, 2014. Published by the Texas State Historical Association.

Ornish, Natalie, "KAUFMAN, DAVID SPANGLER," *Handbook of Texas Online*, (http://www.tshaonline.org/handbook/online/articles/fka12), accessed January 02, 2014. Published by the Texas State Historical Association.

Ramsey, Jack, Jr. *Thunder Beyond the Brazos*. Austin: Eakin Press, 1985.

Siegel, Stanley. *The Poet President of Texas*. Austin: Jenkins Publishing Company, The Pemberton Press, 1977.

Silverthorne, Elizabeth. *Ashbel Smith of Texas: Pioneer, Patriot, Statesman, 1805–1886*. College Station: Texas A&M University Press, 1982.

Spellman, Norman W., "FOWLER, LITTLETON," *Handbook of Texas Online*, (http://www.tshaonline.org/handbook/online/articles/ffo25), accessed January 02, 2014. Published by the Texas State Historical Association.

Texas. *The Laws of Texas, 1822–1897*. Compiled and arranged by H. P. N. Gammel. 10 vols. Austin: Gammel Book Company, 1898. Supplementary vols. 11–31 cover the years 1897–1939. All volumes and the index are available at the University of North Texas Portal to Texas History, http://texashistory.unt.edu/explore/collections/GLT/. Page numbers in the notes refer to online page numbers.

Weir, Merle. "WHARTON, WILLIAM HARRIS," *Handbook of Texas Online*, (http://www.tshaonline.org/handbook/online/articles/fwh08), accessed January 02, 2014. Published by the Texas State Historical Association.

PART I:
FINANCING

3

THE EARLY YEARS OF THE UNIVERSITY OF TEXAS AND THE PERMANENT UNIVERSITY FUND

T he speech President Lamar made to the Congress of the Republic in 1838 began what would be a long and difficult path to opening the University of Texas on September 15, 1883. One important reason forty-five years elapsed between the two events was the political turmoil in Texas during that time. In the last few years leading up to the opening of the university, a number of organizational issues were finally addressed, including forming a board of regents, holding a statewide election to select a site for the university, obtaining enough money to build and equip facilities, and hiring a competent faculty. The center of attention for the first board of regents was learning to understand and manage the university lands for the best possible benefit of the institution.

It is helpful to understand some of the commonly used terms in the chapters that discuss the Permanent University Fund. The Permanent University Fund includes ownership of all university assets, money, stocks, bonds etc., and all university lands. The term Available University Fund is the money that can be spent in support of the designated colleges; it would include such items as money from sale or lease of lands, royalties from oil and gas, income from stock and bonds, or the sale of other assets. The excess money in the Permanent University Fund would be transferred by the Regents to the Available University Fund to be used in operating the universities.

The University Fund was a term used in the beginning years of the funds; it held the money and bonds that had been placed there by the legislature.

* * * * *

To fully understand the beginnings of state support for higher education in Texas, it is important to have a general understanding of the Texas constitutions. The first constitution of Texas came about on March 1, 1836. After meeting for fifteen days while the Battle of the Alamo was taking place, the delegates were expedient in what they chose to adopt because they were short of time and needed to address the war. They, in effect, adopted most of the U.S. Constitution, perhaps influenced by the fact that it has only 4,500 words. This first constitution had some familiar features:

1. A brief preamble
2. Separation of governmental powers into three branches: legislative, executive and judicial
3. A bicameral legislature
4. Checks and balances on the powers of each branch
5. A Bill of Rights
6. Democratic selection of government office holders (restricted to free, non-aboriginal males)

This constitution was silent on education.[1] But it was clear that Africans could not hold office.

The second constitution was adopted in 1845 when Texas became the twenty-eighth state to join the Union. According to the *Handbook of Texas Online* this constitution has been called the most respected because of its simplicity and directness. Even U.S. Senator Daniel Webster, an opponent of Texas statehood, commented that it was the best of the state constitutions. As had the Constitution of 1836 it featured a separation of powers into three branches. It reflected the changes that were needed for the state to join the Union. Even though the Congress of the Republic had earlier granted fifty acres of land for the establishment of a university, this constitution did not mention it.[2]

The third constitution was drafted after voters supported the proposal for secession from the United States. The Texas Secession Convention of 1861 wrote a new constitution that followed the Constitution of 1845 with changes made to replace the references to the United States of America, emphasize the constitutionality of slavery, and assert states' rights. Interestingly it did not provide for the resumption of the African slave trade. In regard to higher education it also did not include provision for the fifty leagues of land for the university.[3]

The fourth constitution was made in 1866 and was dictated by the federal government after the end of the Civil War. This constitution was written to conform to U.S. laws and the U.S. Constitution. While many citizens of Texas were unhappy with this constitution, it did provide maintenance of the University Fund and directed the legislature to make provisions for the organization and operation of a university.[4]

After Reconstruction, Texans were anxious to replace the 1866 constitution, and another constitution in 1869 also included provisions for the university. The sixth (since independence from Mexico), final, and current constitution is the Constitution of the State of Texas (1876), which included the instructions on the university lands and the University of Texas. Despite all the turmoil in state governance, the university lands and the idea of a state university had prevailed.

In regard to higher education the Constitution of the State of Texas (1876):

1. Established the Permanent University Fund (PUF) consisting of all lands, income thereof, and grants that had been set aside, appropriated, or otherwise accrued for the establishment and maintenance of a state university.
2. Called for the creation of the University of Texas, which, although authorized in 1858, had yet to be located or organized.

3. Mandated that the A&M College of Texas be a branch of the University.
4. Expressly prohibited the levying of a tax or appropriation from the General Revenue Fund for construction of buildings at the University of Texas.
5. Directed that the PUF be invested in State of Texas bonds, or if those were unavailable, United States bonds.
6. Took away the prime lands bordering the railroads (one section for every ten) that were granted but never conveyed by the Act of 1858 and gave in lieu thereof 1,000,000 acres in West Texas.[5]

The Act of 1858 refers to the passage of a bill that set up the University of Texas and provided for railroad lands to be placed into the Permanent University Fund. These lands had originally been given to the railroads in an effort to induce them to build track across Texas. Some had been given back to the state because the railroad considered it too worthless to justify paying for a survey. Because the lands surrounding the railroads were beginning to be developed, the state legislature believed it was better to give the Permanent University Fund land that had not already been developed.[6]

In his report to the governor for the fiscal year ending August 31, 1880, the Texas Land Commissioner commented on the passage of a bill by the legislature in 1879 that required the commissioner to appoint a surveyor, or surveyors, to locate and survey, in sections, the one million acres of university land. The commissioner complained that the bill did not include a provision for advertising for competitive bids, and especially that the legislature had not stated how much could be spent to have the land surveyed. The commissioner invited various survey companies to submit bids. He received ten bids and selected the lowest bidder, who agreed to do the work for $4.25 per acre. When these surveys were completed, the information was submitted to the Texas General Land Office, and the commissioner reported that the best available university lands were in Tom Green, Pecos, and Crockett counties.[7]

On March 30, 1881, the legislature ordered a statewide popular election for the purpose of choosing a location for the University of Texas, and it established a governing board of eight regents authorized to set policy and oversee the affairs of the university.[8] The legislature also specified how the university was to be run. Two items were particularly interesting:

> Section 20. No religious qualification shall be required for any office or privilege in the university. Section 21. The board of regents shall report to the board of education annually, and to each regular session of the Legislature, the condition of the university, setting forth the receipts and disbursements, the number and salary of the faculty, the number of students, classified in grade and departments, the expenses of each year, itemized, and the proceedings of the board and faculty stated.[9]

On April 1, 1881, the first regents were nominated by Governor O. M. Roberts and approved by the state senate. The board of regents held its first meeting on November 15, 1881, and Ashbel Smith was elected president of the board. Smith sought to create a university modeled after the University of Virginia, and has been called the "Father of the University of Texas" because of his early efforts on behalf of the institution.[10] Smith's desire to use the University of Virginia as a model was common in Texas, and he may have known that when the Texas senate considered the legislation founding the University of Texas, it discussed that very idea.[11]

Smith wrote an article in 1881 for the *Texas Journal of Education* in which he gave his views about the location of the state university. In her biography of Smith, Elizabeth Silverthorne notes that he "considered Austin the only suitable location for the main branch of the state university; it was 'preeminently healthy,' was easily accessible by railroad from every part of the state, and, being the seat of government, would give the students the advantage of observing the running of the state first hand."[12]

By popular election on September 6, 1881, the City of Austin was selected as the location for the University of Texas, and Galveston was selected for the university's Medical Branch. At its meeting on November 16, 1881, the board of regents passed a resolution requesting the governor provide it with information on the status of the university funds, lands, and money borrowed from the PUF. It also requested that any money borrowed previously be returned to the PUF with interest.[13]

On August 17, 1882, the board received a letter from the state comptroller stating that the Permanent University Fund contained $34,464.34 in interest-bearing bonds.[14] After reading the letter, the board voted to sell the bonds at the highest possible price. The board members were worried, no doubt, about having enough cash to open the university the next year. It is evident from the early financial information that the university had little cash and perhaps no credit. The hard assets that belonged to the university at the time were of little value—the most redeeming quality of the university land was its sheer quantity.[15]

On November 17, 1882, the cornerstone of the Main Building at the University of Texas was laid. President Smith proved prophetic in his remarks: "Texas holds embedded in its rocks and minerals which now lie idle because unknown, resources of incalculable industrial utility, of wealth and power. Smite the earth, smite the rocks with the rod of knowledge and fountains of unstinted wealth will gush forth."[16]

On April 10, 1883, the legislature added 1,000,000 acres of land in West Texas to the Permanent University Fund. This land came from two million acres the Texas & Pacific Railroad had returned to the state as being of such low value that it was too worthless to survey. (The legislature reserved the other one million acres to the Permanent School Fund—the fund to support primary education in the state.) The legislature also appropriated $256,272.57 to repay the PUF for assets diverted by the state for other purposes during the Civil War.[17]

This must have been a strange time for the regents trying to open a new university. They knew they had significant land assets, but they knew little about what type of lands were held or even where they were located. Finances were a major problem in the early years, and the regents spent decades trying to stretch a small budget to meet the demands of a university.

In November 1883, the comptroller sent the governor a letter containing a rendering of the university's account since 1860; he had provided an early copy of the information to the regents and they had discussed it at their June 1883 meeting. Because the new constitution of 1876 had set out in clear detail both the Permanent University Fund and the Available University Fund (see Table 3.1), the comptroller's letter gave the regents a precise picture of where things stood. It provides a fascinating look into the history of the Permanent University Fund. The fund's beginning balance was $130,684.26. Of this, $100,000 was from an earlier appropriation by the legislature. What the legislature could give, it could take away as evidenced by the years of the Civil War when, between 1860 and 1862, the legislature took $145,761.28 from the account, reducing the balance to worthless Confederate notes and a little over $16,000 in warrants (a form of stock security). The money was, however, returned by the legislature in 1866. One surprising item to note about the time is the very good land sales the PUF experienced from 1874 to 1881. The land office was able to sell $255,905 worth of land at a time when the per acre price was very low.[18]

While it was informative for the regents to know how much money was in the Permanent University Fund, what they really needed to know was what money would be available to open the University of Texas on September 15, 1883. After all of the accounting adjustments were made by the comptroller, the amount available as of January 1, 1883 (for use by the university in September), was $47,025.14, plus the $150,000 the previous legislature had appropriated for the opening of the university. It was this $197,025.14, along with money from land sales, that was used to open the University of Texas in September 1883.[19]

By 1886, because of a major emphasis by the board of regents, money was beginning to flow to the university. On June 15, 1886, the board's finance committee noted that there was $101,257.69 in the Available University Fund. By this time, they were collecting interest on land sales, matriculation fees from students, and money from leasing some of the grazing land. The income from all of these sources totaled $48,524.38 for the year.[20]

Early land sales were not of holdings in West Texas but of those located in McLennan, El Paso, and Collin counties. These tracts were not contiguous to the university lands, so the board decided to sell them.[21]

* * * * *

Several points are critical to a more complete understanding of the financial condition of the university. First, the board of regents was always dealing with relatively small amounts of money. Not only was it trying to open a university with very little money, it had very little income to support it once it was open. For example, the total interest earned on the land notes for the entire year of 1883 was only $4,114.07. Economic conditions at the time affected both land sales and lease income. This meager financial situation would not improve for many decades.

Second, the West Texas land was only good for grazing and the ranchers who leased the land were dependent upon a reasonable amount of rainfall. When it did not rain, there was no grass for the cattle and cattle had to be sold off, and in those years there was little use for the land. This resulted in cattlemen not paying their leases, or if they had purchased university land, not paying their notes. No income for the ranchers meant no money going back to the university fund.

Finally, it also must be kept in mind that at this time the legislature had no intention of providing appropriations for the university because of the widely held belief that the land would provide all the income the university would ever need to cover its operations. This discussion would continue for many years as we shall see in later chapters.

Table 3.1 Critical Events in the Establishment of the Permanent University Fund

1876	New constitution established the Permanent University Fund (PUF).
	A University Fund had first been established in the 1836 constitution, but some intervening constitutions had failed to include it.
	The 1876 constitution specified use of both a Permanent University Fund and an Available University Fund. Funds in the latter could be spent, while only income earned on the holdings in the Permanent University Fund could be spent.
March 30, 1881	Legislature ordered an election to choose a location for the University of Texas.
April 1, 1881	First Board of Regents of the University of Texas nominated by Governor O. M. Roberts and approved by the state senate.
September 6, 1881	City of Austin selected as location for the University of Texas.
	Galveston selected for university's Medical Branch.
November 15, 1881	First Board of Regents meeting. Ashbel Smith elected president of the board.
November 16, 1881	Board of Regents requested status of university funds, land, and money borrowed from the PUF, and asked that any money borrowed previously be returned with interest.
August 17, 1882	Regents advised by state comptroller that the PUF contained $34,464.34.
November 17, 1882	Cornerstone of University of Texas Main Building laid.
April 10, 1883	State legislature added 1,000,000 acres of land in West Texas to the PUF, and appropriated $256,272.57 to repay the PUF for assets diverted during Civil War.
September 15, 1883	University of Texas opened.
November 1883	Governor advised by state comptroller that the PUF contained $191,429.17 in actual and contingent funds.

NOTES

1. Texas Constitutions 1824–1876, Texas Law, Tarlton Law Library, Jamail Center for Legal Research, https://tarltonapps.law.utexas.edu/constitutions/.
2. Ibid.
3. Ibid.
4. Charles R. Matthews, "The Early Years of the Permanent University Fund" (Ed.D. thesis, University of Texas, Austin, 2006), 17.
5. Tex. Const. of 1876, chap. LII, § 1, in Gammel's *Laws of Texas.*
6. Chapter 116. An Act to establish the University of Texas (1858), in Gammel's *Laws of Texas,* (1898) vol. 4, 1020–23; Berte R. Haigh, *Land, Oil and Education* (El Paso: Texas Western Press, 1986), 33.
7. Commissioner of the General Land Office, *Report for the Fiscal Year ending August 31, 1880.* (Galveston: Galveston News Book and Job Office).
8. 1881 Texas General Laws, p. 80.
9. 1881, Texas General Laws. March 30, 1881, p. 82.
10. Elizabeth Silverthorne, *Ashbel Smith of Texas: Pioneer, Patriot, Statesman, 1805–1886* (College Station: Texas A&M University Press, 1982), 210.
11. Silverthorne, *Ashbel Smith of Texas,* 218; Journal of the Senate (Texas), 7th Legislature, 1857, Part 1, page 78, http://www.lrl.state.tx.us/collections/journals/journalsSenate7.cfm.
12. Quoted in Silverthorne, *Ashbel Smith of Texas,* 210, [from *Texas Journal of Education* (March 1, 1881): 148–49].
13. The three cities among which voters chose were Austin, Galveston, and Waco. University of Texas Board of Regents Minutes, 1881. Retrieved December 13–17, 20, 2004, from http://www.utsystem.edu/bor/. (Hereafter referred to as UTBOR.)
14. UTBOR, 1882.
15. UTBOR, August 17, 1882.
16. Silverthorne, *Ashbel Smith of Texas,* 219.
17. Matthews, "The Early Years of the Permanent University Fund," 24.
18. UTBOR, 1883e, June 5, pp. 48–59
19. UTBOR, 1883e, pp. 48–59.
20. UTBOR, 1886, pp. 172–75.
21. UTBOR, 1886b, June 12, pp. 172–75.

BIBLIOGRAPHY

Beckham, John L. "The Permanent University Fund: Land, Oil and Politics." MS, Dolph Briscoe Center for American History, University of Texas at Austin, 1981.
Clark, Edward. "The Permanent University Fund: A Foundation for Greatness." Unpublished manuscript, LBJ Library, Austin, 1976.
Commissioner of the General Land Office, *Report for the Fiscal Year ending August 31, 1880.* Galveston: Galveston News Book and Job Office.
Ferguson, Walter Keene. *Geology and Politics in Frontier Texas: 1845–1909.* Austin: University of Texas Press, 1967.
———. *History of the Bureau of Economic Geology: 1909–1960.* Austin: Bureau of Economic Geology, 1981.
Fort Worth Petroleum Club. *Oil Legends of Fort Worth.* Dallas: Taylor Publishing Co., 1993.
Haigh, Berte R. *Land, Oil and Education.* El Paso: Texas Western Press, 1986.
Hogan, William Ransom. *The Texas Republic: A Social and Economic History.* Austin: University of Texas Press, 1969.
Lang, Aldon Socrates. *Financial History of the Public Lands in Texas.* Baylor Bulletin 35, no. 3. Waco: Baylor University, 1932.

Matthews, Charles R. "The Early Years of the Permanent University Fund from 1836 to 1937." Ed.D. thesis, University of Texas, Austin, 2006.

Silverthorne, Elizabeth. *Ashbel Smith of Texas: Pioneer, Patriot, Statesman, 1805–1886.* College Station: Texas A&M University Press, 1982.

Smyrl, Vivian Elizabeth. "PERMANENT UNIVERSITY FUND." *The Handbook of Texas Online* (http://www.tshaonline.org/handbook/online/articles/khp02), accessed December 31, 2014. Uploaded on June 15, 2010. Published by the Texas State Historical Association.

Texas Constitutions 1824–1876, Texas Law, Tarlton Law Library, Jamail Center for Legal Research, https://tarltonapps.law.utexas.edu/constitutions/.

Texas. *The Laws of Texas, 1822–1897.* Compiled and arranged by H. P. N. Gammel. 10 vols. Austin: Gammel Book Company, 1898. Supplementary vols. 11–31 cover the years 1897–1939. All volumes and the index are available at the University of North Texas Portal to Texas History, http://texashistory.unt.edu/explore/collections/GLT/. Page numbers in the notes refer to online page numbers.

University of Texas System Office of the Controller. *Available University Fund and Permanent University Fund: Report to the Legislature and Governor Pursuant to Rider No. 5 to Available University Fund Appropriations.* Austin: University of Texas, 2000.

United States. Congress. Petroleum Investigation: Hearings before the House Committee on Interstate and Foreign Commerce. Subcommittee on Petroleum. Washington, DC: Government Printing Office, 1943.

Warner, C. A. *Texas Oil and Gas Since 1543.* Houston: Gulf Publishing Co., 1939.

4

THE FIGHT FOR CONTROL OF UNIVERSITY LANDS

On three different occasions, Texas appropriated what became a total of slightly more than 2,000,000 acres of land to provide funding for a university. First, in 1839 the Congress of the Republic set aside fifty leagues, or 221,400 acres. Second, in 1876 the citizens of the state ratified a new constitution that stipulated an additional one million acres; and finally, in 1883 the state legislature added another one million acres. Chapters 2 and 3 examined the circumstances surrounding the first gift of fifty leagues, the establishment of the University Fund, and the problematic relationship between the University of Texas Board of Regents and the General Land Office. This chapter will look at the 1876 and 1883 land appropriations in some detail, and at the fight for control of these lands that continued to be waged between the board of regents and the commissioner of the General Land Office, a fight that continued for many years.[1]

★ ★ ★ ★ ★

A lack of information about the university lands led the regents in 1883 to appoint a committee to work with the General Land Office to ascertain the amount of land in the Permanent University Fund (PUF). The General Land Office had been in charge of the university lands since the fund came into being in 1876. On May 1, 1883, the regents passed a resolution asking the commissioner of the General Land Office to designate and set apart the land that belonged to the PUF from the two million acres that had originally been designated for both the Public School Fund and the PUF. The regents also asked for maps and plats of the land. On that same day, the land commissioner, W. C. Walsh, met with the regents and provided them with valuable information about the lands. He said they were supposed to be good for grazing sheep and cattle but did not have much surface water, and they might be more valuable in the future. Walsh also confirmed something the board already knew—the lands were in various parts of Texas although the bulk was in far West Texas an area unknown to most Texans.[2]

The regents wanted as much information as possible about the university lands, but the General Land Office was slow in providing it. In June 1883, one of the regents, T. D. Wooten, reported to the Board that he had talked to the land commissioner and been told that he had not been able to provide the requested information because his office was understaffed. The commissioner was, however, trying to speed up the leasing of the university lands and had begun using newspaper advertising to make public its availability. Wooten then visited with Governor John Ireland who suggested the commissioner hire an additional draftsman. The next day, Walsh told the board he had hired an additional draftsman who would work on the maps and plats for the PUF. He also informed the board that none of the PUF land was in the Panhandle, but was most probably in Tom Green, Pecos, Crockett, and Presidio counties.[3]

The state legislature continued to pass laws during 1883 that were important to the university and the PUF. On April 12, it created the State Land Board—made up of the governor, attorney general, comptroller, treasurer, and land commissioner—to lease and sell public lands. On April 14, the legislature passed an act stipulating that "all minerals in the Public School, University, Asylum and public lands of the State of Texas . . . shall be used and disposed of for the benefit of the respective funds for which said lands are now set apart as hereinafter prescribed." Both of these laws were to have a major impact on the PUF.[4]

The slow response the board of regents received from the General Land Office spawned many conversations among the regents about the feasibility of managing the university lands themselves. The first positive action from the land office came as a result of a meeting that happened just before the board of regents meeting of January 29, 1886. Professor Leslie, chairman of the faculty, was present at a meeting of the State Land Board at which that board gave a qualified control over part of the university land to the board of regents when it passed the following resolution:

> It is agreed by the State Land Board that the Board of Regents of the University of Texas shall have the power to lease University lands under such regulations and price and time and matter of payments as the State Land Board has already adopted or may hereafter adopt it in regard to said lands. It is further agreed that the Board of Regents many select said agent, fix his compensation and term of office and define his duties so that in all aspect, except being governed by the regulations of the State Land Board above mentioned, he shall be the agent of the Board of Regents and not the agent of the Land Board.[5]

Upon hearing this news during their January 29 meeting, the board of regents asked the university president to contract with a land agent to be paid a salary of $2,500 per year. The regents also gave specific instructions about fencing the leased tracts of land using five wires and galvanized posts set not more than thirty feet apart. Yearly leases were to be six cents per acre, with a credit of up to two cents per acre given against the lease payment for costs of fencing and putting stock watering tanks in place.

In June, the board received a long and instructive report from the new land agent, O. W. Williams. Among other things, he told them the frontier lands were generally in Tom Green, Pecos, and Reeves counties, and there was little or no surface water, but water could be obtained by digging to moderate depths.[6]

In 1886, the land commissioner's annual report to the governor discussed some of the difficulties he had encountered in running his office:

> It is perhaps well to call attention to the fact that the remunerative work of this department is rapidly diminishing, while the amount of clerical labor remains the same. This, in view of the constitutional requirement that the office must be self-sustaining, will soon present a difficult question for solution. If the surplus, over expenses, collected and paid into the treasury for the past few years can be credited to the future expenditures, the issue may be postponed for some years.
>
> The sale and lease of School lands, notwithstanding this clerical force provided for the special work, adds largely to the labors of this office and entails expense for which there is no provision of fees. During the past eight years the disposition of these lands had been an absorbing question and a brief glance at the experimental legislation of that without cost for collecting.
>
> University Lands amounting to one million acres were surveyed under authority of an act on April 10, 1883, upon what was then supposed to be the best of the vacant land reserved under former acts. Subsequently, in the adjustment of the Texas and Pacific eighty-mile reserve and correction of survey, good pasturelands were discovered in El Paso County, superior in every respect to much of the first selection. On learning these facts I consulted with the Regents, and through them arranged for the survey of sufficient of this land to replace what was found in the original survey to be sandy and in conflict. This work has now been completed and maps and field notes of the blocks returned and filed with this office. It might be well for the Legislature to confirm this exchange and restore the rejected portions of the first survey to the reserve.[7]

The commissioner had probably been feeling some pressure from the continuing concerns of the regents, and in this report he attempted to explain why his office had been doing such a poor job of overseeing the university lands. He noted that while the legislature had continued to give him more and more duties, it had neglected to give him the necessary money to properly carry out all those duties.

The regents were concerned with the management of the university lands by the land office and, regardless of who was at fault, the records concerning the university property had been poorly maintained. The board had discussed this issue many times. It hired Theodore Roziene to help clean up the records.[8] Roziene reported to the board on March 13, 1887, in a letter to the chairman of the board's land committee, Colonel George W. Brackenridge:

> Dear Sir!
> The work in the General Land Office and in the Office of the Land Board is finished. I am now at work in the State Treasurer's Office. The records of the several offices do not agree, still, I can make a very correct statement of facts tracking the disposition and present status of the old 50 League donations. The field notes and maps on file in the General Land Office are very much mixed, and required much patience study, on account of the numerous corrections of surveys made from time to time. I have been governed by latest files. The records of the Land Office are not very reliable. No true statement can be made on these alone. The Land Board records omit a great many tracts, besides giving wrong descriptions. They ought to be recompiled. The Ledgers and Books in the Office of the State Treasurer's Office, showing the sales of those lands and payments made thereon are in good shape, and without them we could never get to the bottom of our examinations. I had to lay a foundation for my work. And the proper way to begin was to get the latest and most correct field notes. It took time to hunt them up. Some were filed away in pigeonholes and not readily found. They should have been recorded, but are not. So with the patents issued, but as final payments are made almost every few days to the Treasurer the facts are not known to the other offices except by special inquiry. Many have final receipts, and want no patents, probably for the purpose of evading the taxes. But in the Treasurer's office I get all this from the day I begun till [sic] I finish

my examination—within a space of a few days. My work will differ considerable [sic] with the report of Mr. Walsh of December 10, 1886. I account for every parcel of land, and give the history or each tract on one single line, showing the survey or part of survey paid for or patented, and to whom etc. And the particular tracts, fully described and easily identified, on which payments are still due, to whom sold, and the time when the last payment of interest was made, thus finding the forfeited lands. I have found a good many so far—dating back to 1879—and also sales of many tracts that do not appear upon the Land Board Records of the Land Office. I expect to have all the data completed this week, unless something unlooked for should turn up. In the Treasurer's Office I cannot examine more than 200 pages a day, covering 400 separate acc'ts. When I get through here, I will take all notes with me to San Antonio—and put the work in neat and proper shape as a record for future reference.

Please do me the favor to advise First National Bank to pay me $50.00. I want the money to pay any board bills and pay expenses here and at home.[9]

Brackenridge acknowledged Roziene's report in an October 22, 1887, letter to T. D. Wooten, who had become president of the board. This must have been good news to both men because, for the first time, the university would have accurate information regarding the university lands.[10]

In a report to Governor L. S. Ross in 1888, Land Commissioner Richard M. Hall produced some interesting information about the difficulties his office had experienced in obtaining good, reliable information on public lands, and he stated that there were "approximately 398,876 acres," unaccounted for. Some of these could be attributed to survey error. With three million acres in the public domain, that meant an error rate of about 10 percent. Hall further stated that the poor records and poorer survey results caused almost incalculable trouble, which had led to many lawsuits. Like Walsh before him, Hall complained about increasing duties without proper funding.[11]

In the same report, Hall noted that only 77,437 of the two million acres of university lands had been leased. The result for the public school land was much better, primarily because most of the school properties were located next to desirable lands that had already been homesteaded. When those school lands were made available, neighboring ranchers leased them quickly. University lands were different: they were large blocks, in very remote areas, without permanent surface water, and, for the most part, were too distant from other water sources to be used for raising livestock. All of this made it very difficult to lease them. The commissioner suggested one of two plans to deal with the situation. The first was to greatly reduce the lease payments on the land; he suggested a reduction from six cents to three cents per acre per year. In addition, the lessor must be induced to develop the water availability by digging wells or installing stock tanks to catch the runoff from occasional rains. Or perhaps, he suggested, the state should furnish the money to develop the water. His second plan was to give control of the university lands to the regents, something the regents had wanted for some time.[12]

In 1891, the state legislature again dealt with many issues affecting the university lands. In a bill entitled "Lands—Sale and Lease of School and Other Public Lands" it laid out the method by which a purchaser was obligated to make interest payments. The borrower was given a grace period of five months to pay the interest on purchased land. If the interest were not paid at the end of that time, a 20 percent penalty would be charged. The legislation also gave the land commissioner the right to foreclose on property without judicial proceedings. In an effort to speed up the leasing of the land, the legislation also stipulated the terms on which the university lands could be leased, for three cents per acre per year and not for more than ten years. The law restated that all dealings regarding the university lands were to be with the land commissioner.[13]

On June 18, 1894, the regents addressed an issue that may have been the result of earlier annual faculty reports when they took action to collect some of the past due interest on land sales by adopting the following:

> Resolved that the Chairman of the Faculty and Professor Batts be authorized to make such steps as may be necessary to have collected the interest on the land notes and leases belonging to the University of the sales of lands made under the Act of the Legislature of 1874 to the end that the same be realized and the lands recovered back for the University and to take such steps as may be necessary to protect the interest of the University in such lands.[14]

Later in the year, Batts reported to the Board that he had not been able to finish his investigation of the lands near El Paso known as the San Elizario lands. There was a three-way dispute over those lands that involved the people of El Paso, the San Elizario estate, and the university. Land Commissioner Walsh had at one time suggested that the legislature substitute other land for this disputed property, but that had not been done. Batts said it appeared that the lands were worth between $5 and $20 per acre. However, if they could be irrigated, they would be worth much more and could be used to grow the fine "mission grapes" that were produced in the region.[15]

At the board meeting on June 18, 1894, Regent Wooten said that he and the other regents had been working on the issue of control of the university land for some time and had hired an agent, Mr. Williams, to look into the issue. The regents had tried to get the state attorney general to take some action but had been unsuccessful. During this long board meeting, questions were asked as to why the board of regents did not have control of these lands. Regent William L. Prather responded that Governor Ross had always objected to it because there was already a land board in place at the General Land Office, and the governor did not think that another board should be created. It was discussed that even though Commissioner Walsh had told the board he was interested in turning over control of the university lands to them, he had recently testified before the legislature that he opposed the transfer. The confusion about who should be in charge would eventually cause the legislature to take action to resolve the dispute.[16]

Also in the June 18 meeting, Batts told the Board that a large amount of university lands were encumbered by the fact that there were state contracts of sale that were in default and had not been rescinded. This made it impossible to give good title to a new buyer. In an effort to deal with all of these issues, the board unanimously adopted a resolution asking Batts to put together a presentation to the legislature stating the need for these issues to be resolved.[17]

In 1895 the regents received good news when the legislature passed an act allowing the board of regents to control and manage the university lands. At last it had the formal authority for which its members had worked so hard for so many years. No longer would they have to go through the burdensome process of working with the land office. With passage of the act, the regents stepped up their efforts to collect the money that was past due on both leases and land notes.[18]

In a meeting in March 1895, the regents discussed their new responsibilities for managing the university lands and reached several important conclusions. First, they would need additional appropriations from the legislature to pay the expenses that would be incurred in managing the lands. Second, they agreed that they needed to make every effort to keep management of the lands in the hands of the board and not rely on outside agents. They also discussed the need to have firsthand knowledge about the lands. There are numerous stories in the board minutes that illustrate just how difficult it was to manage a property located in a remote area. For example, one story concerns a rancher who was trying to lease some of the land at a low price by saying the land had no water on it. It was later discovered that there were in fact two good wells already on the land, and while the rancher was leasing some land, he was also occupying one hundred sections of other university lands without paying any lease.[19]

By the May 1895 board meeting, maps from various sources had been furnished to the board, but because none of them were from the General Land Office, it made it more difficult for the regents to develop a good understanding of the land. Regent Brackenridge insisted that the only way the board would ever have a true understanding of the university lands was for the regents themselves to visit them. There appears to have been a lack of enthusiasm for his suggestion, although he made it many more times in subsequent years. Discussion at the May 1895 meeting centered on the fact that the regents had been given the new duties, but had not been given any money to accomplish them. The legislature had in actuality appropriated more money, but the governor had vetoed that bill, no doubt a reflection of his earlier stated opposition to the board managing the lands. Brackenridge wryly noted that it appeared the politicians kept control of the lands when it was desirable to have control. During the time the General Land Commissioner had control over the land, cattle prices were low and there was little demand for grazing land. Also at this May meeting the board decided that Regent Brackenridge should be appointed as a committee of one to find and employ someone to make an examination of the lands.[20]

At the board's first meeting of 1896, it hired a new land agent, a Mr. Lee, for one year at a salary of $125 per month plus traveling and stationery expenses. His duties were to investigate all available sources to learn the actual condition and character of the university lands and put the information into a systematic form to be presented to the board. The regents also voted to give the board's land committee the power to sign and execute all deeds and leases.[21]

At the August meeting that year an event occurred that demonstrated the difficulty of managing the lands. It was brought to the regents' attention that a rancher was requesting to lease an additional one hundred sections of land in spite of the fact that he was already three years delinquent on the land he was currently leasing from the university. Lee, the land agent at the time, explained in detail about the land the rancher, E. R. Jackson, was leasing and told the board that Jackson owed the university $3,000. It happened that Jackson was at the meeting and asked the board for permission to speak. He explained that his fences had been down because of the recent drought, and he could not afford to pay two cents per acre for further use of the land. He said he had paid the lease during the first two years of the drought, but he could not afford to pay any more. Jackson then proposed to the board that he lease forty-four sections for eight years at two cents per acre.[22]

Regent Ball asked him about his delinquent payments. Jackson replied, "I understand that I am liable for two years lease of some 60 sections for about $3,000, but if you got the law against us, we can't stay there," meaning that if the board sued him, he would have to leave the land. The board then asked him if he could pay $1,000 of the past due money if they forgave the balance. He replied that he would have to think about it. Of course, that was the last time they heard from him and the land reverted back to the PUF.[23]

These discussions around trying to collect past due payments occurred for many years and the board struggled to obtain enough money to properly fund the university. The budget for the 1905–1907 biennium showed how small the sums from the lands were. It was estimated by the regents that the income from land leases would amount to $72,567.44 per year, and land notes were estimated to bring in $2,000 per year. The small amount of land sale income illustrates that, despite many discussions, a very wise policy of not selling any more university lands was followed.[23] When oil was discovered on the lands some twenty years later, it became evident why this had been such a wise decision.[24]

At its October 1910 meeting, the board received a report stating that the recent reorganization of all state departments by the legislature had again left the General Land Office short staffed. The staff had been reduced and the office given the additional duty of receiving lease money from the university lands. Thus the legislature had again changed its mind and taken that duty from the regents and returned it to the land commissioner. The reduction in staff at the land office prevented it from collecting the payments and providing proper receipts. A bad situation had become worse.[25]

The board continued to look for ways to increase the university's income. In a 1911 meeting, Regent Brackenridge, chairman of the land committee, reported that he had sent national experts, along with a university instructor, to examine the university lands for underground water. If significant water could be found, the regents believed they could increase the income from the lands.[26] Surface or potential well water was of such significance because of the lack of annual rainfall in West Texas.

At a later meeting that year, George W. Littlefield, as the new chairman of the land committee, gave the following report:

> At your last meeting you appointed a committee to inspect the University lands of Andrews County. That committee composed of our Chairman and your Land Committee.
>
> We did not have Capt. Faust of the land committee with us as he was in a Sanitarium at Milwaukee, Wisconsin, nor Mr. Stark, he having been absent from the state and his business was such that he could not join the committee. Col. Ousley and myself, accompanied with Mr. Saner, the Land Agent, met in Ft. Worth on the 10th and put in the 11th and 12th in looking over the lands. Owing to the heavy sandy roads we could not go in automobiles over all the lands laying in the extreme West part of the County, but I can assure you on what I know of that portion and what good citizens of the State have told me, that is the poorest portion of the University land in Andrews County. There are no streams or running water on the lands. Wells are from one hundred to one hundred and fifty feet deep with only a moderate supply of water. On the western blocks of land it is said to be difficult to find water. Some wells have been sunk five hundred feet and no water found.
>
> As to the settlement of the County, the only lands [sic] I saw that showed much chance to be farmed was that in the Eastern portion. In my opinion that about 120,000 of the 311,000 acres only could be looked upon as having any showing to ever become agricultural lands, and from my experience in that Western county, the crops would have to be confined to Kafir corn, milo maze, Sugar Millet and cotton occasionally may be made. The cotton crop would depend

upon getting rain in May to secure a stand. Later than that the season being so short you could not expect maturity of the bolls. Often rain does not fall until the last of June, when there would be no chance for a cotton crop, yet Maze and Millet could be matured before frost. This usually comes from the 15th to the 25th of October. The irrigation from wells cannot be relied upon, as water is simply limited and only a small orchard and garden could be considered. Its being so far west from cities of any considerable size and railroads so distant from those lands, it would be useless to consider vegetables or fruit crops for market, I believe. The hard lands of the plains country will be settled by stock farmers. These sandy lands are more adapted to cotton, fruits and vegetables and cannot be profitable stock farms. The character of the grass they produce is not that which is good feeding during the winter. They principally have sedge grass and shin oak growth on them. Sand from one foot to eighteen inches deep to red clay. Those lands are now being leased and bring an annual rental of seven cents per acre. You cannot expect to increase that rental very much for it requires about twenty to twenty-five acres for the support of an animal for twelve months.

Should we sell the lands for the figure offered, you will then receive an income per annum equal to twenty-five cents per acre. Five years interest paid in advance would be available and can be used in a manner that I wish to submit later to the Regents, which in my mind will result in the greatest good for the University.

Such is my report on the Andrew County property and I recommend its sale.[27]

This report painted a dark financial picture for the Board of Regents.

As we will see, Littlefield later changed his mind about selling the land, but we do not know why. Perhaps he held out hope that some of the university land might contain oil. Certainly, after the famous Spindletop well was discovered in 1901, many Texans hoped that oil would be discovered on their property.[28]

In a lengthy act in 1913, the legislature gave back to the commissioner of the General Land Office the duty and responsibility of leasing the minerals on the university lands. It is not clear from the board minutes or the legislative record why the legislature did this.[29] By that time, oil had been discovered in many parts of Texas, and some had been discovered on land owned by the Public School Fund. Since that fund was administered by the land office, the commissioner was experienced in dealing with mineral issues. Perhaps the legislature was concerned that if oil were discovered on university lands, the regents would not have the same level of expertise.[30]

Income from the university lands was a constant concern for the board. At its meeting on April 25, 1916, the chairman of the land committee reported that the university had now leased 2,067,106 acres of grazing land and would receive $145,983.06 in annual lease money, the most ever received. At the October meeting, he reported lease income would grow to $182,000, another new high. The board had obviously become more adept at leasing the land, as this was a far cry from the early days when the annual lease income rarely exceeded $20,000. This success made the board members more and more certain that they had made the correct decision when they decided not to sell additional land.[31]

A discussion that involved Littlefield at a board meeting may have played a role in that decision because of an event that had occurred in 1901 when Judge Rogan, an Austin lawyer, represented a client who had been for some time attempting to purchase some of the university land located in Andrews County. When the judge asked the board if they were ready to sell, Mr. Littlefield replied: "I think we should not sell it, it would cut up the property into fragments, the terms are too long, the interest rate too low, and the price too small." The board voted to not sell the land.[32]

In those early days, with the exception of the sale of unconnected lands, most of the money from the lands came from leasing the property to ranchers for grazing rights. The lease rate ranged from four to ten cents per acre per year. Because a large amount of the land was not suitable for grazing, the income remained modest. In 1916 it totaled $205,000.[33]

The land commissioner had begun leasing mineral rights on some of the university land for ten cents per acre per year. The board voted in 1923 to request the commissioner to stop leasing mineral rights to university land. The commissioner replied that the law required him to lease land to any applicant as long as that applicant complied with the law, and that almost all of the land within fifty miles of "the new well in Reagan County" had already been leased. The commissioner must have been talking about the new Santa Rita oil well that had started the boom on university land. For an oil company to be able to lease land where there was a good prospect of finding oil was not a good thing for the university, and with discovery of oil in the region, the price should have been much higher than the ten-cent rate.[34]

With management of the university lands once again under the control of the General Land Office, the speed with which it was leasing the mineral rights and lessees were drilling wells on the lands made it very difficult for the commissioner to maintain sufficient staff to monitor the activities of the oil operators. This staffing problem caused additional friction between the board and the commissioner. In his biannual report to the governor for the years 1924–1926, the commissioner's dismay at the conflict was evident:

> Until oil was found on University land May 28, 1923, it seemed
> the matter was of but little concern to the University authorities,
> but since then, and especially since the royalty amounts to about a
> quarter million dollars a month, they have for some reason become
> so enthusiastically interested that they have even employed lawyers to
> attack the validity of the law, and if successful there will not be authority
> for anyone to collect the royalty. If they would leave the present system
> alone it is believed in ten years the University would have a permanent
> endowment from this source alone of some thirty to fifty million
> dollars. However, I am now in the same attitude that I was during the
> last Regular Session of the Legislature when I informed those speaking
> for the University that I would be glad if they would devise a better
> and more efficient system for handling the subject and take over its

administration; that I would in good faith tender my services in the endeavor to aid in preparing a bill and encourage its enactment because it was much desired by the Land Office that the University authorities would either take over the whole thing and administer it or that they quit meddling with it while its administration is in the Land Office.[35]

This dispute continued to be discussed in the Texas Legislature. Between 1923 and 1937 there were four more legislative sessions that affected this relationship. In 1929, the legislature passed a bill that addressed for the first time the sale of oil and gas leases on university lands. It created the Board for Lease of University Lands to deal with surveying, dividing, and marking of the lands, and it authorized the employment of geologists, mineralogists, and other needed employees. It also set out the duties of the General Land Office and the board of regents.[36] In addition, the bill established that the Board for Lease of University Lands was to be made up of the Commissioner of the General Land Office and two members of the board of regents. It directed that when the lease board had approved the signing of an oil and gas lease, the lease was to be signed by the commissioner, and all royalty payments were to be made to the General Land Office.[37]

The regents believed that further changes were needed regarding the administration of the university lands and that only the legislature could make those changes. It had become obvious that the land office had been given too many duties by the legislature and that profitable management of the university lands was not a high priority for the office. It had always been the highest priority for the regents to correctly manage the university lands and to quickly increase the income because the revenue was necessary for the successful operation of the university. On March 29, 1929, S.B. 82 was passed, and chapter 282 of the act put the board of regents in charge of the university lands.[38] In his book *Land, Oil, and Education*, Berte Haigh notes that:

> Robert L. Holiday, one of the authors of the Act, discussed the
> intention of the Board of Regents Legislative Committee and

supporters in the legislature . . . said it was their intention to remove as much jurisdiction over oil and gas matters in the Permanent University Fund lands from the Land Commissioner and his staff as the Constitution of 1876 would permit. It was also the intent of the Board of Regents and the authors of the act that the University through its members on such board should have the balance of power on the Board of Lease.[39]

In 1931 the legislature again dealt with this issue by amending chapter 87 of the *General Laws of Texas*. This vested to the regents the authority to lease the university lands. In addition, the act gave the regents the authority to hire staff to deal with the management of the lands, and it appropriated money to do the work.[40]

The legislature tried to treat the General Land Office fairly in all of this legislation and said that all lease bids were to go the land office and the commissioner had the responsibility for executing the leases. The Board for Lease also had its duties further outlined: it was to adopt proper forms, regulations, rules, and contracts to protect lease income. Because the Board for Lease had only three members and two were members of the Board of Regents, the legislature had in the end given control of the lands to the regents.[41]

* * * * *

The dispute between the regents and the land commissioner expended a great deal of political capital for both parties over the years. Because of the continued fighting, the legislature felt compelled to keep addressing the issue. In truth, the size and the remote location of the university lands made it difficult for either party to manage them, but in the end, the regents gained control and this enabled them to begin to accumulate wealth in the Permanent University Fund.

NOTES

1. Charles R. Matthews, "The Early Years of the Permanent University Fund" (Ed.D. thesis, University of Texas, Austin, 2006), 42.

2. University of Texas Board of Regents (UTBOR) Minutes, 1883a (May), pp. 34–37. Retrieved December 13, 2004; http://utsystem.edu/board-of-regents/meetings/archive/1881-1949.

3. Ibid.

4. Texas General Laws, p. 85.

5. Berte R. Haigh, *Land, Oil and Education* (El Paso: Texas Western Press, 1986), 72–73.

6. UTBOR Minutes, 1886b (June 12) p. 163. Retrieved December 14, 2004; http://utsystem.edu/board-of-regents/meetings/archive/1881-1949.

7. Commissioner of the General Land Office. *Report to the Governor of Texas for the year ending December 31, 1886* (Austin: Triplett & Hutchings State Printers, 1886).

8. Matthews, "The Early Years of the Permanent University Fund," 47.

9. Matthews, "The Early Years of the Permanent University Fund," T. Roziene to Colonel George W. Brackenridge, March 13, 1887, 48.

10. Matthews, "The Early Years of the Permanent University Fund," 48; John J. Lane, *History of the University of Texas: Based on Facts and Records* (Austin: Henry Hutchings, State Printer, 1891), 82–85.

11. Commissioner of the General Land Office. *Report to the Governor of Texas for the Two Years Ending August, 31, 1888* (Austin: Eugene Von Boeckmann State Printers, 1888).

12. Ibid.

13. S.H.B. 481. Under Chapter 114, entitled Lands—Sale and Lease of School and Other Public Lands, Section 11.

14. UTBOR Minutes, 1894a (June 18), p. 414. Retrieved December 15, 2004; http://utsystem.edu/board-of-regents/meetings/archive/1881-1949.

15. UTBOR Minutes, 1894b, (December, no date), pp. 2–3. Retrieved December 15, 2004; http://utsystem.edu/board-of-regents/meetings/archive/1881-1949.

16. UTBOR Minutes, 1894a (June 18), p. 414. Retrieved December 15, 2004; http://utsystem.edu/board-of-regents/meetings/archive/1881-1949.

17. UTBOR Minutes, 1894a (June 18), p. 414. Retrieved December 15, 2004; http://utsystem.edu/board-of-regents/meetings/archive/1881-1949.

18. UTBOR Minutes, 1895b, (March 26), pp. 29–32. Retrieved December 13, 2004; http://utsystem.edu/board-of-regents/meetings/archive/1881-1949.

19. UTBOR Minutes, 1895c (May 16), pp. 43–44. Retrieved December 15, 2005; http://utsystem.edu/board-of-regents/meetings/archive/1881-1949.

20. Ibid.

21. UTBOR Minutes, 1896a (January 14), pp. 71–72. Retrieved December 15, 2004; http://utsystem.edu/board-of-regents/meetings/archive/1881-1949.

22. Ibid.

23. In the *Biennial Report* Ball's name appears with the initials T. W. and F. W., but no other information about his first name has been located; UTBOR Minutes, 1896a (January 14), pp. 71–72. Retrieved December 15, 2004; http://utsystem.edu/board-of-regents/meetings/archive/1881-1949.

24. UTBOR Minutes, 1896a (January 14), pp. 71–72. Retrieved December 15, 2004; http://utsystem.edu/board-of-regents/meetings/archive/1881-1949.

25. UTBOR Minutes, 1910b (October 22), p.7 7. Retrieved December 17, 2004; http://utsystem.edu/board-of-regents/meetings/archive/1881-1949.

26. UTBOR Minutes, 1911c (October 17), p. 187. Retrieved December 17, 2004; http://utsystem.edu/board-of-regents/meetings/archive/1881-1949.

27. Ibid.

28. Dianna Olien and Roger M. Olien, *Oil in Texas: The Gusher Age 1895–1945* (Austin: University of Texas Press, 2002), 23.

29. Tex. Gen Laws, 1913, p. 409.

30. Matthews, "The Early Years of the Permanent University Fund," 66.

31. UTBOR Minutes, 1916b, p. 13. Retrieved December 17, 2004; http://utsystem.edu/board-of-regents/meetings/archive/1881-1949.

32. UTBOR Minutes, 1916b, p. 13. Retrieved December 17, 2004; http://utsystem.edu/board-of-regents/meetings/archive/1881-1949.

33. UTBOR Minutes, 1917a (June 12), p. 68. Retrieved December 17, 2004; http://utsystem.edu/board-of-regents/meetings/archive/1881-1949.

34. UTBOR Minutes, 1923 (July 10), p. 143. Retrieved December 20, 2004; http://utsystem.edu/board-of-regents/meetings/archive/1881-1949.

35. Haigh, *Land, Oil and Education*, 171.

36. Senate Bill 82.

37. Journal of the Senate, 41st Session, 1929, p. 617.

38. Journal of the Senate, 41st Session, Tex. 1929, p. 617.

39. Haigh, *Land, Oil and Education*, 28.

40. Chapter 87, 42nd Legislative Session, p. 193.

41. Ibid.

BIBLIOGRAPHY

Cook, W. Bruce. *From Wasteland to Wealth: The Incredible Story of the State of Texas Permanent University Fund*. Austin: University of Texas Investment Management Company, 1997.

Haigh, Berte R. *Land, Oil and Education*. El Paso: Texas Western Press, 1986.

Lane, John J. *History of the University of Texas: Based on Facts and Records*. Austin: Henry Hutchings, State Printer, 1891.

Matthews, Charles R. "The Early Years of the Permanent University Fund." Ed.D. thesis, University of Texas, Austin, 2006.

Olien, Dianna, and Roger M. Olien. *Oil in Texas: The Gusher Age 1895–1945*. Austin: University of Texas Press, 2002.

Texas State Historical Association. *The New Handbook of Texas*, Vol. 5. Austin: Texas State Historical Association, 1996.

5

THE FOUNDING OF TEXAS A&M AND THE DISPUTE BETWEEN THE UNIVERSITY BOARD OF REGENTS AND THE TEXAS A&M BOARD OF DIRECTORS

The story of Texas A&M College begins with efforts by the federal government in the 1850s to establish colleges that would be responsible for teaching the industrial arts, a term that in the nineteenth century meant programs that provided training in wood and metal work along with engine repair and maintenance and some level of engineering training. U.S. Senator Justin S. Morrill of Vermont became the driving force in Congress for the idea of land-grant colleges that would focus on agriculture and the mechanical arts. In 1857 he introduced what became known as the Morrill Act, which provided 30,000 acres of federal land times the number of members of a state's congressional delegation. The land was then sold by the state and the proceeds used to fund public colleges that would emphasize agriculture and the mechanical arts. It was a struggle to get the bill passed, but finally in 1862, President Abraham Lincoln signed it into law. Of course, as part of the Confederacy, Texas could not participate until after the Civil War ended in 1865. On November 1, 1866, the Texas Eleventh Legislature approved a joint resolution "to accept the provisions of the Act of Congress of the United States, approved July 2, 1862, entitled an Act to donate public land to the several States and Territories which may provide Colleges for the benefit of Agriculture and the Mechanic Arts."[1]

However, Texas did not contain any federal lands because when the state was admitted to the Union it had been allowed to keep all of its unappropriated land—the only state to be given that right. This presented a problem that was resolved when the federal government granted Texas 180,000 acres of land in Colorado that was then sold for seventy-five cents per acre. Because of these special circumstances, Texas A&M became both a federal and a state land-grant college.[2]

* * * * *

On April 17, 1871, the Texas legislature approved a bill providing for the organization of the Texas Agricultural and Mechanical College (Texas A&M) and appropriated $75,000 for the construction of academic buildings and suitable accommodations. Governor Edmund J. Davis appointed a committee of three to find a suitable location for the college on a site of not less than 1,280 acres. That committee selected a site near Bryan after the citizens of the city donated 2,416 acres of land for the college.[3]

The state Constitution of 1876 specified that the college was to be a branch of the University of Texas, which was not yet in operation. The new college opened on October 4, 1876, with 106 students and a faculty of 6, making Texas A&M College the first public college established in Texas.[4]

One of the most interesting aspects of the next forty-five years in Texas was the long-lived dispute between the regents of the University of Texas and the directors of Texas A&M College. There were a number of reasons for this conflict. Texas A&M, which opened before the University of Texas, had a primary mission to support agricultural and mechanical education. Because the early Texas economy was based on agriculture, it is easy to understand how the small farming communities that made up most of early Texas had a natural affinity for Texas A&M. This affinity was reflected in the various governors who served during the years of the dispute. Time and time again, Texas governors from Colquitt to Hogg intervened on behalf of Texas A&M College in its dispute with the University of Texas regents.[5]

The original mission of the University of Texas was to be a more traditional institution of higher education based on the model set down by Thomas Jefferson at the University of Virginia. When ordinary Texans heard some of their early political leaders talk about modeling a Texas university after one in Virginia, there was undoubtedly some skepticism about establishing an institution seemingly disconnected from the important business of agriculture. The constitution of 1876 had made Texas A&M College a branch of the University of Texas, and being part of and subordinate under the law must have been very difficult for the Texas A&M directors.[6]

As discussed in chapter 4, the legislature had set up the land assets that were part of the Permanent University Fund (PUF) as the primary funding source for higher education. But, while the fund was rich in land, it was poor in revenue. The primary source of income from the lands was the lease of grazing land; this income was very modest and could not support two institutions. At the beginning of this period, the directors of Texas A&M College realized how poor was the prospect for revenue from the PUF, so they requested the regents give them $500 annually from the PUF, and said they would request additional funds from the legislature for operating expenses. Thus the essential message sent by the A&M directors to the University of Texas regents was: when it comes to funding, let each of us go our own way. In the first years, it was clear the directors had made a wise decision because of the political makeup of early Texas and the strong support they had in the legislature, and it was in the best interests of both institutions.[7]

When oil was discovered on the university lands and income to the PUF increased rapidly, the A&M directors realized they needed to be receiving a larger share. The directors also believed that they needed to have a say in how the PUF was managed. As the fund began its rapid growth in income and assets, the directors grew increasingly agitated. However, they found themselves in a weak negotiating position for several reasons. First, the state constitution clearly stated that Texas A&M College was a branch of the University of Texas. Second, the University of Texas regents controlled the management of the PUF. These two issues made negotiating an equitable financial arrangement difficult and added immeasurably to the time it took to resolve these issues. This conflict eventually played itself out during the meetings of both institutions' leaders and can be followed in the minutes of those meetings.[8]

The first move was made by the A&M directors during their March 8, 1887, meeting when they adopted a resolution appointing a committee to meet with the University of Texas regents to discuss the proper share of money to be given to Texas A&M College from the fund. This appears to be the earliest discussion by the directors about their fair share of the PUF, and it was a discussion that went on for decades.[9]

Also during this meeting, the directors discussed the fact that they had a member of the legislature who would introduce a bill to allow Texas A&M to receive 25 percent of the Available University Fund. This had come about because in January 1887 the directors had received word from the regents that the revenue coming from the PUF was needed to maintain the university and at that time there was insufficient revenue to also provide for the college; the regents thus encouraged the directors to ask the legislature for separate funding. The legislation, however, did not pass.[10]

Later in March 1887, a committee of directors met with a committee of regents to discuss points of controversy between the two schools. The committee came to an agreement that called for 20 percent of all income from the Available University Fund to be paid to Texas A&M and for the board of regents to remain in control of the management of the PUF. But the regents on the committee reminded the directors that their votes were not binding and approval of the agreement would require the support of a majority of the full board of regents. When a vote was taken, the board did not approve the agreement.[11]

There was little doubt on the part of either institution that there was insufficient revenue from the PUF to support both schools. In 1890 the regents announced that the land office had leased 167,040 acres of land for three cents per acre per year; the income from that transaction would be $4,011.20, certainly not enough money for the maintenance of two colleges.[12]

There is evidence in the minutes of both boards that in spite of their differences, they did look for ways to cooperate in dealing with the legislature. The regents asked the directors to come to Austin to discuss efforts to get the legislature to approve a bill giving one half of the remaining land in the public domain to the Permanent University Fund. This meeting occurred on June 19, 1893, and involved several members from each board. The bill they discussed would have given the University of Texas (and its branches) and the public schools each one-half of the remaining public vacant and unappropriated land. At the time of this proposal there were about six million acres of land that had not been appropriated. This legislation also did not pass.[13]

Later, as evidenced by the following letter, the directors of Texas A&M College were anxious to again meet with the regents to discuss the issues between the two bodies:

> Dear Sirs,
>
> The Board of Directors of the A&M College at their recent meeting (this month) passed a motion unanimously inviting the Board of Regents of the University to meet with us at the A&M College, on the 29th and 30th. Please so notify your Board.
>
> Judge Beauregard Bryan, of your body will explain why this meeting is desired. We trust you will find it both convenient and desirable to be with us. We promise to do all we can to make the meeting mutually pleasant and profitable.

> We offer a cordial welcome, an airy office for business, cool well
> ventilated rooms in which to sleep, and plenty to eat, etcetera, all
> which will be free, though not as hot as the summer sun.
> We hope you will come.[14]

A joint meeting of the regents and the directors was held in College
Station on June 30 and July 1, 1896. The first item of business was to
form a Joint Committee on the Revision of Curricula. This committee
was to study the advisability of revising the curriculum of the university and its branches in an effort to cut costs. The committee was to
report back to the two boards by January 1, 1897. While this effort
did not bear fruit, it shows the beginnings of working together for
the best interests of higher education in general and the institutions
in particular.[15]

A review of the minutes of both boards reveals that discussion
of PUF issues was mostly dormant in the early twentieth century.
However, in a 1911 meeting of the Texas A&M directors, a question of a constitutional amendment to separate the College from the
University was again discussed. The Democratic state convention
had passed a resolution calling for the separation of the two institutions. In addition, Governor O. B. Colquitt in his address to the
Thirty-second Legislature had also called for such a separation. As a
result of these discussions, a resolution was passed by the legislature that laid out in great detail how each of the two institutions was
to receive 50 percent of the Permanent University Fund. Later, at a
joint meeting of the two boards an A&M director made a motion to
support the bill that was adopted. The meeting adjourned until later
in the evening, and when it reconvened, Director Summers speaking
on behalf of the A&M board said:

> The report that I have been instructed to make to the Joint meeting
> is that the Board of Directors are willing to yield as to a donation
> of one half of the land of the Permanent University Fund, but the
> Board of Directors wants it understood in the connection, that
> its understanding of Agreement No. 2 of the joint meeting of the

former Board of Regents and the former Board of Directors, which
is as follows: A special tax rate to raise sufficient revenues for the
maintenance and the building and equipment needs of the A&M
College, in lieu of any interest of the College in the University
permanent fund.[16]

The directors wanted the support of the regents to get a tax
passed in support of Texas A&M. The regents countered with a new
proposal that would transfer land notes and other securities in an
amount that would generate annual revenues of $2,600 to be paid to
the College.[17]

On the second day of the joint meeting, Summers, again speaking on behalf of his board, said that A&M would compromise and
give up their request for half of the land from the PUF in return
for the support of the regents for taking a bill to the legislature
asking for a statewide tax to provide income for both schools that
would be called the Higher Education Fund. Continued discussion
brought up yet another proposal, one for a constitutional amendment that would allow the University to transfer land notes or other
securities that would yield an annual income of $8,000 and would
formally separate the two institutions. All of these efforts of the
joint meeting failed to gain sufficient legislative support, so no bill
was passed.[18]

The ongoing dispute caused Governor Colquitt to intervene.
He prepared a resolution stating what he believed to be the fair-
est resolution of the differences. A copy of his resolution with a
cover letter was sent to both boards and resulted in this letter from
the A&M directors which contains a summary of the governor's
resolution:

> We endorse the resolution prepared by Governor Colquitt, subject to
> the following amendments and pledge ourselves to support it in all
> proper ways:
> Eliminate the fifty thousand dollars in bonds transferred from
> the University to the Agricultural and Mechanical College, leaving

them in the possession of the University. Transfer the asylum lands and proceeds there-from the estimated amount of five hundred and ninety thousand dollars ($590,000) from the Agricultural and Mechanical College to the University.

Transfer from the University to the Agricultural and Mechanical College four hundred thousand acres of the University lands of average value to be determined and selected by a commission composed of one representative from the University, one representative from the Agricultural and Mechanical College, to be chosen by their respective boards, and one member chosen by the Governor of the State; or transfer from the University to the Agricultural and Mechanical College the equivalent in securities the four hundred thousand acres of land, at the option of the Agricultural and Mechanical College.

This agreement is made in final satisfaction of any claims of the Agricultural and Mechanical College to any part of the permanent fund of the University to any part of the appropriations made by the Federal government on behalf of agricultural and mechanical arts.

This agreement is reached after a careful estimate of the total endowment and the permanent income of each institution capitalized at an estimated valuation agreed to, and acceptable to both institutions. The total capitalization is thus divided in the ration of approximately sixty-seven for the University and thirty-three for the Agricultural and Mechanical College.[19]

Once again nothing came of the proposal, and it provides evidence of the increasing frustration on the part of the A&M directors; regardless of their proposals and best efforts, nothing changed. On the other hand, it is obvious that the regents did not want to split up the Permanent University Fund. As long as the Texas Constitution of 1876, which made Texas A&M a branch of the University of Texas, was not amended, the regents knew they did not have to compromise. From 1914 until 1915, four more proposals were offered by one side or the other without any resolution. Despite the disagreement and frustration, it is interesting to note that both boards were extremely polite to each other in public statements. In response to the last proposal by the directors on November 24, 1913, the regents passed a resolution telling the directors how they appreciated their suggestions and would be glad to meet at some future date to discuss all matters. Yet no date was set and the issue continued to fester.[20]

On December 27, 1918, Governor W. P. Hobby called a joint meeting of the Texas A&M Board of Directors and the University of Texas Board of Regents. At the opening of the meeting, the governor said he was interested in getting advice from both boards on legislation that would affect the two institutions. He said that in his mind the great question was the university lands, and he wanted them to become a more liquid asset for the benefit of both schools. After some discussion, it was decided to appoint a committee made up of three members from each board to properly format the issues and conduct a future meeting with the governor to propose legislation.[21]

A subsequent joint meeting of both boards was held on January 29, 1919. Out of that meeting came a resolution asking the Texas Legislature to consider taking over the lands in the Permanent University Fund for the sum of $10 million, with the money to be divided two-thirds to the University of Texas and one-third to Texas A&M College. The cash would come from a sale of bonds by the state and be put into the PUF to be invested in the same manner as the Permanent School Fund. It was also suggested that both colleges be allowed to sell bonds and use the income from the permanent fund as security on those bonds. The proceeds from the bond sales were to be used only for permanent improvements at the two institutions.[22]

In addition, the joint committee suggested that the state sell the lands but retain the mineral rights. It was suggested that if the sale of the lands or the mineral deposits that might be discovered on the lands brought more than $10 million, that money would go to the institutions. The joint committee suggested a fixed property tax for the purpose of supporting institutions of higher education.

The committee also suggested that the two institutions be separated by constitutional amendment. Once again, nothing came from this initiative.[23]

Five years later on November 26, 1924, the Texas A&M board met in Austin and the president of the college read a resolution on the advisability of separating the two institutions. The directors also agreed that the disposition of the university lands should be two-thirds to the University and one-third to the College. Later that same day both boards joined in a meeting where they discussed the issues. The University of Texas regents introduced their new president to the A&M directors, and after a polite exchange the new president said he needed time to study the issues, which were new to him. Both groups agreed they would get together again for further discussions at a later date.[24]

This meeting demonstrated once again that the board of regents was made up of skilled negotiators. In spite of the fact that these two boards had been discussing these issues for over forty years, the regents were able, without much apparent effort, to convince the A&M directors to once again give them more time to evaluate the issues, proving the old adage that "the one with the gold always wins." The university regents controlled the PUF with its ever-increasing oil revenues, and the A&M directors had little leverage in these negotiations.

After another six years of discussion between the two boards there was another joint meeting of representatives of both boards, and this group came to an agreement about a settlement to be presented to each board. The details of the agreement were discussed during the Texas A&M directors meeting on March 8, 1930; but, a few days later, word reached the directors that the full board of regents had already rejected the settlement their representatives had favored.[25]

The issues surrounding the management of the Permanent University Fund were finally resolved in 1937. In that year, President F.M. Law of the A&M board of directors approached his cousin Jubal R. Parten, a regent of the University of Texas, about sharing in the management of the oil lands. Parten in an interview conducted in 1981 told the following story:

> I thought about it early one morning, and it flashed on me what to do—if I could get the consent of my colleagues and other Board members—just forthrightly go to my friend Law and say "We doubt very seriously if we can make sense of two boards being charged with the responsibility for that. We think it would be logical and fairly feasible if we simply combine these two boards; then we will have overall responsibility. . . . Combine A&M and the University of Texas . . . I sold Benedict [president of the university] and the board on it. Then I went down to see him [Law]. Well, he said that does make sense; or something like that. You couldn't argue with it. And that was the end of it. As expected. . . . Because I know that they thought they'd be meeting all the time in Austin."[26]

At that point the A&M directors agreed to continue having their own board and splitting the Permanent University Fund two-thirds to the University and one-third to A&M.[27]

The interview with Parten describes his version of the final settlement of the dispute between the two institutions. By this time, the regents thought they knew the A&M directors pretty well. They believed the directors would not surrender their college to the administrative control of the University of Texas regents. Parten used that knowledge to negotiate a better deal for the University of Texas. It is impossible to estimate the time and talent that was expended by both sides in this very long debate. Clearly, the regents always had the upper hand in the negotiations, primarily because the state constitution made A&M College a branch of the University.[28] In the end, the regents remained in control of the university land and funds, and have ever since distributed the money in the agreed upon manner. To date the constitution has never been amended to split the two institutions.[29]

★ ★ ★ ★

The formation of the Texas university system and the role of the state's vast land holdings in fueling that system are only a piece of the story of higher education in Texas—critical yes, but still only a piece. Certain groups in Texas had a vested interest in better-educated citizens and would step in to fill, first, the dearth of schools, and then later gaps in schools for certain types of education as well as for certain groups of citizens. Even then some citizens because of their race were not able to or were not allowed to attend any schools of higher education, much less the state's two big universities. As important as the two big universities are, there are other equally important parts of the system—smaller universities and colleges, normal schools, private colleges, and community colleges. Two important entities that would work hard to establish other schools were religious groups and those supporting teacher training. Across all these types of higher education institutions three groups of citizens—women, African Americans, and Hispanics—would experience serious roadblocks in their path to obtaining a college education. The remainder of the book will look at some of the groups that founded schools and some of the groups that wanted to attend schools.

NOTES

1. Henry C. Dethloff, *Texas A&M University, 1876–1976* (College Station: Texas A&M University Press, 1975), 15; The Library of Congress, Web Guides, Primary Documents in American History, Morrill Act, https://www.loc.gov/rr/program/bib/ourdocs/Morrill.html (Accessed December 1, 2015).

2. Randolph B. Campbell, *Gone to Texas: A History of the Lone Star State*, 2nd ed. (New York: Oxford University Press, 2012), 280.

3. Dethloff, *Texas A&M University, 1876–1976*, 14–15.

4. Dethloff, *Texas A&M University, 1876–1976*, 15.

5. Charles R. Matthews, "The Early Years of the Permanent University Fund" (Ed.D. thesis, University of Texas, Austin, 2006), 79–80.

6. Journal of the Senate, 7th Session, 1857, p. 780.

7. Berte R. Haigh, *Land, Oil and Education* (El Paso: Texas Western Press, 1986), 46.

8. Matthews, "The Early Years of the Permanent University Fund," 76.

9. Board of Directors of Texas A&M College Minutes, 1879.

10. Board of Directors of Texas A&M College Minutes, 1879.

11. Board of Directors of Texas A&M College Minutes, (1880c, June 8), 27–29.

12. University of Texas Board of Regents Minutes, (1890), 258. Retrieved December 14, 2004, from http://www.utsystem.edu/bor/.

13. Board of Directors of Texas A&M College Minutes, (1883, January 18), 140.

14. Board of Directors of Texas A&M College Minutes, June 16, 1896.

15. Board of Directors of Texas A&M College Minutes, (1896a, June 30), 181–82; (July 1, 1896b), 104–105.

16. Board of Directors and University of Texas Joint Meeting Minutes, 1911, 242–46; Board of Directors of Texas A&M College Minutes, (1911a), 98–108; (1911a), 235–41; (1911a, April 6), 88–108; (1911b).

17. Board of Directors and University of Texas Joint Meeting Minutes, (1911), 242–46.

18. Board of Directors and University of Texas Joint Meeting Minutes, (1911), 242–46; University of Texas Board of Regents Minutes, (1911), 161; Matthews, "The Early Years of the Permanent University Fund," 83.

19. Board of Directors of Texas A&M College Minutes, 1913a, 51–59; Matthews, "The Early Years of the Permanent University Fund," 83–84.

20. University of Texas Board of Regents Minutes, (1913), 338–39.

21. Matthews, "The Early Years of the Permanent University Fund," 90–91.

22. University of Texas Board of Regents Minutes, (1919a, June 29), 283.

23. University of Texas Board of Regents Minutes, (1919a, June 29), 283.

24. Board of Directors of Texas A&M College Minutes, (1924, Nov. 26), 26–27.

25. Board of Directors of Texas A&M College Minutes, (1930b, March 8), 138–41; Board of Directors of Texas A&M College Minutes, (1930c, May 30), 150.

26. David F. Prindle, "Oil and the Permanent University Fund: The Early Years," *Southwestern Historical Quarterly* 86, no. 2 (October 1982): 295.

27. Board of Directors of Texas A&M College Minutes, (1937, April 1), 82.

28. Matthews, "The Early Years of the Permanent University Fund," 98.

29. Ibid.

BIBLIOGRAPHY

Campbell, Randolph B. *Gone to Texas: A History of the Lone Star State.* 2nd ed. New York: Oxford University Press, 2010.

Clark, Edward. "The Permanent University Fund: A Foundation for Greatness." Unpublished manuscript, LBJ Library, Austin, 1976.

Dethloff, Henry C. *Texas A&M University, 1876–1976.* College Station, TX: Texas A&M University Press, 1975.

Ferguson, Walter Keene. *Geology and Politics in Frontier Texas: 1845–1909.* Austin: University of Texas Press, 1967.

Haigh, Berte R. *Land, Oil and Education.* El Paso: Texas Western Press, 1986.

Matthews, Charles R. "The Early Years of the Permanent University Fund from 1836 to 1937." Ed.D. thesis, University of Texas, Austin, 2006.

Prindle, David F. "Oil and the Permanent University Fund: The Early Years." *Southwestern Historical Quarterly* 86, no. 2 (October 1982): 277–98.

Richardson, Susan R. "Oil, Power and Universities: Political Struggle and Academic Advancement at the University of Texas and Texas A&M, 1876–1965." PhD diss., Pennsylvania State University, State College, PA, 2005.

PART II:
GROWTH AND EXPANSION

★ 6 ★

RELIGIOUS COLLEGES IN TEXAS

Religion played a critical role in the early development of institutions of higher education in Texas. Chapter 2 looked at how the Congress of the Republic was motivated by President Lamar's December 1838 speech and in 1839 passed a bill setting aside land to provide support for schools at all levels. Yet, it was not until 1876 that Texas A&M College opened and the state government was actually operating a college. Demand for higher education existed in early Texas, but elected officials, in spite of their vocal support, were slow to move. It was religious colleges that filled the thirty-eight-year void.

★ ★ ★ ★ ★

The first colleges in Texas were almost all organized by churches belonging to many different Christian denominations. Reading about these many institutions suggests that among their founders was a clear sense of purpose as well as an understanding of the need for higher education in the state. These early colleges were supported by donations, mostly cash, from church members, at a time when money in Texas was scarce; this generosity was a critical element in the schools' establishment.

These institutions were known by many names—university, college, academy, institute, seminary, collegiate institute—but these terms were, for the most part, too generous in describing the quality of education offered. It could be said, however, that the names reflected institutional aspirations. When most of them were organized in the early 1800s, there were no established statewide educational standards; and, regardless of name, all of the institutions had to operate within both available finances and the supply of qualified instructors. Many of these schools in the early days did not even possess a library or a laboratory, and the level of education offered was rudimentary.[1]

These schools received the authority to organize and operate first from the republic and later from the State of Texas in the form of public charters to issue degrees. These charters were given alike to academies, universities, institutes, and even high schools. In almost all of the schools that existed prior to the Civil War, the instruction constituted primary education, and there was little in the way of secondary schools. Thus students came to college without the basic skills, which had to be taught before they could do more advanced work. Because of this, few of these colleges provided real college training. Many Texans who had somehow acquired the basic skills wanted more advanced training and they left the state to obtain it elsewhere, for the most part attending colleges in the East. None of this slowed the efforts of small communities and churches—which were very proud of their local institutions—to continue supporting and growing their schools, even though very few of their graduates would be able to pass the sixth grade in today's schools.[2]

Especially active among the denominations founding early colleges were the Methodists, Baptists, Presbyterians, and Catholics, all of whom provided education for white students. The Methodists laid out their policies regarding education in a General Convention held in 1840, where the bishops of the church made a plea for the maintenance of Methodist institutions and pointed out the need for Christian education. The Methodist Church had as part of its general principles accepted by members that it was the duty of the church to educate and enlighten the human mind, encourage sound learning, and establish a reasonable number of educational institutions. Critical to include in the teaching was an understanding of Christianity to support the belief that a well-rounded education was necessary for the clergy and that the knowledge they gained would help them develop God-fearing citizens.[3]

Baptists, led in part by Robert E. B. Baylor, organized the Texas Baptist Educational Society in 1841 within the Texas Union Baptist Association for the purposes of starting a school for the training of young men who were studying to be ministers and bringing together the entire Baptist community behind one school in Texas.[4]

Presbyterians also had an early interest in Christian education and, while they had an interest in women's education, their main focus was on providing educational opportunities for a learned clergy. The founders described the overall objectives of their first college as social, moral, spiritual, and intellectual. The social aim was to increase the refinements and culture of society as a whole. The moral and religious values spoke to the spiritual teachings of the church, and the intellectual aim was to attain the highest mental culture possible.[5]

Ultimately, there were more than 107 of these early colleges and 39 of them are still in business today. We will look closely at two of the first to be established, as they are broadly representative of the group as a whole. Following that is a brief review of the rest of the institutions, grouped by religious affiliation.

* * * * *

To Rutersville College in LaGrange belongs the distinction of being both the first college and the first of the denominational colleges in Texas. In 1837, Dr. Martin Ruter, who at the time was president of Berea College in Kentucky, came to Texas to attend a Methodist General Conference. As he traveled around the state, he concluded there was a need for a denominational school. Soon thereafter he contracted a fever and died, but both his presence and his ideas had such an impact on his fellow Methodists that they decided to follow through on his ideas and open a college, called Rutersville College in his honor.[6]

The college was granted a charter by the first Congress of the Republic of Texas on February 5, 1840. The charter called for the school to have both a male and female department, and in it the congress granted the college four leagues of land and stated that it was established for the "promotion of the arts, literature, and science in general and for no other purpose whatever." This charter is of a curious nature but one that reflected the ideas of the time, particularly evident in the concern of elected officials that a denominational or religious college could grow too wealthy for the good of the state. The congress had passed a law the preceding year calling for the establishment of two "first class" public colleges and perhaps congress was worried about the potential competition from a religious college. The charter only granted a right for the new college to operate for a period of ten years and stated that total value of the college could not exceed $25,000.[7]

Rutersville College began operation in January 1841 with sixty students. The Rev. Chauncey Richardson and his wife opened the male and female departments at the same time. By the end of its first year the college had 100 students, and by 1850 the college could claim an enrollment of 800 students who attended at least part-time during the year. After several more years the enrollment begin to decline and the college was merged with the Texas Monument and Military Institute located in nearby Bastrop. The failure of the college in 1856 came about primarily because of disputes about the control of the institution between local authorities and the denominational authority of the church.[8]

The University of San Augustine was the second institution to receive a charter and several leagues of land from the Congress of the Republic of Texas. The town of San Augustine was well located in southeastern Texas not far from the Louisiana border. Under the republic it became the county seat and an important town as its population increased. Calling itself the "Athens of Texas," it wanted to be known both as a commercial town and for its learning.[9]

To get started, the college traded a league of the land it received from the republic for a two-story frame building in town and on September 5, 1842, it was opened by the Reverend Marcus A. Montrose. The college had decided not to charge tuition, so in an effort to control costs, Montrose used a form of mutual instruction. He would teach a group of students and then they were required to teach what they had learned to another group of students. The organizational structure comprised a grammar school for children under twelve, a female department, and then the college itself. A very aggressive advertising campaign and a reputation for good instruction made the college a quick success. Laboratory work in science was required, and it was the first institution in the republic to install a chemical laboratory and organize a mineralogical cabinet. Among the other subjects taught at San Augustine were Latin, Greek, history, astronomy, navigation, rhetoric, logic, mathematics, political economy, natural philosophy, chemistry, botany, and geology. That there was only one professor at the institution made this an even more ambitious curriculum.[10]

In 1845 in a dispute with the university's board of directors, Montrose was removed from office and succeeded by James Russell, who was a graduate of the University of Edinburgh and a Scottish Presbyterian. The school had not been organized originally as a denominational college although it had been mostly under the influence of members of the Presbyterian faith. Later, a dispute broke out in the town of San Augustine between Methodists and Presbyterians over which of them should control the college. The dispute caused the Methodists of the community to organize a new institution: Wesleyan College. The rivalry between the two schools over time became quite heated and one day the president of the University of San Augustine was assassinated and the murder was attributed to the dispute. For a while, both colleges prospered, but the dispute continued and eventually led to the schools' demise in 1847. In an effort to save both colleges, supporters of higher education in the community attempted to consolidate the two into a single entity called the University of Eastern Texas, for which a new charter was granted in 1848, but the attempt was unsuccessful and that school soon closed and was superseded by San Augustine Masonic Institute. The various disputes demonstrated how difficult it often was to maintain cooperation between two different religious denominations in matters of higher education.[11]

It should be noted that Baylor University in Waco is the first college in Texas to have obtained a charter that still exists today. As noted above, it was first established in 1845 in the town of Independence under the leadership of R. E. B. Baylor and several others as a school for training young men to be ministers. The university is discussed in more detail later in this chapter.

Beginning in the 1880s, the various Christian denominations throughout the state began to build colleges at a prolific pace. All of them understood how important it was to have a well-educated clergy to staff their churches, men who had a good grasp of theology and an excellent knowledge of the Bible. These pastors were leaders who played an important role in most rural communities. They were the ones who oversaw the schools that taught their members reading, arithmetic, and perhaps some Latin, and most were the first schoolteachers in their communities. The widely felt need in Texas for colleges to provide education for the clergy meant that was one of the first goals of these early colleges, yet it was not long before curriculums expanded to provide educational opportunities for other Texans. It was from these denominational colleges that the first efforts to teach medicine and law were made.[12]

These first institutions of higher education were established by a large number of religious organizations. The work and financial contributions of many of their members played an important role in providing higher education to Texans, and in many cases members still do today. Their donations, no doubt encouraged by their ministers, supported over 100 institutions, paying for facilities, faculty, and administrative costs along with providing scholarships for deserving students. This record of support of higher education by Texans in the earliest years of the republic and the young state gives an indication of how strong that support was from the beginning.

★ ★ ★ ★ ★

The following provides brief examinations of all these institutions, organized according to the denominations that established them.

AFRICAN METHODIST EPISCOPAL (AME) CHURCH

Paul Quinn College was founded in 1872 by a group of AME pastors "to educate freed slaves and their offspring." It was first located in Austin, but in 1877 it moved to Waco and was renamed Waco College. The school expanded its physical plant and course offerings and in May 1881 it received a charter from the state and changed its name to Paul Quinn College. By the mid-1980s, the college was having difficulty competing for enrollment with the larger colleges and it moved again in 1990, this time to Dallas when there was an opportunity to use the closed campus of Bishop College.[13]

ASSEMBLY OF GOD CHURCH

Southwestern Assemblies of God University is a coeducational, liberal arts institution owned and operated by seven districts of the church, including the three Texas districts. The school developed from the merger of three previously independent church-related institutions, and later moved to Houston. By 1941, these three schools, which had functioned not as a true college but as private elementary and high schools, had moved to Fort Worth, where they were unified under the name Southwestern Bible Institute. In 1943 the school was moved to Waxahachie, its present home.[14]

During the 1944–1945 school year, a junior college was added. In 1946 the college began preparations to become a four-year institution. In 1954 the Institute was designated a regional Assemblies of God school, brought under the ownership and control of the seven districts of the church, and renamed Southwestern Assemblies of God University. By 1963 the institution had stopped offering elementary and high school education and began to emphasize the junior college, which offered courses in ministerial and missionary education. Courses in these fields were later offered in the Southwestern College of the Bible. In 1968 the junior college was renamed the Southwestern Junior College of the Assemblies of God. Then in 1987 the two divisions were united under the name, Southwestern Assemblies of God College, which began offering four years of postsecondary education leading to a bachelor's degree. In 1994 the board of regents changed the name back to Southwestern Assemblies of God University.[15]

BAPTIST CHURCH

Baylor University was established in 1845 by the Union Baptist Association of Travis County, which had created the Texas Baptist Educational Society in 1841 in order to establish a Baptist university in Texas. The ninth Congress of the Republic of Texas granted a charter for a Baptist university on February 1, 1845, and Baylor opened in Independence in 1846. In 1886, the Baptist General Association of Texas and the Baptist State Convention, under whose control Baylor University had been operating since 1848, merged and as a result, Baylor University and Waco University were combined under the name of Baylor University. The university moved its campus to Waco in 1887.[16]

The 1845 charter for Baylor University called for a female department, which became Baylor Female College at Independence, the oldest college for women west of the Mississippi River. For its first twenty years the female department provided only college preparatory work, but as the desire grew in Texas for more educational opportunities for females, Baylor began to offer full college courses in the department. In 1886, Baylor Female College moved to Belton, and in 1934, Baylor Female College became Mary Hardin-Baylor College, deriving its name from Mary Hardin, a benefactor of the college.[17]

Bishop College was founded in 1881 under the temporary name South-Western Baptist College as a school for black Baptists in Marshall, where there was a small startup college—Centennial College—that within the year became part of Bishop College. In 1925, the Texas State Board of Education gave the college senior status, which meant at the time that they could grant four-year degrees. In the early years, the college had financial difficulties, but despite setbacks, in later years its religious program drew the attention of prominent religious leaders such as Martin Luther King Jr. and Jesse Jackson. In 1957, the college received multiple donations to help it move to Dallas, and the new college campus opened in 1961. However, in 1988, the school closed and sold its buildings to Paul Quinn College.[18]

Burleson College opened in Greenville in 1895 with S. J. Anderson as its first president. The college became a junior college in 1899 and closed in 1930.[19]

Butler College was founded in 1905 in Tyler as Texas Baptist Academy, a coeducational junior college for blacks. In 1931, the college began receiving support from the Texas Baptist Convention. After World War II, the college slowly expanded its course offerings, and in 1951 became a senior college with the ability to grant four-year degrees; but, because it was unable to become accredited, the college began to lose enrollment, and in 1972 it closed.[20]

Centennial College was founded in Marshall in 1881. It began as an elementary school for blacks, and was the predecessor of Bishop College.[21]

Central Texas College was founded by black Baptists in 1902 in Waco. The school began by offering instruction from first grade through college, and in 1907 it became a full-time college. It remained small with a mainly part-time faculty. In 1931, financial difficulties caused it to close.[22]

Dallas Baptist University is the modern iteration of Decatur Baptist College, which began life as Northwest Texas Baptist College. Northwest Texas Baptist College was founded as a junior college in 1891 in Decatur, which was chosen specifically for its central location and healthful climate. Financial problems led to the school's closure and the auction of its property in 1896. In 1897 the college was purchased by the Baptist General Convention of Texas and the name changed to Decatur Baptist College. In 1965 the school moved to its current location in Dallas and became Dallas Baptist College. In 1968 it became a four-year institution and in 1985 it began offering graduate degrees in education, religion, and business administration, and changed its name to Dallas Baptist University.[23]

East Texas Baptist University was founded in Marshall in 1859 as the College of Marshall. The school opened in 1917 as a two-year junior college and academy. In 1944 it became East Texas Baptist College. Of the six academies and colleges in Marshall, it was the leading higher education institution in 1859. In 1917 the trustees changed the school's name to East Texas Baptist University.[24]

Hardin-Simmons University began life as the Abilene Baptist College in 1891 when it was founded by the Sweetwater Baptist Association. Its name was changed to Simmons College in 1925 in honor of a donor, and in 1934 to Hardin-Simmons University, again for the same reason. The Baptist General Convention assumed control of the university in 1941.[25]

Houston Baptist University was organized by the Baptist General Convention of Texas when it opened its doors in 1963 as Houston Baptist College. It grew rapidly, and after adding graduate courses the name was changed to Houston Baptist University in 1973.[26]

Howard Payne University was founded in Brownwood in 1899 by Dr. John D. Robnett and the Pecos Valley Baptist Association. The college motto was "Economy, more and more for less and less: patriotism in the heart of Texas and in the hearts of Texans; democracy, the college where everyone is somebody." Daniel Baker College merged with the university before 1950.[27]

Jacksonville Baptist College began as a college with an enrollment of eighty-two students in 1899. From 1919 to 1930, the institution operated as a junior college. Since 1939 the college has been a senior college.[28]

Mary Nash College was begun by Jesse G. and Mary Louise Nash with the sponsorship of the Baptist Church. The college started in Sherman in 1877. Known as Sherman Female Institute, it was well known for its music program. The school closed in 1901 and the property was sold to Kidd-Key College.[29]

Sabine Baptist College was founded in Milam in 1858 with the aid of the Central Baptist Association. The college closed during the Civil War but reopened in 1868 with the help of the Bethlehem, Mount Zion, New Hope, and Sabine Baptist Associations. The school closed in 1870 because of financial difficulties.[30]

Simmons College was the successor to Abilene Baptist College in 1891. It was named after James S. Simmons. The school later became Hardin-Simmons College.[31]

South Texas Baptist College was started in Waller in 1898 by the South Texas Educational Conference. The college was intended to provide Baptist education to local residents after Baylor moved to Waco. In 1900, the Galveston hurricane damaged the school's one building, which prompted the school to close.[32]

Texas Baptist College was established by the Baptist Missionary Association of Texas in 1904. The school was located in Dallas and offered a bachelor's degree in addition to a college preparatory course. Financial difficulties caused the school to close in 1912.[33]

The *University of Corpus Christi* was organized because the Baptist Church in South Texas was dissatisfied with the lack of colleges in its region after the relocation of Baylor to Waco in 1882 and Baylor Female College to Belton in 1886. The City of Corpus Christi invited the General Baptist Convention of Texas to locate the Arts and Technology College in Corpus Christi in 1947. The school became part of the Texas A&M University System in 1973.[34]

The *University of Mary Hardin-Baylor* was formerly Baylor Female College in Independence. It moved to Belton in 1886. In 1971 it became coeducational. In never merged with another institution and is still operating under its original charter received from the Republic of Texas in 1845.[35]

Waco University, originally called Trinity River High School, was founded in 1856 by the Trinity River Baptist Association. The Waco Baptist Association changed the school's name to Waco Classical

School in 1860 when it purchased the property. Its growth was slowed by the Civil War. In 1866, it began to admit women. The university was transferred to the Baptist General Association in 1881 and merged with Baylor University in 1886.[36]

Wayland Baptist College began in 1908 in Plainview as Wayland Technological and Literary Institute. The name was changed in honor of J. H. Wayland to Wayland Baptist College in 1910.[37]

CATHOLIC CHURCH

Dominican College was founded in Houston by the Catholic Congregation of the Sacred Heart in 1945 as an extension of its religious training program. It was originally built as a junior college, and became a senior college in 1948. Despite having an international reputation for excellence, especially in nursing, the college closed in 1975.[38]

Our Lady of the Lake University was established by the Sisters of Divine Providence in Castroville in 1868. The college moved to San Antonio in 1896. From 1912 until 1919, it operated as a junior college, and in 1919 it became a senior college.[39]

Our Lady of Victory College was opened in Fort Worth in 1910, and chartered by the state and authorized to confer degrees in 1911. The college was dedicated to training young women who had already completed high school. It was the predecessor of the University of Dallas.[40]

St. Basil's College was founded in 1899 by the Basilian Fathers in Waco. The main purpose of the school was college preparation, to which were added business courses, Romance languages, and a few music courses. By 1915, enrollment had declined and the institution was taken over by the Sisters of Namur, but it soon closed.[41]

St. Edward's University was founded outside of Austin in 1878 by the priests of the Congregation of the Holy Cross. The current name was approved in 1925. It is a coeducational liberal arts institution with a wide variety of courses and programs.[42]

St. Mary's University opened as St. Mary's Institute in 1852. Later the name was changed to St. Louis College. In 1923 the college was moved and changed its name again, to St. Mary's College and, as course offerings expanded, it became St. Mary's University.[43]

The *University of Dallas* opened its campus on 1,000 acres of land in 1956. This Catholic institution is managed by a group of lay people. The first chancellor was Bishop Thomas K. Gorman, bishop of Dallas. The faculty consists of members of the Cistercian Fathers, Sisters of Namur, Dominican Fathers, and members of the laity.[44]

The *University of St. Thomas* was organized in 1947 by Bishop Christopher E. Byrne of Galveston, and it opened in Houston. It is under the direction of the Basilian Fathers.[45]

University of the Incarnate Word was started by the Sisters of Charity of the Incarnate Word in 1881 as the Academy of the Incarnate Word, a Catholic college for women. In 1897, the sisters purchased George W. Brackenridge's 280-acre estate and, in 1910 opened the academy at the motherhouse of the Brackenridge Villa. In 1909 the name was changed to College of Incarnate Word. In 1971 it became coeducational, and in 1996 changed its name to the University of the Incarnate Word.[46]

CHURCH OF CHRIST

Abilene Christian University was chartered as Childers Classical Institution in 1906. The college was accredited as a junior college in 1916 and as a senior college in 1920. In February 1976, the college changed its name to Abilene Christian University. Since its founding, the college has been governed by a board of trustees composed of members of the Church of Christ.[47]

Amberton University began as a branch of the Abilene Christian College in 1971 and was called ACC Metrocenter. Before it opened its own campus, most of the classes were held at the campus of the by then defunct Christian College of the Southwest. When it moved to a new campus in Garland it changed its name to Abilene Christian College at Dallas. On June 1, 1981, it became a separate institution named Amber University. The name was changed to Amberton University in 2001.[48]

Christian College of the Southwest was originally named Garland Christian College when it opened in 1952 as a two-year school. It changed its name to Christian College of the Southwest in 1963, and in 1970 it became a four-year college. In 1971, despite an increase in enrollment, the school closed and its properties were acquired by Abilene Christian University.[49]

Clebarro College was established in 1909 by the Church of Christ in Cleburne. The school offered college courses in addition to elementary and secondary education, but closed in 1919.[50]

Lockney Christian College was founded in 1894 in Lockney under the control of the church. It offered only elementary and high school courses for the first ten years. In 1906, a new president raised funds for construction of a college building and the establishment of four-year college courses, but the school closed at the end of World War I in 1918.[51]

Lubbock Christian University was opened in 1957 as Lubbock Christian College. First a junior college, in 1987 it became a four-year institution.[52]

CHRISTIAN CHURCH (DISCIPLES OF CHRIST)

Burnetta College, named for Burnetta Barnes, was located in Venus and operated from 1896 until 1906. The college built a four-story frame building with $500 from the citizens of the town and $5,000 from the college's first president. Later, the building burned and, although it was rebuilt, the school closed and its property was given to the Venus public school system.[53]

Carlton College was founded in 1865 in Kentuckytown by Charles Carlton. It was the first college in Texas recognized as a church school but not financed or controlled by the church. Carlton moved the college to Bonham in 1867. After his death in 1913, enrollment began to decline and the college was merged with Carr-Burdette College in Sherman.[54]

Carr-Burdette College in Sherman was founded by Mrs. O. A. Carr in 1894. The college was a seminary to train ministers for the Christian Church and closed because of financial problems in 1929.[55]

Hereford Christian College was established in Hereford in 1902, and was transferred to the church in 1904 because of financial difficulties. It opened the next year and the name was changed to Panhandle Christian College. In 1909 the name was changed back to Hereford Christian College. In 1912 the school closed permanently due to a lack of financial support.[56]

Jarvis Christian College in Hawkins began as Jarvis Christian Institute in 1912. It has been affiliated with the church since its founding. In the beginning it offered high school-level education to "members of the Negro race." In 1927, it became a junior college, and in 1937 it became a senior college. In 1950, it was recognized as the only black college in the region with accreditation when the Southern Association of Colleges and Schools added the school to its "Approved List of Colleges and Universities for Negro Youth."[57]

Midland Christian College was started as a result of efforts by Texas Christian University to establish a junior college in southwest Texas. The university selected Midland, and a charter was granted in 1909. The college offered the usual junior college courses in addition to religious training. The school was closed in 1921, and in 1922 it moved to Cisco and became Cisco Christian College; later it was renamed Randolph Junior College.[58]

Pan-Handle Christian College began as Hereford College and Industrial School in Hereford in 1902. By 1905 it was known as Pan-Handle Christian College, and from 1909 to 1911 it was known as Hereford College. It closed in 1911.[59]

Texas Christian University in Fort Worth began as Add-Ran Christian University, which had begun as Add-Ran College. The college was started when Randolph Clark, on a visit to Fort Worth in 1873, bought property to establish a school at Thorp Spring. The school became Add-Ran Christian University in 1890 when the Christian

Churches of Texas took over the property, and in 1895 it was moved to Waco. The university experienced economic hardships from 1895 to 1902. In 1902, Add-Ran University became Texas Christian University, although its Department of Arts and Science kept the name Add-Ran College of Arts and Sciences. In 1910 a fire destroyed part of the campus. The college moved to Ft. Worth in 1911. The university believes that religion is an indispensable part of education.[60]

Thorp Spring Christian College went through several iterations in the late 1900s and early twentieth century. It began as Thorp College in 1871, but by 1873 had become Add-Ran Male and Female College. The school became Jarvis Institute in 1896, after Add-Ran was moved to Waco in 1895 and became Texas Christian University in 1902. The original facilities in Thorp Spring became the Jarvis Institute, which became Add-Ran Jarvis College. On March 1, 1910, Add-Ran Jarvis handed over its properties to the newly founded Thorp Spring Christian College because the college lacked support. The college moved to Terrell in 1928 where it was called Texas Christian College. The college closed and the property was sold to the city of Terrell in 1937.[61]

CONGREGATIONAL CHURCH

Tillotson College was located in Austin. It was a senior college for blacks built and maintained by the American Missionary Society of Congregational Churches. It was chartered in 1877 and named for George Jeffrey Tillotson, who planned the school, selected the site, and raised $16,000 for its establishment. Its predecessor was Tillotson Collegiate and Normal Institute opened in 1881. In 1925 the school became a junior college, and in 1931 senior college standing was achieved. On October 24, 1952, it was merged with Samuel Huston College to form Huston-Tillotson College.[62]

EPISCOPAL CHURCH

St. Mary's Hall was founded as a girl's school in San Antonio by the Episcopal Church in 1860. In 1866 the school closed because of a cholera epidemic. It reopened in 1879 as the West Texas College for Girls. In 1889 and 1890 the college offered primary academic and college work. In 1924 Ruth Coit became president and upon her retirement in 1937 the school changed its name to the Ruth Coit School. It reverted to St. Mary's Hall in 1945, and the school now offers a preschool Montessori program and a lower, middle, and upper school.[63]

St. Phillips College was started by the Episcopal Church in San Antonio in 1898 and was one of only four black colleges started by the Episcopal Church. It later came under the control of the American Institute for Negroes. It was unique because it was not a liberal arts college but emphasized vocational courses. Today it operates as a junior college.[64]

LUTHERAN CHURCH

Clifton College was organized on May 6, 1896, as the *Lutheran College of Clifton, Texas*, and its first building was dedicated on October 14, 1897. The school was financially supported by the Norwegian Lutheran Churches of America and opened as Clifton High School on October 28, 1897. The Missouri Synod of German Lutherans helped support the school from 1902 to 1914. In 1922 it began offering courses on the junior-college level and in 1945 became Clifton Junior College. In 1952 it changed its name to Clifton College, and in 1954 merged with Texas Lutheran College in Seguin.[65]

Colorado College was established in 1857, and is reputed to be the first Lutheran college in Texas. It was first established in Columbus under the control of twenty-five trustees, with a majority required to be members of the Evangelical Lutheran Church. The college remained open until 1886.[66]

Concordia University was started in the late nineteenth century, when Texas Lutherans were determined to build a school to prepare their young men for the ministry. There were three short-lived attempts—at New Orleans (Texas) in 1883, at Giddings in 1894, and at Clifton in the early nineteenth century. After World War I they were finally successful in establishing the Lutheran College of Texas in Austin. A junior college was established in 1951, and by 1955 women were matriculating. The name was changed in 1965 to Concordia Lutheran College. High school classes were discontinued in 1967, and the college was accredited by the Southern Association of Colleges and Schools in 1968. In 1979 the Texas Lutherans under the Missouri Synod authorized Concordia to become a four-year institution, and the first bachelor's degrees were awarded in 1982. In 1996 it began offering graduate degrees and the name was changed to Concordia University.[67]

Evangelical Lutheran College was the first of two colleges by the same name. This first one was founded in 1870 at Rutersville. It experienced little success and was closed by 1878.[68]

Texas Lutheran University began in Brenham as Evangelical Lutheran College in 1891; it later moved to Seguin where it was called the Lutheran College of Seguin. It opened as an academy in 1912 then became a junior college in 1928. In 1948 it became a senior college. The American Lutheran Church then decided to make Texas Lutheran College its senior college in the Southwest. The Augustana Lutheran Church, Evangelical Lutheran Church, and the United Lutheran Church in America all cooperated with the American Lutheran Church to maintain and govern Texas Lutheran College. In 1954, Clifton College was merged into the college, and in 1966 the name was changed to Texas Lutheran University.[69]

METHODIST CHURCH

Andrew Female College was established at Huntsville in 1852. The college closed after the creation of Sam Houston Normal Institute at Huntsville since the public school made Andrew Female College unnecessary.[70]

Centenary College was founded by the Methodist Church in 1883 in Lampasas. Marshall McIlhaney served as its first president. According to an 1888–1889 school catalogue, the college had five faculty members and 180 students. It closed in 1897.[71]

Chappell Hill Female College was originally part of the Chappell Hill Male and Female Institute, founded in 1852. By August 29, 1856, the Methodist Texas Conference decided to split the college between the male and female departments and Chappell Hill Female College was chartered as a separate school (see also, *Soule University* below). During the 1890s enrollment began to drop, and the college closed in 1912.[72]

Clarendon College was sponsored by the Methodist Conference in 1898. The school reached its highest enrollment in 1927 with 340 students. The same year a special commission of the Methodist Conference closed the college. Later the citizens of Clarendon voted to purchase the college plant for a local municipal junior college.[73]

Coronal Institute was not originally founded as a Methodist college. The Institute was established by O. N. Hollingsworth and was a "pioneer" private institution in Southwest Texas. Later Hollingsworth sold the school to R. H. Belvin, who in turn sold it to the Methodist Church in 1876. The buildings and grounds were sold to the city of San Marcos when the school closed in 1918.[74]

Fort Worth University began as Texas Wesleyan College in 1881, but an amended charter in 1889 changed the name. Controlled by the Northern Methodist Church, Fort Worth University was forced to close after it attempted to establish schools of law and medicine and graduate courses simultaneously without the appropriate financial ability. The university then became part of the Methodist Episcopal University in Oklahoma City in 1889.[75]

The *Holding Institute* was founded in Laredo by the Methodist Church for the purpose of educating Mexican children in 1880. Of the 11,000 children who attended the school before it closed for lack of funds in May 1983, 35 percent were from Mexico.[76]

McMurry University was founded in Abilene by the Northwest Texas Conference of Methodist Churches and opened in 1923. Named for Bishop William Fletcher McMurry, its first president was James Winfred Hunt who had been president of Stamford College in Stamford (Texas), which had closed in 1918. The first senior class of four students graduated in 1926, and in that same year the college was accredited as a senior college by the Texas Association of Colleges and the Educational Board of the Methodist Church. Though it was originally founded as a liberal arts college, it added teacher training and business administration during its first ten years. It served the Methodist Church by training potential clergy, and its ties with the Methodist Church remain strong.[77]

Paine Female Institute was founded by the citizens of Goliad with the aid of the Methodist Church. It opened in 1856. Conflicts between the church and the local citizens led to the closing of the college, and the building was sold to Goliad High School in 1885.[78]

Polytechnic College was founded by the Methodists in Fort Worth and opened in 1891. A smallpox scare closed the school in 1899.[79]

Rutersville College was once located in Rutersville. Dr. Martin Ruter, a linguist and author nicknamed the "Apostle of Methodism in Texas" was the first to initiate the founding of a denominational college in Texas. The establishment of the college in 1840 by legislative charter marked the establishment of the first Protestant college in Texas. During its existence, the school enrolled more than 800 students. In 1856 it became a private school called Texas Monumental and Military Institute.[80]

Seth Ward College was opened by the Methodist Church in 1910 near Plainview. There were two major fires, the last one in 1916. The Trustees closed the college in 1929.[81]

Soule University was formed from the Male Department of the Chappell Hill Male and Female College. When Rutersville College and Wesleyan College at San Augustine failed, a convention of delegates from the Texas Conference of the Methodist Church assembled at Chappell Hill in 1855 and established Soule University. In 1856, the school received its charter and began offering college courses. Soule operated from 1855 until 1888. By the end of the Civil War, the college was dilapidated and "without furniture, apparatus, assets, endowments, library, faculty or students." The university had reopened in 1865, but was forced to close temporarily in 1866 because of an outbreak of yellow fever. Enrollment declined and the school permanently closed in 1888.[82]

Southern Methodist University was founded in Dallas after a Conference of the Methodist Church appointed an Educational Commission. The Methodist General Conference and Annual Conferences in Texas, Oklahoma, Louisiana, Missouri, Arkansas, and New Mexico chose a board of trustees to govern the university. The university began its first session in 1915 with an enrollment of 700 students.[83]

Southwestern University, in Georgetown, was formed from four early Methodist colleges: Rutersville, Wesleyan, McKenzie, and Soule. After Soule closed, Francis Asbury Mood, the former president of Stamford College, decided to lead a project to consolidate these four institutions and establish a single institution outside the "fever belt." Five Methodist Conferences adopted Mood's project and located the new school at Georgetown, calling it Texas University. It opened in 1873; in 1875 the school changed its name to Southwestern University.[84]

Stamford College, originally called Stamford Collegiate Institute and located in Stamford, was opened in September 1907. Founded by the Northwest Texas Methodist Conference, the college grew and the name was changed to Stamford College. After World War I, enrollment began to decline, and the school closed in 1918 after a fire destroyed the administration building.[85]

Texas Wesleyan College was established by Swedish Methodists in Austin; it was to be a Swedish Methodist college. It received its name in honor of John Wesley, the founder of Methodism. The college opened its doors on January 9, 1912. The 1930s saw a movement away from things ethnic and movement to be more "American." Interest in the college began to decline. In May 1935 the name was changed to Texas Wesleyan Academy. When the Academy failed, the assets were place into a fund for scholarships for descendants of Swedes. The last of the funds were awarded in the 1976–1977 school year and the operation ceased.[86]

Waco Female College was chartered in Waco in 1860 as a result of a consolidation of Waco Female Seminary and Waco Female Academy. The college closed because of financial difficulties in 1895. Its properties were purchased by Add-Ran Christian University, a forerunner of Texas Christian University.[87]

Wesleyan College was organized because of the Methodists' interest in locating a college in San Augustine in 1842. Later, the board consolidated the college with the University of San Augustine, and that institution became the University of Eastern Texas.[88]

METHODIST EPISCOPAL CHURCH

Central College was founded by the Methodist Episcopal Church-South in 1883. The college originated as Sulphur Springs District Conference High School in 1877. In 1884, a Central College professor from Indiana, H. P. Eastman, bought the school and changed its name to Eastman College and Conservatory of Music and Art. The institution operated under his leadership until it was destroyed by fire in 1900.[89]

Huston-Tillotson University began as Samuel Huston College, which was established by the Methodist Episcopal Conference in 1900 as a coeducational facility serving blacks in Austin. The college grew and in 1943 the state recognized it as a Class A senior college. In 1952, it merged with the Congregational Church's Tillotson College to become Huston-Tillotson College, which remained under the control of the Methodist Episcopal Conference. It became a university in 2005.[90]

Kidd-Key College was opened in 1878 as a fine arts college and grew into the North Texas Female College and Kidd-Key Conservatory of Music. When the Methodist Church withdrew its support in 1935, the college closed.[91]

Marvin College in Waxahachie was established by the Northwest Texas Conference of the Methodist Episcopal Church in 1868. The school immediately experienced financial difficulties and closed in 1878.[92]

San Antonio Female College was started in 1894 by Dr. J. E. Harrison and backed by the West Texas Conference of the Methodist Episcopal Church. The University of Texas recognized the college as a junior college in 1916. In 1918, the college changed its name to Westmoreland College, and in 1937 changed it again to the University of San Antonio. In 1942, the University of San Antonio merged with Trinity University.[93]

San Saba Masonic College was established in 1863, in San Saba. By 1879, the Methodist Episcopal Church took control of the school and, in 1885, renamed it San Saba College. In 1886, the college closed only to reopen briefly in the 1890s.[94]

Texas College was established in 1894, by the Colored Methodist Episcopal Church in Tyler. It received junior college status in 1924 and four-year status in 1932. Texas College today focuses its attention on low income students and offers degrees in liberal arts, home economics, and sciences.[95]

Texas Wesleyan University started as Polytechnic College, established in 1891 at Fort Worth by a committee of the Northwest Texas Conference of the Methodist Church. It had suffered an enrollment decline and in an effort to reverse this trend the Trustees made the institution coeducational and the name was changed to Texas Wesleyan College. In 1988 it changed its name to Texas Wesleyan University.[96]

Wiley College is the oldest black college west of the Mississippi River. It was established in Marshall by the Freedman's Aid Society of the Methodist Episcopal Church in 1873. The college offered regular college courses and some vocational training. It offered courses below the college level until 1922, when it began offering only college courses. In 1907, it received the first Carnegie college library west of the Mississippi.[97]

CHURCH OF THE NAZARENE

Central Nazarene College opened in 1911 in Hamlin. The college had various primary, academy, and collegiate departments. An early catalogue mentions a "strong theological course" that required training to read the Bible in the original language. In 1931, the college merged with Bethany Peniel College in Bethany, Oklahoma.[98]

Nazarene Central Plains College was located in Plainview. Because of financial difficulties it was sold to the Methodist Church of Plainview. It was renamed Seth Ward College in 1910. After a fire at the college it was closed and the property sold, the money was loaned interest-free to McMurry College in Abilene.[99]

Texas Holiness University was established in Greenville in 1900. The university offered a four-year collegiate course and courses in music, art, and voice. In 1911, the school was adopted as a church university by the Pentecostal Church of the Nazarene. The church called it Peniel University. In 1917, the name was changed to Peniel College. The school was consolidated with the Oklahoma Holiness University in 1920.[100]

PENTECOSTAL CHURCH OF GOD

Southern Bible College was opened by Worden McDonald in 1958 in Houston. The school was established at the suggestion of the East Texas District of the Pentecostal Church of God of America because the denomination needed its own Bible college. It was owned and operated by the Pentecostal Church to provide programs in minister training and theology. By 1968, the college was a recognized member of the Accrediting Association of Bible Colleges. The school closed in the early 1980s due to financial difficulties.[101]

PRESBYTERIAN CHURCH

Aranama College was established in 1854 as a Presbyterian senior college located in Goliad. The town's gift of the Aranama Mission and twenty-one acres made the school possible. The college was damaged during the Civil War and destroyed by a storm in 1886.[102]

Austin College was established by the Presbytery of Brazos at Huntsville in 1849 after Dr. Daniel Baker secured almost $100,000 for support of the college. It remained open at that location until 1871. Because the college was experiencing some difficulties it was moved in 1876; Austin College again moved, to Sherman in 1878, where the college's first building was completed. Sam Houston State Normal School received the former Austin College building in Huntsville. In 1930, the Texas Synod of the Presbyterian Church ordered its three senior colleges to consolidate with Austin College. One of those colleges, Daniel Baker College, located in Brownwood, decided not to consolidate but to remain a separate institution; however, Texas Presbyterian College at Milford did consolidate with Austin College.[103]

Buffalo Gap College, which began in 1881, was founded as the result of efforts by ministers A. J. Haynes and Alpha Young to establish a coeducational higher education institution. The Buffalo Gap and San Saba Presbyteries of the Cumberland Presbyterian Church controlled the college, which awarded both bachelor of arts and bachelor of science degrees and graduated twelve students in 1898. The college closed in 1902, and its property was given to the Buffalo Gap public schools.[104]

Chapel Hill College opened in 1852 in Daingerfield on land donated to the Cumberland Presbyterian Church. It offered free education for Presbyterian ministers in order to increase enrollment. New buildings were constructed in 1858. Fears of a Union army invasion in 1860 prompted the school to cease college-level education. The school closed in 1869.[105]

Cumberland College was established by the Texas Synod of the Cumberland Presbyterian Church at Leonard in 1911. The college opened with sixty-three students; however, the Synod could not afford to maintain the college and its property was sold in 1918.[106]

Daniel Baker College was founded by the Presbyterian Church at Brownwood in 1889 and became part of a merger with Southwestern University in 1946. In 1950, the college became an Episcopal college in the Episcopal Diocese of Dallas and merged with Howard Payne College in Brownwood in 1953.[107]

Larissa College was founded by Cumberland Presbyterians in 1848; it was one of the earliest institutions of higher education in Texas. For its first seven years, the college provided only elementary education. In 1855, it received a charter from the state legislature.

At that time the female department had forty-six students, and faculty taught courses felt to be essential for the training of young ladies. A declining enrollment and the temporary closing of the Female Department in 1857 caused financial difficulties. By the beginning of the Civil War, the school had recovered, but the outbreak of war caused the school to close. In 1886, the school reopened but the Synod withdrew its financial support in favor of Trinity University, and the school soon closed permanently.[108]

Mary Allen College was a junior college in Crockett. It was started as the Crockett Presbyterian Church Colored Sabbath School. From 1875 until 1885, it was known as Moffatt Parochial School, and was renamed Mary Allen Seminary from 1885 until 1933. Mary Allen College closed during World War II.[109]

Schreiner University was founded in 1917 as the Schreiner Institute by Charles A. Schreiner, who placed $250,000 and 140 acres of land in Kerrville in trust to the Presbyterian Synod of Texas. The school began as a preparatory school and junior college. In 1982 it became a senior college. The name was changed to Schreiner University in 2001. Today it retains its ties with the Presbyterian Church.[110]

Texas Presbyterian College for Girls originated out of a donation of ten acres of land accompanied by a gift of $25,000 and ten acres of land by the city of Milford to the Presbyterian Synod of Texas. The college opened in 1902. Low enrollment caused the college to close in 1929, and its assets were transferred to Austin College.[111]

Texas Presbyterian University was chartered in 1886 but failed to open, in spite of a donation of one hundred acres of land in Dallas's Highland Park by J. S. Armstrong in 1907. The endowment goal was $2 million but it was never reached and the project ended.[112]

Trinity University's history is tied to the Cumberland Presbyterian Church, which established three colleges in Texas prior to 1866. The colleges included Chapel Hill College, which opened in Daingerfield in 1859; Ewing College, which opened in LaGrange in 1852; and Larissa College, which opened in Larissa in 1855. At the time,

Larissa College offered the best science courses of any college in Texas. In 1866, the Brazos, Colorado, and Texas Synod began accepting bids for a location for a central Presbyterian institution. The town of Tehuacana offered to donate 130 acres in the Tehuacana Hills and 1,500 acres in the prairie below for the institution; the locating committee accepted the offer. The name Trinity University was chosen because the Synods had founded three Presbyterian colleges. Trinity University remained in Tehuacana from 1869 to 1902, moved to Waxahachie in 1902, and finally to San Antonio in 1942.[113]

SEVENTH-DAY ADVENTIST CHURCH

Keene Industrial Academy was founded in Keene in 1894. It was the predecessor to Southwestern Adventist College.[114]

Southwestern Adventist University opened in 1894 as Keene Industrial Academy, then as Southwestern Junior College, Southwestern Union College, and finally Southwestern Adventist College. It became a four-year institution in 1977 and a university in 1989.[115]

NOTES

1. Frederick Eby, *The Development of Education in Texas* (New York: Macmillan Co., 1925), 142.
2. Ibid., 141.
3. Eby, *The Development of Education in Texas*, 95.
4. Michael A. White, *History of Baylor University: 1845–1861* (Waco: Texian Press, 1968), 2–4; J. A. Reynolds, "TEXAS BAPTIST EDUCATIONAL SOCIETY," *Handbook of Texas Online* (http://www.tshaonline.org/handbook/kat11), accessed June 22, 2015. Uploaded on June 15, 2010. Published by the Texas State Historical Association.
5. Donald W. Whisenhunt, *Encyclopedia of Texas Colleges and Universities* (Austin: Eakin Press, 1986), 115.
6. Julia Lee Sinks, "Rutersville College," *Texas State Historical Association Quarterly* 2 (1948): 124–33.
7. Eby, *The Development of Education in Texas*, 95.
8. Sinks, "Rutersville College," 124–33.
9. Eby, *The Development of Education in Texas*, 96.
10. Ibid., 9.
11. Nancy Beck Young, "UNIVERSITY OF SAN AUGUSTINE," *Handbook of Texas Online* (http://www.tshaonline.org/handbook/online/articles/kcu06), accessed September 15, 2104. Uploaded on June 15, 2010. Published by the Texas State Historical Association
12. Eby, *The Development of Education in Texas*, 33.
13. June Rayfield Welch, *The Colleges of Texas* (Dallas: GLA Press, 1981), 26.
14. C. E. Evans, *The Story of Texas Schools* (Austin: Steck Co., 1955), 369–70.
15. Ibid.

16. Lois Smith Murray, *Baylor at Independence* (Waco: Baylor University Press, 1972), 21–23.

17. Evans, *The Story of Texas Schools,* 313. See chapter 8 for a discussion of the development of women's colleges in Texas; and, for a more detailed look at the role of Baylor's Female Department in the lives of mid-nineteenth-century Texas women, see Rebecca Sharpless, "Sallie McNeill: A Woman's Higher Education in Antebellum Texas," in *Texas Women: Their Histories, Their Lives,* ed. Elizabeth Hayes Turner, Stephanie Cole, and Rebecca Sharpless (Athens: University of Georgia Press, 2015), 82–104.

18. Jack Herman and Peggy Hardman, "BISHOP COLLEGE," *Handbook of Texas Online,* (tshaolnine.org/handbook/online/articles/kbb11) accessed April 15, 2015, Uploaded on June 12, 2010, Modified on April 7, 2015. Published by the Texas State Historical Association.

19. Evans, *The Story of Texas Schools,* 324.

20. Michael R. Heintze, *Private Black Colleges in Texas, 1865–1954* (College Station: Texas A&M University Press, 1985), 39.

21. Heintze, *Private Black Colleges in Texas,* 31.

22. E. A. Bernhausen, "Development of Education in Waco" (master's thesis, Southwest Texas State University, San Marcos, 1937), 62.

23. Evans, *The Story of Texas Schools,* 364.

24. Evans, *The Story of Texas Schools,* 321.

25. Hugh E. Cosby and John R. Hutto, *History of Hardin Simmons* (Abilene: Hugh E. Cosby Co, 1954), 5; Whisenhunt, *Encyclopedia of Texas Colleges and Universities,* 1, 58, 99, 122.

26. Nancy Beck Young, "HOUSTON BAPTIST UNIVERSITY," *Handbook of Texas Online* (http://www.tshaonline.org/handbook/online/articles/kbh09), accessed November 8, 2011. Uploaded on June 15, 2010. Published by the Texas State Historical Association.

27. Evans, *The Story of Texas Schools,* 315.

28. Evans, *The Story of Texas Schools,* 317.

29. Lisa C. Maxwell, "MARY NASH COLLEGE," *Handbook of Texas Online* (http://www.tshaonline.org/handbook/online/articles/kbm10), accessed November 2, 2011. Uploaded on June 15, 2010. Published by the Texas State Historical Association.

30. Marie Giles, "SABINE BAPTIST COLLEGE," *Handbook of Texas Online* (http://www.tshaonline.org/handbook/online/articles/kbs02), accessed November 2, 2011. Published by the Texas State Historical Association.

31. Cosby and Hutto, *History of Hardin Simmons,* 5; Whisenhunt, *Encyclopedia of Texas Colleges and Universities,* 42, 64.

32. Diane E. Spencer, "SOUTH TEXAS BAPTIST COLLEGE," *Handbook of Texas Online* (http://www.tshaonline.org/handbook/online/articles/kbs26), accessed November 2, 2011. Uploaded on June 15, 2010. Published by the Texas State Historical Association.

33. Marie Giles, "TEXAS BAPTIST COLLEGE," *Handbook of Texas Online* (http://www.tshaonline.org/handbook/online/articles/kbt03), accessed November 2, 2011. Uploaded on June 15, 2010. Published by the Texas State Historical Association.

34. Evans, *The Story of Texas Schools,* 322.

35. White, *History of Baylor University,* 35.

36. John Robert Guemple, "The History of Waco University" (master's thesis, Baylor University, Waco, 1964), 2, 15, 101; Whisenhunt, *Encyclopedia of Texas Colleges and Universities,* 14, 159, 184.

37. Evans, *The Story of Texas Schools,* 320.

38. Sister Antoinette Boykin, O.P., "DOMINICAN COLLEGE," *Handbook of Texas Online* (http://www.tshaonline.org/handbook/online/articles/kbd10), accessed November 2, 2011. Uploaded on June 12, 2010. Published by the Texas State Historical Association.

39. Castañeda, *The Church in Texas Since Independence, 1836–1950,* 315.

40. Castañeda, *The Church in Texas Since Independence, 1836–1950,* 313.

41. Bernhausen, "Development of Education in Waco," 55.

42. Castañeda, *The Church in Texas Since Independence, 1836–1950*, 331.

43. Castañeda, *The Church in Texas Since Independence, 1836–1950*, 300.

44. Sister Lois Bannon, O.S.U. "UNIVERSITY OF DALLAS," *Handbook of Texas Online* (http://www.tshaonline.org/handbook/online/articles/kbu02), accessed September 17. 2014. Published by the Texas State Historical Association.

45. Virginia Bernhard, "UNIVERSITY OF ST. THOMAS," *Handbook of Texas Online* (http://www.tshaonline.org/handbook/online/articles/kbu03), accessed September 17. 2014. Published by the Texas State Historical Association.

46. Carlos E. Castañeda, *The Church in Texas Since Independence, 1836–1950* (Austin: Von Boeckmann-Jones, 1958), 303.

47. Evans, *The Story of Texas Schools*, 354.

48. Lisa C. Maxwell, "AMBERTON UNIVERSITY," *Handbook of Texas Online* (http://www.tshaonline.org/handbook/online/articles/kbaae), accessed September 17, 2014. Published by the Texas State Historical Association.

49. Matthew Hayes Nall, "CHRISTIAN COLLEGE OF THE SOUTHWEST," *Handbook of Texas Online* (http://www.tshaonline.org/handbook/online/articles/kbc19), accessed December 13, 2011. Published by the Texas State Historical Association.

50. David Minor and Nancy Beck Young, "CLEBARRO COLLEGE," *Handbook of Texas Online* (http://www.tshaonline.org/handbook/online/articles/kbc28), accessed November 13, 2011. Published by the Texas State Historical Association.

51. Evans, *The Story of Texas Schools*, 355.

52. Carroll Burcham, "LUBBOCK CHRISTIAN COLLEGE," *Handbook of Texas Online* (http://www.tshaonline.org/handbook/online/articles/kb117), accessed November 8, 2011. Published by the Texas State Historical Association.

53. David Minor, "BURNETTA COLLEGE," *Handbook of Texas Online* (http://www.tshaonline.org/handbook/online/articles/kbb22), accessed January 17, 2012. Published by the Texas State Historical Association.

54. Evans, *The Story of Texas Schools*, 351.

55. Evans, *The Story of Texas Schools*, 352.

56. Colby D. Hall, "HEREFORD CHRISTIAN COLLEGE," *Handbook of Texas Online* (http://www.tshaonline.org/handbook/online/articles/kch06), accessed November 2, 2011. Published by the Texas State Historical Association.

57. Clifford H. Taylor, "Jarvis Christian College" (bachelor's thesis, Texas Christian University, Fort Worth, 1948), 82–86. Donald W. Whisenhunt, *Encyclopedia of Texas Colleges and Universities.* (Austin, Eakin Press, 1986), 2, 68.

58. Evans, *The Story of Texas Schools*, 353.

59. Evans, *The Story of Texas Schools*, 352.

60. Evans, *The Story of Texas Schools*, 351.

61. Rhonda L. Callaway, "THORP SPRING CHRISTIAN COLLEGE," *Handbook of Texas Online* (http://www.tshaonline.org/handbook/online/articles/kbt26), accessed November 18, 2014. Uploaded on June 15, 2010. Modified on January 5, 2011. Published by the Texas State Historical Association.

62. "TILLOTSON COLLEGE," *Handbook of Texas Online* (http://tshaonline.org/handbook/online/articles/kbt27), accessed June 15, 2010, Modified on June 5, 2013. Published by the Texas State Historical Association.

63. Evans, *The Story of Texas Schools*, 363.

64. Evans, *The Story of Texas Schools*, 218–19.

65. Karen Yancy, "CLIFTON COLLEGE," *Handbook of Texas Online* (http://www.tshaonline.org/handbook/online/articles/kbc49), accessed September 18, 2014. Uploaded on June 12, 2010. Published by the Texas State Historical Association.

66. William A. Flachmeier, "COLORADO COLLEGE," *Handbook of Texas Online* (http://www.tshaonline.org/handbook/online/articles/kbc37), accessed September 18, 2014. Published by the Texas State Historical Association.

67. Louann Atkins Temple, "CONCORDIA UNIVERSITY AT AUSTIN," *Handbook of Texas Online* (http://www.tshaonline.org/handbook/online/articles/kbc40), accessed September 18, 2014. Published by the Texas State Historical Association.

68. Evans, *The Story of Texas Schools*, 367.

69. Evans, *The Story of Texas Schools*, 365–66.

70. Evans, *The Story of Texas Schools*, 337.

71. Mark Donitz, "CENTENARY COLLEGE," *Handbook of Texas Online* tshaonline.org/handbook/kbc53), accessed October 19, 2011. Published by the Texas State Historical Association.

72. Carole E. Christian, "CHAPPELL HILL FEMALE COLLEGE," *Handbook of Texas Online* (http://www.tshaonline.org/handbook/online/articles/kbc15), accessed October 19, 2011. Published by the Texas State Historical Association.

73. Evans, *The Story of Texas Schools*, 335.

74. Evans, *The Story of Texas Schools*, 337.

75. Evans, *The Story of Texas Schools*, 339–40.

76. Evans, *The Story of Texas Schools*, 340.

77. Fane Downs, "MCMURRY UNIVERSITY," *Handbook of Texas Online* (http://www.tshaonline.org/handbook/online/articles/kbm17), accessed February 25, 2014. Published by the Texas State Historical Association.

78. Gina Maria Jerome, "PAINE FEMALE INSTITUTE," *Handbook of Texas Online* (http://www.tshaonline.org/handbook/online/articles/kbp01), accessed November 2, 2011. Published by the Texas State Historical Association.

79. Evans, *The Story of Texas Schools*, 332.

80. Eby, *The Development of Education in Texas,* 94–95.

81. Evans, *The Story of Texas Schools*, 335.

82. Carole E. Christian, "SOULE UNIVERSITY," *Handbook of Texas Online* (http://www.tshaonline.org/handbook/online/articles/kbs24), accessed November 8, 2011. Published by the Texas State Historical Association.

83. Marshall Terry, *From High on the Hilltop* (Dallas: Three Forks Press, 2009), 10.

84. Evans, *The Story of Texas Schools*, 328.

85. Evans, *The Story of Texas Schools*, 328.

86. Christianson, James M., "Texas Wesleyan College," *Handbook of Texas Online* (http:/www.tshaonline.org/handbook/online/articles/kbt25) downloaded September 18, 2017. Published by the Texas Historical Association.

87. Bernhausen, "Development of Education in Waco," 46.

88. Evans, *The Story of Texas Schools*, 339.

89. Bob Gilbert and Michelle Gilbert, "CENTRAL COLLEGE," *Handbook of Texas Online* (http://www.tshaonline.org/handbook/online/articles/kbc09), accessed November 8, 2011. Published by the Texas State Historical Association.

90. Heintze, *Private Black Colleges in Texas*, 38.

91. Evans, *The Story of Texas Schools*, 339.

92. Charlie C. Haynes, Jr. "MARVIN COLLEGE," *Handbook of Texas Online* (http://www.tshaonline.org/handbook/online/articles/kbm07), accessed January 22, 2012. Published by the Texas State Historical Association.

93. Evans, *The Story of Texas Schools*, 347.

94. Evans, *The Story of Texas Schools*, 75.

95. Heintze, *Private Black Colleges in Texas*, 34–35.

96. Evans, *The Story of Texas Schools*, 266.

97. Heintze, *Private Black Colleges in Texas*, 23–26.

98. H. Allen Anderson, "CENTRAL NAZARENE COLLEGE," *Handbook of Texas Online* (http://www.tshaonline.org/handbook/online/articles/kbc11), accessed September 18, 2014. Uploaded on June 12, 2010. Published by the Texas State Historical Association.

99. Evans, *The Story of Texas Schools*, 334.

100. Evans, *The Story of Texas Schools*, 368.

101. Diana J. Kleiner, "SOUTHERN BIBLE COLLEGE," *Handbook of Texas Online* (http://www.tshaonline.org/handbook/online/articles/kbs30), accessed October 19, 2011. Published by the Texas State Historical Association.

102. Evans, *The Story of Texas Schools*, 394.

103. Ibid., 348.

104. Ibid.

105. Evans, *The Story of Texas Schools*, 70.

106. Eby, *The Development of Education in Texas,* 348.

107. Evans, *The Story of Texas Schools*, 364.

108. Christopher Long, "LARISSA COLLEGE," *Handbook of Texas Online* (http://www.tshaonline.org/handbook/online/articles/kbl07), accessed November 2, 2011. Published by the Texas State Historical Association.

109. Evans, *The Story of Texas Schools*, 218.

110. Ibid., 145.

111. Eby, *The Development of Education in Texas,* 345.

112. Louise Kelly, "TEXAS PRESBYTERIAN UNIVERSITY," *Handbook of Texas Online*. (http://www.tshaonline.org/handbook/online/articles/kbt22), accessed November 8, 2011. Published by the Texas State Historical Association.

113. Eby, *The Development of Education in Texas,* 347.

114. "ADVENTIST CHURCHES," *Handbook of Texas Online* (http://www.tshaonline.org/handbook/online/articles/iaa01), accessed September 18, 2014. Uploaded on June 9, 2010. Published by the Texas State Historical Association.

115. Ibid.

BIBLIOGRAPHY

"ADVENTIST CHURCHES," *Handbook of Texas Online* (http://www.tshaonline.org/handbook/online/articles/iaa01), accessed September 18, 2014. Uploaded on June 9, 2010. Published by the Texas State Historical Association.

Anderson, H. Allen. "CENTRAL NAZARENE COLLEGE," Handbook of Texas Online. (http://www.tshaonline.org/handbook/online/articles/kbc11), accessed September 18, 2014. Uploaded on June 12, 2010. Published by the Texas State Historical Association.

Bannon, Sister Lois, O.S.U. "UNIVERSITY OF DALLAS," *Handbook of Texas Online* (http://www.tshaonline.org/handbook/online/articles/kbu02), accessed November 17, 2011. Published by the Texas State Historical Association.

Baulch, Joe R. "SCHREINER UNIVERSITY," *Handbook of Texas Online* (http://www.tshaonline.org/handbook/online/articles/kbs16), accessed on March 05, 2012. Published by the Texas State Historical Association.

Behnke, Martin, "BUTLER COLLEGE," *Handbook of Texas Online* (http://www.tshaonline.org/handbook/online/articles/kbb23), accessed November 08, 2011. Published by the Texas State Historical Association.

Bernhard, Virginia, "UNIVERSITY OF ST. THOMAS," *Handbook of Texas Online* (http://www.tshaonline.org/handbook/online/articles/kbu03), accessed September 11. 2014. Published by the Texas State Historical Association.

Bernhausen, E. A. "Development of Education in Waco." Master's thesis, Southwest Texas State University, San Marcos, 1937.

Boykin, Sister Antoinette, O.P. "DOMINICAN COLLEGE," *Handbook of Texas Online* (http://www.tshaonline.org/handbook/online/articles/kbd10), accessed November 2, 2011. Published by the Texas State Historical Association.

Brackenridge, R. Douglas. *Trinity University: A Tale of Three Cities*. San Antonio: Trinity University Press, 2004.

Burcham, Carroll. "LUBBOCK CHRISTIAN COLLEGE," *Handbook of Texas Online* (http://www.tshaonline.org/handbook/online/articles/kb117), accessed November 8, 2011. Published by the Texas State Historical Association.

Callaway, Rhonda L. "THORP SPRING CHRISTIAN COLLEGE," *Handbook of Texas Online* (http://www.tshaonline.org/handbook/online/articles/kbt26), accessed April 13, 2015. Uploaded on June 15, 2010. Modified on January 5, 2011. Published by the Texas State Historical Association.

Castañeda, Carlos E. *The Church in Texas Since Independence, 1836–1950*. Vol. 7 of *Our Catholic Heritage in Texas*. Austin: Von Boeckmann-Jones, 1958.

Christian, Carole E. "CHAPPELL HILL FEMALE COLLEGE," *Handbook of Texas Online* (http://www.tshaonline.org/handbook/online/articles/kbc15), accessed October 19, 2011. Published by the Texas State Historical Association.

———. "SOULE UNIVERSITY," *Handbook of Texas Online* (http://www.tshaonline.org/handbook/online/articles/kbs24), accessed November 8, 2011. Published by the Texas State Historical Association.

Christianson, James M. "TEXAS WESLEYAN COLLEGE," *Handbook of Texas Online* (http:www.tshaonline.org/handbook/online.articles/kbt25) accessed September 18, 2017. Published by the Texas State Historical Association.

Cosby, Hugh E., and John R. Hutto. *History of Hardin Simmons*. Abilene: Hugh E. Cosby Co, 1954.

Crusendorf, Arthur A. "A Century of Education in Washington County, Texas." Ph.D. diss., University of Texas, Austin, 1938.

Dederichs, Sister Joseph A., and Sister Rose Mary Cousins. *Catholic Schools: Dawn of Education in Texas*. Beaumont, TX: Beaumont Printing and Lithographing, 1986.

Downs, Fane. "MCMURRY UNIVERSITY," *Handbook of Texas Online* (http://www.tshaonline.org/handbook/online/articles/kbm17), accessed February 25, 2014. Published by the Texas State Historical Association.

Eby, Frederick. *The Development of Education in Texas*. New York: Macmillan Co., 1925.

Evans, C. E. *The Story of Texas Schools*. Austin: Steck Co., 1955.

Fisher, Don R. "An Analysis of the Historical Development of Senior Colleges and Universities in West Texas." Ph.D. diss., Texas Tech University, Lubbock, 1988.

Flachmeier, William A. "COLORADO COLLEGE," *Handbook of Texas Online* (http://www.tshaonline.org/handbook/online/articles/kbc37), accessed September 18, 2014. Published by the Texas State Historical Association.

Gilbert, Bob, and Michelle Gilbert. "CENTRAL COLLEGE," *Handbook of Texas Online* (http://www.tshaonline.org/handbook/online/articles/kbc09), accessed November 08, 2011. Published by the Texas State Historical Association.

Giles, Marie. "SABINE BAPTIST COLLEGE," *Handbook of Texas Online* (http://www.tshaonline.org/handbook/online/articles/kbs02), accessed November 2, 2011. Published by the Texas State Historical Association.

——— "TEXAS BAPTIST COLLEGE," *Handbook of Texas Online* (http://www.tshaonline.org/handbook/online/articles/kbt03), accessed November 2, 2011. Uploaded on June 15, 2010. Published by the Texas State Historical Association.

Guemple, John Robert. "The History of Waco University." Master's thesis, Baylor University, Waco, 1964.

Hall, Colby D. "HEREFORD CHRISTIAN COLLEGE," *Handbook of Texas Online* (http://www.tshaonline.org/handbook/online/articles/kch06), accessed November 2, 2011. Published by the Texas State Historical Association.

Hart, Brian. "SOUTHWESTERN ADVENTIST UNIVERSITY," Handbook of Texas Online. (http://www.tshaonline.org/handbook/online/articles/kbs39), accessed September 18, 2014. Published by the Texas State Historical Association.

Haynes, Charlie C., Jr. "MARVIN COLLEGE," Handbook of Texas Online (http://www.tshaonline. org/handbook/online/articles/kbm07), accessed January 22, 2012. Published by the Texas State Historical Association.

Heintze, Michael R. Private Black Colleges in Texas, 1865–1954. College Station: Texas A&M University Press, 1985.

Herman, Jack, and Peggy Hardman. "BISHOP COLLEGE," Handbook of Texas Online (http://www. tshaonline.org/handbook/online/articles/kbb11), accessed November 8, 2011. Published by the Texas State Historical Association.

Hesler, Samuel B. "BRYAN BAPTIST ACADEMY," Handbook of Texas Online (http://www.tshaonline. org/handbook/online/articles/kbb18), accessed November 02, 2011. Published by the Texas State Historical Association.

Hornbeak, Samuel L. Trinity University: Project of Pioneers. San Antonio: Trinity University Development Council, 1951.

Jerome, Gina Maria. "PAINE FEMALE INSTITUTE," Handbook of Texas Online (http://www. tshaonline.org/handbook/online/articles/kbp01), accessed November 2, 2011. Published by the Texas State Historical Association.

Kelly, Louise. "TEXAS PRESBYTERIAN UNIVERSITY," Handbook of Texas Online. (http://www. tshaonline.org/handbook/online/articles/kbt22), accessed November 18, 2011. Published by the Texas State Historical Association.

Kleiner, Diana J. "SOUTHERN BIBLE COLLEGE," Handbook of Texas Online (http://www.tshaonline. org/handbook/online/articles/kbs30), accessed October 19, 2011. Published by the Texas State Historical Association.

Long, Christopher. "LARISSA COLLEGE," Handbook of Texas Online (http://www.tshaonline.org/ handbook/online/articles/kbl07), accessed November 2, 2011. Published by the Texas State Historical Association.

Lyndon B. Johnson School of Public Affairs. Texas Atlas of Higher Education. Austin: Lyndon B. Johnson School of Public Affairs, University of Texas at Austin, 1974.

Maxwell, Lisa C. "AMBERTON UNIVERSITY," Handbook of Texas Online (http://www.tshaonline. org/handbook/online/articles/kbaae), accessed March 1, 2012. Published by the Texas State Historical Association.

———. "MARY NASH COLLEGE," Handbook of Texas Online (http://www.tshaonline.org/ handbook/online/articles/kbm10), accessed November 8, 2011. Published by the Texas State Historical Association.

McFarland, Carl L. "CHAPEL HILL COLLEGE," Handbook of Texas Online (http://www.tshaonline. org/handbook/online/articles/kbc14), accessed November 13, 2011. Published by the Texas State Historical Association.

Minor, David. "BURNETTA COLLEGE," Handbook of Texas Online (http://www.tshaonline.org/ handbook/online/articles/kbb22), accessed January 17, 2012, Published by the Texas State Historical Association.

———, and Nancy Beck Young. "CLEBARRO COLLEGE," Handbook of Texas Online (http://www. tshaonline.org/handbook/online/articles/kbc28), accessed November 13, 2011. Published by the Texas State Historical Association.

Murray, Lois Smith. Baylor at Independence. Waco: Baylor University Press, 1972.

Nall, Matthew Hayes. "CHRISTIAN COLLEGE OF THE SOUTHWEST," Handbook of Texas Online (http://www.tshaonline.org/handbook/online/articles/kbc19), accessed December 13, 2011. Published by the Texas State Historical Association.

Odintz, Mark. "CENTENARY COLLEGE," Handbook of Texas Online (http://www.tshaonline.org/ handbook/kbc53), accessed October 19, 2011. Published by the Texas State Historical Association.

Reynolds, J. A. "TEXAS BAPTIST EDUCATIONAL SOCIETY," *Handbook of Texas Online* (http://www.tshaonline.org/handbook/kat11), accessed June 22, 2015. Uploaded on June 15, 2010. Published by the Texas State Historical Association.

Sharpless, M. Rebecca. "CENTRAL TEXAS COLLEGE," *Handbook of Texas Online* (http://www.tshaonline.org/handbook/online/articles/kcc10), accessed November 08, 2011. Published by the Texas State Historical Association.

———. "Sallie McNeill: A Woman's Higher Education in Antebellum Texas." In *Texas Women: Their Histories, Their Lives*, edited by Elizabeth Hayes Turner, Stephanie Cole, and Rebecca Sharpless, 82–104. Athens: University of Georgia Press, 2015.

Sinks, Julia Lee. "Rutersville College." *Texas State Historical Association Quarterly* 2 (1948): 124–33.

Spencer, Diane E., "SOUTH TEXAS BAPTIST COLLEGE," *Handbook of Texas Online* (http://www.tshaonline.org/handbook/online/articles/kbs26), accessed November 2, 2011. Published by the Texas State Historical Association.

Taylor, Clifford H. "Jarvis Christian College." Bachelor's thesis, Texas Christian University, Fort Worth, 1948.

Temple, Louann Atkins. "CONCORDIA UNIVERSITY AT AUSTIN," *Handbook of Texas Online* (http://www.tshaonline.org/handbook/online/articles/kbc40), accessed September 18, 2014. Published by the Texas State Historical Association.

Terry, Marshall. *From High on the Hilltop*. Dallas: Three Forks Press, 2009.

"TILLOTSON COLLEGE," *Handbook of Texas Online* (http://tshaonline.org/handbook/online/articles/kbt27) assessed June 15, 2010, Modified on June 5, 2013. Published by the Texas State Historical Association.

Welch, June Rayfield. *The Colleges of Texas*. Dallas: GLA Press, 1981.

Whisenhunt, Donald W. *Encyclopedia of Texas Colleges and Universities*. Austin: Eakin Press, 1986.

White, Fred A. *The History of Dallas Baptist University*. Dallas: Harty's Press, 1991.

White, Michael A. *History of Baylor University: 1845–1861*. Waco: Texian Press, 1968.

Williams, Michael E., Sr. *To God Be the Glory: The Centennial History of Dallas Baptist University, 1898–1998*. Arlington, TX: Summit Publishing Co., 1998.

Wooster, Robert. "COLD SPRINGS FEMALE INSTITUTE," *Handbook of Texas Online* (http://www.tshaonline.org/handbook/online/articles/kbc33), accessed January 17, 2012. Published by the Texas State Historical Association.

Wrotenbery, Carl R. *Baptist Island College: An Interpretive History of the University of Corpus Christi, 1946–1973*. Austin: Eakin Press, 1998.

Yancy, Karen. "CLIFTON COLLEGE," *Handbook of Texas Online* (http://www.tshaonline.org/handbook/online/articles/kbc49), accessed September 18, 2014. Published by the Texas State Historical Association.

Young, Nancy Beck. "HOUSTON BAPTIST UNIVERSITY," *Handbook of Texas Online* (tsaonline.org/handbook/online/articles/kbh09), accessed November 8, 2011. Published by the Texas State Historical Association

———. "UNIVERSITY OF INCARNATE WORD," *Handbook of Texas Online* (http://www.tshaonline.org/handbook/online/articles/kbu07), accessed March 05, 2012. Published by the Texas State Historical Association.

———. "UNIVERSITY OF SAN AUGUSTINE," *Handbook of Texas Online* (http://www.tshaonline.org/handbook/online/articles/kcu06), accessed September 14, 2014. Uploaded on June 15, 2010. Published by the Texas State Historical Association

STATE NORMAL SCHOOLS AND COLLEGES

To understand how Texas provided for better teachers for
the public schools and how those efforts led to the State
Normal Schools and Colleges it is necessary to understand
the forces at work that caused these events to occur.
The word normal is from a Latin word that means a rule
or a model. So the idea was developed that a place that
developed teacher rules should be called a normal school.
The very first normal institute was established in 1685
in Rheims, France by a religious order planning to offer
primary education to children of the French working class.
In the United States in the 1850's the American normal
school was a subject of skepticism as an institution for the
preparations of teachers. Despite those criticisms normal
schools represented an idea that there was a need for special
preparation for teaching and they were willing to change
with the times.[1]

Prior to the Civil War, the control of schools and teachers in
Texas had been a local matter and the superintendent of public
instruction had been elected in a statewide election. During
Reconstruction many northern politicians moved to Texas with the
express intent of helping to enact laws they perceived to be necessary
for the development of education. The Republican Party dominated
Texas politics from 1870 to 1875. Historian of education Frederick

Eby (1925) refers to the law enacted at that time as the "Radical School Law" of 1871, "radical" because it called for a highly centralized system of public education. Prior to its passage there had been no system of public education in Texas, and its passage made normal schools (teacher training schools) a necessity because the new public schools would need teachers. According to Eby, the law set up the "most imperial system of education known to an American State."[2] The State Board of Education, which consisted of the superintendent of public instruction, the governor, and the attorney general, was empowered to provide for the examination and appointment of all teachers, fix teacher salaries, define the state course of study, and select textbooks and apparatus for schools.[3]

A young Prussian military officer, Jacob C. De Gress, was appointed superintendent of public instruction and charged with making the new centralized system work. For the first time, teachers were employed by the state without local input, and local residents had no say in the conduct of the schools that the law required them to attend. The superintendent also established a rule that no teacher would be allowed to teach in the public schools without a teacher's certificate issued by the superintendent.

At the time, Texas had a serious teacher shortage because the state had only a few private colleges offering programs for teacher training and thus nowhere near enough graduates to fill open positions. Most teachers were from other states or foreign countries and few were educated to teach. In response to the shortage, Superintendent De Gress, in his report to the governor in 1872, suggested the possibility of establishing a normal school, and so began the discussion in Texas.[4]

In comparison with other states, Texas was late in establishing normal schools. From 1839 to 1900, normal colleges (or schools) were organized across the United States in an effort to increase the number of qualified teachers for elementary and secondary schools. Normal schools (called that until 1923) were the predecessor of teachers colleges, which later all evolved into universities while still remaining close to their teacher-training roots. Charles Hunt, who in 1940 was secretary-treasurer of the American Association of Teachers Colleges (a department of the National Education Association) and head of a state normal school in New York, had this to say about these institutions:

> The normal school has become the teachers college. While a few institutions are still called normal schools, these will soon be gone. This transformation, which is much more than a change in name has been amazingly rapid. During the first sixty years of their existence, the normal schools were poorly supported, isolated institutions. They have had, however, a significant central purpose which made them sturdy and fitted them into the American scene. The founders of this nation recognized that education for all the people was essential in a democracy. A citizen who could cooperate with his fellows in making democracy work was essential. It was also implicit in their thought that the individual, and by that is meant all persons, should have an opportunity to become as much of a person as he could be in this new democracy.
>
> When common schools were first established, it soon became apparent that the quality of the experience which children might have in them was dependent upon the quality of the teacher.[5]

The first normal school was started in Lexington, Maryland, on July 3, 1839, with an enrollment of twelve students and an instruction period of one year. By 1850 there were more than fifteen state normal schools around the country. Membership numbers from the American Association of Teachers Colleges show that in 1917 there were forty-seven normal schools that belonged to the association. These institutions had a total enrollment during the regular school year of 15,849 students. During the summer session there were an additional 13,362 students enrolled. By 1926 these original forty-seven institutions were teaching 38,076 students during the regular school year, and an additional 39,414 in summer sessions. During the decade from 1917 to 1926, the increase in enrollment in these institutions was an astonishing 240 percent.[6] According to the *Peabody*

Journal of Education issue of September 28, 1939, the students from these colleges and schools were teaching 97 percent of the elementary and secondary students in the United States—the very institutions that were beginning to educate large numbers of students and increase the number of people in the country who could read and write.[7]

Bruce Payne, president of George Peabody College for Teachers in Nashville, Tennessee, gave an address to the American Association for Teachers Colleges on February 24, 1928, in which he explained just how important was the role played by teachers trained at these colleges:

> I have had the honor, then to talk today with regard to the pipelines of distribution that leads [*sic*] down from the reservoirs of discovered knowledge in the world. There are no other pipelines possible except those which the teachers themselves establish by word of mouth to their own pupils.
>
> This, then—the teacher college—is the only type of institution which, in any very large and appreciable way, stands as a sort of hopper into which every grain of truth, when poured, may be sent down to the eager minds of all the people, and especially the ninety-seven percent who never go to college or university.[8]

In its quest to improve education in the South, the Peabody Education Fund employed Dr. Barnas Sears, fifth president of Brown University, as general agent. Sears first visited Texas in 1869, where he discovered an education system in chaos because of the political turmoil immediately following the Civil War and the state's struggle over how to proceed in public education. Because of the turmoil, Sears at the time advised the Peabody Education Fund trustees not to invest in Texas. The need for qualified teachers in Texas was well known as the growing state tried to make up for years of neglect and antipathy towards its public schools, and Sears returned to Texas ten years later. He came at the invitation of Governor Roberts, to attend a meeting of teachers in Austin to investigate the school law at the time and make suggestions to improve it. At that meeting, it was proposed to Sears that the Peabody Fund board provide assistance to the state in establishing a teacher training school. Sears offered $6,000 if the legislature would appropriate an additional $14,000.[9]

Finally, on April 21, 1879, Texas Governor Oran M. Roberts signed the bill establishing Sam Houston Normal Institute in Huntsville, the first school for the training of white teachers in the state. Roberts had worked for some time in cooperation with the Peabody Education Fund to begin the normal school movement in Texas. The Fund gave Sam Houston Normal Institute $6,000 the first year and continued to give it smaller amounts for a number of years. This support was a direct result of the interest in helping Texas schools expressed by wealthy New England merchant George Peabody when he established the fund in 1867.[10]

Sam Houston Normal Institute was located at the site previously occupied by Austin College, which the Presbyterian Synod had moved to Sherman in 1878. This was the first tax-supported teacher training institution in Texas. The legislature gave control of the institute to the State Board of Education with the provision that it appoint three Huntsville citizens as the local board of directors. The legislation establishing this institute was unlike other bills that established public colleges in that it called for admittance of two students from each of the state senatorial districts and six from the state at large, all to be admitted by competitive examination. These "state students" were given scholarships that obligated them to teach in their home senatorial districts when they completed their schooling. That policy ended in 1910.[11]

In a faculty address given at Southwest Texas State Normal on June 17, 1890, former Governor Roberts offered a definition of normal schools and described the intent behind the series of laws that had established the seven public state normal institutions:

> The normal schools are the creatures of the Legislature, and are not mentioned in the Constitution. They were instituted to train the teachers of the time, that there was no uniformity in the mode

of teaching in the common schools throughout the State. They were not intended to be schools for teaching pupils, further than to perfect them in the best modes of teaching, and in learning the common school branches. For that purpose, provision was made to collect them from all parts of the State, and give them such training at the public expense, and send them back obligated to teach in the public schools. They are emphatically an adjunct, and part of the public free school system of the State, and should be kept so. Would it not have been a strange and unheard thing, to establish a school in this State to teach a select body of young men and young women with free tuition, free board and lodging, with books and stationery furnished free at the public expense? If the object had been merely to educate them, that is, to make them better scholars, such partiality to them would have been an outrage upon common sense and common justice. There was no such design. They were established to train teachers to teach in the public schools, and inaugurate the best mode of teaching uniformly throughout the State. That was and still is the true consideration for the liberal outlay of money by the State for their support.[12]

Every two years the Superintendent of Public Instruction was required by law to issue to the governor a biennial report on the state of education at both the public schools and the institutions of higher education. Superintendents were the state leaders when it came to proposing state education policy. Members of the legislature, along with the governor, used the superintendent's ideas to propose legislation that affected education across the state. Superintendent Benjamin Baker issued the "Fifth Biennial Report" in 1886, and in it he commented on the status of the teaching profession:

The State has the best reason to be proud of the progress of her teachers. I attribute their advancement in a large way to the fact that the most recent changes of school law have encouraged them to become professional teachers. Some of the provisions of the law of 1874 bore so unjustly upon them that there were few who looked

upon themselves as in the work for life. The provisions of that law
making teachers' salary dependent upon the attendance of pupils was
a relic of barbarism. Its repeal and the advance in maximum salaries
allowed by the law of 1884 give promise of adequate remuneration
to the teacher and encourages him to regard the profession
as not wanting in dignity. The State normal schools and the
summer normal, so generously provided, have also been powerful
instruments in advancing the profession. It is probable now that no
State can boast of a better qualified, more conscientious corps of
public school teachers.[13]

Prior to this, much that was reported about the teaching
profession was negative, in part because teachers were not properly
trained and were not treated by the local schools as professionals.
At the time of the report there were only two public normal institutions, and Baker commented on both. About Sam Houston
Normal Institute he said, "It has done wonderful work for Texas
and if liberally supported will increase in usefulness each succeeding year. Teachers who have attended this institution may be found
in every county and in almost every city. In every instance they
are worthy and competent." At the time Sam Houston only served
the white population.[14]

Prairie View Normal School was the school that trained teachers
for the black schools. About Prairie View, Baker said, "It has a most
excellent faculty, and is doing splendid work. It has accomplished
much in elevating the standard of the colored teachers of the State."[15]
In praising the work done by both institutions he reported that the
two institutions could not provide enough graduates to staff all of
the public schools, and he asked that the legislature consider adding
additional normal schools.[16]

When Sam Houston Normal Institute opened on October 10,
1879, it was a two-year school with 110 students. Among the first
graduating class two years later were seven students who would
have outstanding careers. They included H. F. Estill, later president of the Institute; Allison Mayfield, who would be elected to

the powerful Texas Railroad Commission; T. U. Taylor, who for many years was head of the engineering school at the University of Texas; Anna Hardwicke Pennybacker, a well-known teacher and historian; Anna's husband Percy V. Pennybacker, also a well-known educator; and J. S. Brown, who became head of the math department at Southwest Texas State Teachers College.[17]

The Institute's main building was dedicated on September 22, 1890. By 1911 it was possible to receive training for four years at the Institute, with the last two years providing a junior college degree, and in 1915 it began offering a four-year bachelor's degree. In 1911 the school was put under the control of the Normal School Board of Regents, which was eventually succeeded by the Texas State University System Board of Regents.[18]

Superintendent of Public Education Oscar H. Cooper in his 1890 biennial report to the governor discussed the need for more teachers. He estimated the shortfall of trained teachers to be about three thousand, and in the report he described the sources of teachers for Texas public schools:

> The agencies established by the State through the law for the improvement of teachers may be grouped under four heads:
> I.   County Institutes
> II. Summer Normals
> III. State Normal Schools
> IV. County and City Examination

In his report Cooper explained the role of each of the four sources. The county institutes were one-day, monthly meetings of teachers conducted by the county judge or local superintendent. Cooper complained that one day was not enough time and posed a hardship on the teachers who had to travel to the county seat for the meetings. Cooper's solution was to follow the example of other states where county institutes met for an entire week. The report recommended to the governor that Texas change its law to mandate a one-week monthly meeting of teachers.

The summer normal schools were short-term normal schools with a primary duty to instill professionalism in the attending teachers and provide insight into improved methods of instruction. They also conducted examinations for teaching certificates. In 1890 there were forty-five of these schools in operation.

State normal schools Cooper called the most important source for training teachers, and he cited the good work being done by Sam Houston Normal Institute for white teachers and Prairie View Normal Institute for black teachers.

The fourth source of teachers was county and city examinations. These had been authorized by the legislature so those entities could conduct examinations to ascertain the quality of teacher candidates for their local school districts and issue certificates to those who passed the examination. The certificates were only good in the county in which the candidate took the exam and were good for only one year.[19]

None of these four methods were producing the number of qualified teachers needed. The new Superintendent of Public Instruction, J. M. Carlisle, again addressed the continuing shortage in his 1893 report. He described Sam Houston Normal Institute as running at full capacity and, while praising the quality of its graduates, lamented the fact that they were only able to produce 225 teachers a year, woefully short of the number needed. Carlisle also wrote about the new normal department that had recently been established at the University of Texas and was intended to produce additional good teachers. While he applauded the efforts of the administration, he noted that the worthy efforts would only produce a small number of teachers. He called on the governor and the legislature to increase the number of normal schools.[20]

East Texas Normal College is considered to be the second normal school established in Texas. The school was originally founded by W. L. Mayo as a private college at the town of Cooper in 1889. In 1894 Mayo moved the college to the town of Commerce. By 1917, under Mayo's leadership it had become one of the largest private colleges in the South, and he was widely regarded for the great interest he took in the students who attended his school:

> He was a friend to the friendless, a father to the fatherless, a guide to the blind, and a benediction to all. Education for the masses was his doctrine. Education for leadership as associated with the aristocratic idea of education had no place in his thinking.[21]

Attendance at the college during the 1895–1896 school year was eighty-eight students. In the 1900–1901 school year the enrollment was 324. In 1917, the college's last year as a private school, there were 2,400 students in attendance during the regular and summer sessions. That same year, the state legislature passed a bill to purchase the college and rename it East Texas State Normal College.[22]

Eighteen years earlier, on May 19, 1899, the legislature had passed a bill establishing Southwest Texas Normal School, to be located at San Marcos. The citizens of San Marcos donated eleven acres of land and in 1901 the legislature appropriated $25,000 for the first building. The State Board of Education, which oversaw the school, wanted the new building to be a duplicate of the main building at Sam Houston Normal School. Southwest Texas Normal School opened on September 9, 1903, and by 1918 it had become a senior college and changed its name to Southwest Texas State Normal College.[23]

The same act of May 19, 1899, also established the North Texas Normal College, and the legislature appropriated the money to open it in 1901. The college really began in 1890 when Joshua C. Chilton and the citizens of Denton founded Texas Normal College and Teacher's Training Institute as a private college to train teachers. Chilton and the citizens who operated the Institute did not receive their state charter until 1891, by which time the group had purchased a permanent campus. The first classes had been held in September 1890 in a corner of the hardware store located on the Denton town square. The city of Denton financed the first new building of the college and 185 students attended in the first year it was open. The school soon began to have financial difficulties and a request was made to the legislature to create a normal school. On March 31, 1899, Governor Joseph D. Sayers signed a bill doing just that. Under state ownership, the college received senior status by 1917 and began conferring bachelor's degrees, and by 1923, when its enrollment reached 4,736, it had become the largest teacher training institution in the southwestern United States. On August 29, 1961, it became North Texas State University and in 1988, it assumed its current name of the University of North Texas.[24]

In 1909 the legislature established West Texas State Normal College in the city of Canyon, which donated forty acres of land and $100,000 toward construction of the college. The school opened in 1910 as a two-year school and by 1919 it was granting four-year degrees. It was the first of the teachers colleges to grant a master's degree. W. M. Thornton, in an article written for the *Dallas Morning News* in November 1918, described the location:

> An asset which the Canyon college publishes to the world is the near-by Palo Duro Canyon, a Grand Canyon in miniature. It is proclaimed as the greatest out-of-door asset of that place, being of such rare beauty. It is becoming a shrine to those who frequent it, since it furnishes an ideal recreation ground, a field of study for the student of geometry, geology, ornithology, or biology, and is the delight to the artist. The college encourages the students to make the canyon their playground.[25]

In 1917 the legislature established Stephen F. Austin Normal College. A committee consisting of the governor, the superintendent of public instruction, and the regents of the normal colleges was charged with finding a city for the college. They chose Nacogdoches, which had an early history as a site for a college since the by then defunct Nacogdoches University had been founded there in 1845. Thornton noted that during A. W. Birdwell's tenure as president of the school (1923–1942):

> Most of the students at Nacogdoches are drawn from the farms of East Texas, and Dr. Birdwell is of the opinion that Texas will always

have its rural life and that, therefore, the colleges should recognize that fact and serve it, as they are endeavoring to do in teacher training. He says that Anglo-Saxons love agriculture and it will ever be with us, make rural communities indigenous and permanent.[26]

Also in 1917, the legislature passed a bill establishing Sul Ross Normal College at Alpine in Brewster County. The bill required the county to donate a minimum of 100 acres of land for the school, while the legislature appropriated $40,000 for operating expenses and $200,000 for construction of the buildings. When the buildings were completed the college opened in June 1920. In 1923 the legislature changed the name of the school to Sul Ross State Teachers College, and in 1949 to Sul Ross State University.

Sul Ross State College is situated on one of the most commanding locations in Texas. Its position is unequaled by that of any other state or private institution. The college is placed on a small level spot half the distance up a tall mountain. It is far above the town of Alpine, and the view commands the whole county, except to the rear, where the mountain continues upward. On this great slope the students have made the college monogram in white stones, the letters being 150 feet in length. From Alpine and from the San Antonio–El Paso Highway the letters appear to be about fifteen feet long, so great is the elevation.[27]

The 1917 law also proposed a teacher college to be located in South Texas, but the location and the opening were postponed because of World War I. In 1923 the locating committee chose the town of Kingsville for South Texas State Teachers College. It opened in 1925, and in 1929 the legislature changed the college's role to that of a technical college and its name to Texas College of Arts and Industry. In 1967 the name was changed again to Texas A&I University. Although it was given additional duties, teacher education continued to be part of its mission.[28]

From 1879 until 1913, course work at the Texas state normal colleges covered a maximum of three years, and the senior year was the only time when college level courses were part of the curriculum. Then during 1915 to 1918 the colleges' requirements included two years of college level courses, and from 1918 until 1921 this increased to the degree granting level of four years. During the period from 1922 to 1925 all the schools became accredited members of the Association of Texas Colleges and the Southern Association of Colleges and Secondary Schools (SACSS). By 1931 the first of them began offering graduate degrees, and by 1937 all were doing so.[29]

National accreditation was an important and time-consuming process that began with a review of course material, equipment, laboratories, library accommodations, and faculty scholarship at each school, conducted by faculty from the University of Texas. These reviews helped facilitate later review by the Southern Association of Colleges and Secondary Schools and helped to prepare the way to accreditation.[30]

In January 1951, twenty-three distinguished educators from other states, including New York, California, Kansas, Missouri, Oklahoma, and Mississippi, acting for the SACSS evaluated only Southwest Texas State Teachers College in San Marcos. This evaluation was part of an effort by SACSS to upgrade teacher education in the nation by reviewing 245 members of the organization. The SACSS had developed new standards and inspection protocols for this review. The entire program at Southwest Texas was reviewed and evaluated—every department and every agency. The result was an official report that paid tribute to the work being done at the college to train quality teachers.[31]

A survey conducted in Texas in 1933 reviewed the distribution of students in the teaching colleges and found that 62.7 percent of the students attending the seven teaching schools lived within 100 miles of the school they were attending. The legislature was interested in where students were coming from and this information was used in discussions about the feasibility of having so many of these schools in the state.[32]

CONTROL OF THE NORMAL SCHOOLS

From 1899 until 1911, control of the teaching schools was under the auspices of the State Board of Education, but in 1911 a bill was enacted that established the Normal School Board of Regents whose members were to be appointed by the governor. This new board enacted the following changes for all of the normal schools:

1. Uniform entrance requirements
2. Uniform courses of study
3. Increased study from three to four years
4. Established six distinct curricula for teacher training: agriculture, industrial arts, language, science, primary, and art.[33]

At the same time, the schools began training teachers in home economics; manual training, which included various industrial arts, such as woodworking; music; and kindergarten.[34]

The Conference for Education in Texas was a business-led organization with the primary goal of increasing the quality of rural public schools. In the fifth general session, held in April 1912, the state superintendent of public instruction provided an excellent description of the role of the state normal schools:

> The primary object of the State Normal Schools is to prepare
> and train teachers for the common public schools. The function
> of the normal schools, therefore, is to improve the scholarship
> of teachers, to increase their zeal, to augment their professional
> efficiency, and through its work to provide genuine leaders among
> the public school teachers of Texas. No work would be more
> important than that undertaken by the State Normal Schools
> of Texas. The public schools of Texas are each year demanding
> approximately 4000 new teachers, and it's the business of the
> State Normal Schools to respond to this demand, in a large,
> sound and professional spirit. It is but just to say that the State
> Normal Schools of Texas have done their part in the great work of
> education for the masses of people.[35]

As part of an effort to reform state government and cut costs, the legislature in 1931 appointed a special committee—the Joint Legislative Committee on Organization and Economy—and one element of its charge was to investigate the public universities and colleges for economic and governmental efficiency and to make recommendations to the entire legislature on how to improve the schools' performance. The committee was made up of three members of the House appointed by its speaker and two members of the state Senate appointed by the lieutenant governor. It was staffed by an experienced outside consultant group that helped perform the review.[36]

The committee issued its report on December 15, 1932. *Part 10. Education, Teachers Colleges* contained the review of all of the normal schools along with a review of the teacher education programs offered by other public colleges and universities. It made suggestions about reducing class sizes and discontinuing classes that were attracting only small groups of students. It recommended that the open admission enrollment in the normal schools be eliminated and that institutions use increased selectivity in their admissions. The report suggested better cooperation with local public school districts to increase the use of practice teaching programs as a recognized way to increase the performance of new teachers.

The portion of the report that caused the most concern for the normal schools was where it called for some consolidation of the schools, in particular where there were public colleges in close proximity to each other. These recommendations caused local communities to engage their own legislative delegations and make a strong case for the economic importance to local and regional economies that these schools continue to exist and grow stronger in both size and educational importance. The end result of all of the work of the Efficiency and Economy Committee was that little change came from the full legislature. The normal colleges, however, began to institute changes to improve the quality of both their student bodies and their faculties. The committee's report had an impact on the schools even without any major action from the legislature.[37]

During its first regular session, the Fifty-first Legislature in 1949 enacted three bills that effected a completed reorganization of the Texas public school system. These laws made sweeping changes in the administration of the system and the methods of school finance. The three bills that put into place this reorganization were known as the Gilmer-Aikin bills, after the Gilmer-Aikin Committee, which in 1947 had been given the charge by the legislature to survey the education system and recommend changes to improve the public schools of Texas.[38]

Senate Bill 116 was the longest and most complicated of the three bills. Among other issues it addressed a state minimum base salary for those holding a bachelor's degree, increase in pay based on years of service, and additional salary for those with a master's degree. It also put into place a payment schedule for school superintendents.[39]

The Gilmer-Aikin bills truly began to have an impact on the teaching profession by putting into place a method of providing for the public funding of public education and addressing various salary issues, including offering the incentives for teachers to obtain bachelor's and master's degrees.[40]

The Gilmer-Aikin programs, in fact, quickly showed positive results. The new system eliminated many uncooperative school districts, improved school attendance, placed a premium on academic excellence, and encouraged thousands of the state's teachers to go back for more schooling.[41]

There was a series of events that caused normal schools to grow to four-year senior colleges, and then universities when they began to add graduate degrees. In 1923 all of the Texas normal schools were renamed as state teachers colleges, which followed a national trend. These schools had, in fact, been allowed to begin offering bachelor's degrees several years earlier.[42]

Texas colleges and universities benefited from New Deal programs during the presidency of Franklin D. Roosevelt. Between 1935 and 1943, the National Youth Administration made it possible for thousands of young people to attend college. The first head of this program in Texas was Lyndon Johnson, who aggressively promoted the program. He was a graduate of Southwest Normal School and seemed to have an affinity for the normal colleges. Any needy student who applied to the program could earn up to $15 a month— the hourly wage was 25 cents—but at the time that was enough for a student to pay their way to a state college.[43]

Use of the GI Bill by the soldiers returning from World War II caused massive growth in college enrollment in Texas and throughout the country. The Texas Legislature in an effort to help returning solders took several steps to increase opportunities in the normal schools. In 1949 the state normal colleges were allowed to broaden their curriculum. This influx of students caused the colleges to quickly upgrade their offerings in an attempt to attract as many new students as possible. After these veterans graduated there was a decline in enrollment in all of the colleges.[44]

Beginning in 1955, teacher certification required holding at least a bachelor's degree and completing a state-approved teacher education program. This caused enrollment at the state teachers colleges to increase again.[45]

When Lyndon Johnson became president he continued his support for education. He appointed a task force in 1964 headed by John W. Gardner, which, with the full support of Johnson, resulted in Congress passing the Higher Education Development Act. The Act provided grants to colleges for innovated academic programs, and grants to "emerging graduate schools." These efforts had a great impact on the state teacher colleges.[46]

In 1987 in a continuing effort to improve these colleges in a response to criticism that students were focusing on education courses and not enough on academics, the Texas Education Agency issued standards stating: "The best preparation for teaching is a high quality, well rounded education that includes a grasp of the humanities, the natural and social sciences, mathematics and the fine arts." Today teachers must meet minimum semester-hour requirements in their college programs, or demonstrate competency in English, speech, American history, political science, mathematics, computing and information technology, and the fine arts. They must complete at least sixty hours from those areas in addition to a foreign language. Thus, fully half of the 120 hours required for a degree is directed towards making the student well-rounded in their educational experience.[47]

* * * * *

Texas responded to the need for better-qualified teachers by passing legislation that established the state normal schools. Those schools' growth, in both size and prestige, was aided by the interest of its citizens in receiving a good public school education. Many organizations and groups worked hard to make their voices heard by the elected officials of Texas, including the governor and members of the legislature. Those efforts led to a series of laws that continued to improve these educational institutions. Much credit must be given to the Normal School Board of Regents and the presidents of the various institutions under its control. Those presidents, in turn, have relied on administrative staff and faculty members to play major roles in increasing the professionalism of public school teachers in Texas. Their collective success is evident today in the quality of the universities that began as normal schools.

While this chapter has focused on the state normal schools and their impact on the increase in knowledge and professionalism among Texas teachers, they are not the only schools that have worked to achieve that goal. Thus, the focus here should not detract from the important role other institutions of higher education in the state have also played. All the state universities and many of Texas's private colleges maintain education departments that help train teachers at all levels and have played long-term, critical roles in providing quality college graduates to fill the ranks of the state's teaching corps.

NOTES

1. George A. Dillingham, *The Foundation of the Peabody Tradition* (Lanham, MD: University Press of America, 1989), 87–88.

2. Chara Haeussler Bohan and J. Wesley Null. "Gender and the Evolution of Normal School Education: A Historical Analysis of Teacher Education Institutions" *Educational Foundations* 21, no. 3–4 (Summer-Fall 2007), 7.

3. Texas. *The Laws of Texas, 1822–1897*. Compiled and arranged by H. P. N. Gammel. 10 vols. (Austin: Gammel Book Company, 1898), 6: 960. Supplementary vols. 11–31 cover the years 1897–1939 (hereafter referred to as *Gammel's Laws of Texas*); An Act to Organize and Maintain a System of Public Free Schools in the State of Texas, General Laws of the Twelfth Legislature of the State of Texas, First Session, 1871, 57.

4. Donna Lee Younger, "Teacher Education in Texas, 1879–1919" (PhD diss., University of Texas, Austin, 1964), 63–65.

5. Charles W. Hunt, "From Normal School to Teachers College," *College and Research Libraries* 1, no. 3 (June, 1940): 246.

6. Rebecca C. Tansil, "Steps in the History of Standardization of Normal Schools and Teachers Colleges," *Peabody Journal of Education* 7, no. 3 (Nov. 1929): 68.

7. Charles C. Sherrod, "The Contribution of the Normal Schools and Teacher Colleges," *Peabody Journal of Education* 17, no. 2. (Sep. 1939): 102–104.

8. Tansil, "Steps in the History of Standardization of Normal Schools and Teachers Colleges," 70.

9. Bohan and Null, "Gender and the Evolution of Normal School Education," 7; Mitchell, "Sears, Barnas."

10. C. E. Evans, *The Story of Texas Schools* (Austin, TX: Steck Co., 1955), 286; Martha Mitchell, "Sears, Barnas," in *Encyclopedia Brunoniana* (Providence, RI: Brown University Library, 1993). http://www.brown.edu/Administration/News_Bureau/Databases/Encyclopedia/search.php?serial=S0100.

11. *Gammel's Laws of Texas*, Sixteenth Legislature, pp. 181–82; Evans, *The Story of Texas Schools*, 288.

12. Ben Wilson, Jr., "History of Teacher Education at Southwest Texas State University" (PhD diss., Baylor University, 1977), 39–40.

13. Benjamin M. Baker, *Fifth Biennial Report of the Superintendent of Public Instruction for Scholastic Years Ending August 31, 1885, and August 31, 1896* (Austin, TX: State Printing Office, 1886), 7.

14. Baker, *Fifth Biennial Report of the Superintendent of Public Instruction*, 15.

15. Ibid., 15–16.

16. Ibid., 16.

17. J. M. Bledsoe, *The Old Mayo School* (Dallas: Harben-Spotts Co., 1946), 35; Evans, *The Story of Texas Schools*, 287.

18. Evans, *The Story of Texas Schools*, 288.

19. Oscar H. Cooper, *Seventh Biennial Report of the Superintendent of Public Instruction for the Scholastic Years Ending August 31, 1889, and August 31, 1890* (Austin, TX: State Printing Office, 1890), 20–21.

20. J. M. Carlisle, "Eighth Biennial Report of the State Superintendent of Public Instruction for the Scholastic Years Ending August 31, 1891, and August 31, 1892," Austin, TX: Ben C. Jones & Co. State Printer, 1893, 16–17.

21. Evans, *The Story of Texas Schools*, 285.

22. William M. Thornton, *How Texas Trains Its Teachers: A Series of Fifteen Articles* (Dallas: Dallas News, 1928), 45; Evans, *The Story of Texas Schools*, 245.

23. Thornton, *How Texas Trains Its Teachers*, 54; June Rayfield Welch, *The Colleges of Texas* (Dallas: GLA Press, 1981), 130–31.

24. Thornton, *How Texas Trains Its Teachers*, 51; Robert S. La Forte, "UNIVERSITY OF NORTH TEXAS," *Handbook of Texas Online*, (http://tshaonline.org/handbook/online/articles/kcu53), accessed July 09, 2014. Uploaded on June 5, 2010. Published by the Texas State Historical Association.

25. Evans, *The Story of Texas Schools*, 297–96.

26. Ibid., 295.

27. Ibid., 297–96.

28. Welch, *The Colleges of Texas*, 146.

29. Evans, *The Story of Texas Schools*, 283.

30. Evans, *The Story of Texas Schools*, 284.

31. Ibid., 284.

32. Crutsinger, *Survey Study of Teacher Training in Texas*, 67.

33. Evans, *The Story of Texas Schools*, 284.

34. Ibid.

35. F. M. Bralley, "Organization for the Enlargement by the State of Texas of its Institutions of Higher Education," in *Proceedings of the Fifth General Session of the Conference for Education in Texas* (Austin: A. C. Baldwin & Sons, 1912), 44–45.

36. Harry N. Graves, Texas Legislature Joint Legislative Committee on Organization and Economy, and Griffenhagen and Associates, *Part 10. Education, Teachers Colleges*, Part 10 of *The Government of the State of Texas: Report of the Joint Legislative Committee on Organization and Economy and Griffenhagen and Associates, Specialists in Public Administration and Finance* (Austin: A.C. Baldwin & Sons, 1932–33), 1; J. Horace Bass, "GRIFFENHAGEN REPORT," *Handbook of Texas Online* (http://www.tshaonline.org/handbook/online/articles/mkg01), accessed June 14, 2015. Uploaded on June 15, 2010. Published by the Texas State Historical Association.

37. Graves, et al., *Part 10. Education, Teachers Colleges*, 11.

38. Rae Files Still, *The Gilmer-Aikin Bills: A Study in the Legislative Process* (Austin: Steck Co., 1950), 1–3.

39. Still, *The Gilmer-Aikin Bills*, 608.

40. Alan W. Garrett, "TEACHER EDUCATION," *Handbook of Texas Online* (http://tshaonline.org/handbook/online/articles/kdtsj). Accessed December 09, 2014. Uploaded on June 15, 2010. Published by the Texas State Historical Association.

41. Donald W. Whisenhunt, *Texas: A Sesquicentennial Celebration* (Austin, TX: Eakin Press, 1984), 397.

42. V. R. Cardozier, "Higher Education," *Handbook of Texas Online* (http://tshaonline.org. handbook.online.articles/khhxr). Accessed June 25, 2016. Uploaded on June 25, 2010. Modified on August 21, 2012. Published by the Texas State Historical Association.

43. Ibid.

44. Ibid.

45. Texas Education Agency, "Teacher Certification in Texas," Bulletin 573, 1955.

46. Janet C. Kerr, "From Truman to Johnson: Ad Hoc Policy Formulation in Higher Education," *ASHE Reader* (Needham Heights, MA: Ginn Press, 1989), 512–22.

47. Texas Education Agency, "Teacher Certification in Texas."

BIBLIOGRAPHY

Baker, Benjamin M. *Fifth Biennial Report of the Superintendent of Public Instruction for Scholastic Years Ending August 31, 1885, and August 31, 1896*. Austin, TX: State Printing Office, 1886.

Bass, J. Horace. "GRIFFENHAGEN REPORT," *Handbook of Texas Online* (http://www.tshaonline. org/handbook/online/articles/mkg01), accessed June 14, 2015. Uploaded on June 15, 2010. Published by the Texas State Historical Association.

Bledsoe, J. M. *The Old Mayo School*. Dallas: Harben-Spotts Co., 1946.

Bohan, Chara Haeussler, and J. Wesley Null. "Gender and the Evolution of Normal School Education: A Historical Analysis of Teacher Education Institutions." *Educational Foundations* 21, no. 3–4 (Summer-Fall 2007): 3–26.

Bralley, F. M. "Organization for the Enlargement by the State of Texas of Its Institutions of Higher Education." In *Proceedings of the Fifth General Session of the Conference for Education in Texas*. Austin: A. C. Baldwin & Sons, 1912.

Brown, Sarah Drake, and John J. Patrick. *History Education in the United States: Study of Teacher Certification and Staff-Based Standards and Assessment for Teachers and Students*. Washington, DC: American Historical Association and Organization of American Historians, 2004.

Brown, Ronald C. *Beacon on the Hill: Southwest Texas State University, 1903–1978*. Dallas: Taylor Publishing, 1979.

Cardozier, V. R. "Higher Education" *Handbook of Texas Online*, (http://tshaonline.org.handbook. online.articles/khhxr). Accessed June 25, 2016. Uploaded on June 25, 2010. Modified on August 21, 2012. Published by the Texas State Historical Association.

———. *Colleges and Universities in World War II*. Westport, CT: Praeger, 1993.

Carlisle, James M. *Eighth Biennial Report of the State Superintendent of Public Instruction for the Scholastic Years Ending August 31, 1891, and August 31, 1892*. Austin, TX: Ben C. Jones & Co. State Printers, 1893.

———. *Ninth Biennial Report of the State Superintendent of Public Instruction for the Scholastic Years Ending August 31, 1893, and August 31, 1894*. Austin, TX: Ben Jones & Co., State Printers, 1895.

———. *Tenth Biennial Report of the State Superintendent of Public Instruction for the Scholastic Years Ending August 31, 1895 and August 31, 1896*. Austin, TX: Ben C. Jones & Co., State Printers, 1897.

Cooper, Oscar H. *Seventh Biennial Report of the Superintendent of Public Instruction for the Scholastic Years Ending August 31, 1889, and August 31, 1890*. Austin, TX: State Printing Office, 1890.

———. *Sixth Biennial Report of the Superintendent of Public Instruction for the Scholastic Years Ending August 31, 1887 and August 31, 1888*. Austin, TX: State Printing Office, 1988.

Cousins, R. B. *Fifteenth Biennial Report of the State Superintendent of Public Instruction for the Years Ending August 31, 1905, and August 31, 1906*. Austin, TX: Von Broeckmann & Schutze, State Printers, 1906.

Crutsinger, George M. *Survey Study of Teacher Training in Texas, and a Suggested Program*. Contributions to Education, no. 537. New York: Teachers College, Columbia University, 1933.

Dillingham, George A. *The Foundation of the Peabody Tradition*. Lanham, MD: University of America Press, 1989.

Eby, Frederick. *The Development of Education in Texas*. New York: Macmillan Co. 1925.

Evans, C. E. *The Story of Texas Schools*. Austin, TX: Steck Co., 1955.

Fraser, James W. *Preparing America's Teachers*. New York: Teachers College Press, 2007.

Funkhouser, Charles W. *Education in Texas: Policies, Practices and Perspectives*. 9th ed. Upper Saddle River, NJ: Prentice-Hall, 2000.

Garrett, Alan W. "TEACHER EDUCATION," *Handbook of Texas Online*. (http://tshaonline.org/ handbook/online/articles/kdtsj), accessed December 09, 2014. Uploaded on June 15, 2010. Published by the Texas State Historical Association.

Graves, Harry N. Texas Legislature Joint Legislative Committee on Organization and Economy, and Griffenhagen and Associates. *Part 10. Education, Teachers Colleges*. Part 10 of *The Government of the State of Texas: Report of the Joint Legislative Committee on Organization and Economy and Griffenhagen and Associates, Specialists in Public Administration and Finance*. Austin: A.C. Baldwin & Sons, 1932–33.

Hunt, Charles W. "From Normal School to Teachers College." *College and Research Libraries* 1, no. 3 (June 1940): 246–50.

Kendall, J. S. *Twelfth Annual Report of the State Superintendent of Public Instruction for the Scholastic Years Ending August 31, 1899 and August 31, 1900*. Austin, TX: Von Broeckmann, Moore & Schutze, State Printers, 1900.

Kerr, Janet C. "From Truman to Johnson: Ad Hoc Policy Formulation in Higher Education." In *ASHE Reader*. Needham Heights, MA: Ginn Press, 1989.

King, Kelly M. "Called to Teach: Percy and Anna Pennybacker's Contributions to Education in Texas, 1880–1899." *American Educational History Journal* 39, no. 1 (2012): 87–105.

Lafferty, H. M. "Of Time and the Teachers Colleges: In Texas." *Peabody Journal of Education* 42, no. 1 (July 1964): 14–22.

La Forge, Marguerite, and Clementine Faseler. "Southwest Texas State Teachers College, San Marcos." *Peabody Journal of Education* 22, no. 1 (July 1944): 7–9.

La Forte, Robert S. "UNIVERSITY OF NORTH TEXAS," *Handbook of Texas Online*, (tshaonline.org/handbook/online/articles/kcu53), accessed July 09, 2014. Uploaded on June 5, 2010. Published by the Texas State Historical Association.

Lefevre, Arthur. *Thirteenth Biennial Report of the State Superintendent of Public Instruction for the Scholastic Years Ending August 31, 1901, and August 31, 1902*. Austin, TX: Von Broeckmann, Schutze & Co. State Printers, 1902.

Mears, J. W. "Teacher-Training Programs of Seven Texas State Teachers Colleges." PhD diss., University of Texas, 1948.

Mitchell, Martha. "Sears, Barnas." In *Encyclopedia Brunoniana*. Providence, RI: Brown University Library, 1993. http://www.brown.edu/Administration/News_Bureau/Databases/Encyclopedia/search.php?serial=S0100.

Sheppard, Lorna Geer. *An Editor's View of Early Texas*. Austin, TX: Eakin Press, 1998.

Sherrod, Charles C. "The Contribution of the Normal Schools and Teacher Colleges." *Peabody Journal of Education* 17, no. 2. (Sept. 1939): 102–104.

Still, Rae Files. *The Gilmer-Aikin Bills: A Study in the Legislative Process*. Austin: Steck Co., 1950.

Tansil, Rebecca C. "Steps in the History of Standardization of Normal Schools and Teachers Colleges." *Peabody Journal of Education* 7, no. 3 (Nov. 1929): 164–67.

Texas Education Agency. "Teacher Certification in Texas." *Bulletin* 573, 1955.

Texas. *The Laws of Texas, 1822–1897*. Compiled and arranged by H. P. N. Gammel. 10 vols. Austin: Gammel Book Company, 1898. Supplementary vols. 11–31 cover the years 1897–1939. All volumes and the index are available at the University of North Texas Portal to Texas History, http://texashistory.unt.edu/explore/collections/GLT/.

Texas Education Agency, "Teacher Certification in Texas," *Bulletin* 573, 1955.

Thornton, William M. *How Texas Trains Its Teachers: A Series of Fifteen Articles*. Dallas: Dallas News, 1928. (Reprint of staff correspondence. *Dallas Morning News*, November 11–25, 1928.)

Welch, June Rayfield. *The Colleges of Texas*. Dallas: GLA Press, 1981.

Weltzin, J. Frederick. "Authority of Normal-School Boards to Establish Teachers' Colleges." *Elementary School Journal* 32, no. 1 (Sep. 1931): 44–52.

Whisenhunt, Donald W. *Texas: A Sesquicentennial Celebration*. Austin: Eakin Press, 1984.

Wilson, Ben, Jr. "History of Teacher Education at Southwest Texas State University." PhD diss., Baylor University, 1977.

Younger, Donna Lee. "Teacher Education in Texas, 1879–1919." PhD diss., University of Texas, Austin, 1964.

★ 8 ★

COMMUNITY/JUNIOR COLLEGES

For a long time, many perceived the United States as a land of opportunity. The European countries from which a great number of immigrants came were class-based societies, but America was seen as a place where, with hard work and some ability, one could achieve a financial reward based on merit. The rise of large corporations around the time of the Civil War began to change those perceptions as many felt it was more difficult for ordinary people to achieve success. This helped foster a discussion in the late nineteenth century about a new pathway that could provide greater chances for success for individuals. In 1885, in a widely reported speech made at Curry Commercial College in Pittsburgh, well-known industrialist Andrew Carnegie said that "the growth of 'immense concerns' had made it harder and harder . . . for a young man without capital to get a start for himself."[1]

Carnegie suggested that perhaps the way to improve the opportunities for the ordinary citizen was to follow the examples of educational benefactors such as Peter Cooper and Leland Stanford who with uncommon foresight had begun to endow colleges to provide new opportunities for success. Carnegie called them "ladders upon which the aspiring can rise."[2] He felt that there was no educational system in place to provide the skills necessary for a successful economic life; in the late nineteenth century, getting ahead in American was a matter of skill in the marketplace, not in the classroom.

In fact, at the time "getting a good education" was not mainstream thinking for most Americans. There were many reasons for this but one was certainly that there was no uniform structure in the country's educational system. While there were common schools in many communities, their primary purpose was to train citizens for life in a democratic society, not to train workers. To meet the new challenge, the educational system needed a new structure. To help create the ladders of ascent that Carnegie advocated, the educational system in the United States needed to be transformed from the loose array of high schools, colleges, and universities that served the relatively small number of students who continued their education beyond elementary school. By 1920, the stratified educational system that remains today began to appear, and a link began to develop between the labor market—which had in the past depended upon the self-made man—and the educational system that gave new life to the idea of equality of opportunity to those willing to climb those ladders. Out of that milieu the educational system in the United States was transformed and the two-year junior college came into being.[3] Of course, in the beginning, access to even this level of education was seldom extended to women and people of color. Here we will look at both how the institution began and grew and how access and opportunities would change over time.

* * * * *

In the late nineteenth century, William Rainey Harper, founding president of the University of Chicago, developed a plan to separate the first two years of college from the last two years; with this plan he revolutionized higher education. Harper's idea was modeled on Germany's "Gymnasium," and it involved creating two-year colleges, which he called junior colleges, with the intent that they would teach lower-level preparatory material. Junior colleges were designed to increase access to higher education without burdening existing four-year institutions, and they were generally defined as any institution accredited to award the associate in arts or associate in science as the highest degree. That definition included comprehensive two-year colleges and many technical institutes, both public and private.[4]

By 1940 the public school system had stabilized as a twelve-year program in most states. As large numbers of students completed four years of high school, increasing numbers of them sought admission to college. Most four-year colleges had never envisioned themselves as responsible for the education of the majority of high school graduates. Their education programs, at least in theory, were based upon restricted admissions designed to prepare their graduates for the professions or for advanced scholarly pursuits. In addition, a four-year college was beyond the financial reach of most students. The two-year colleges filled this void.[5]

While today's community college is a product of twentieth-century America, this modern idea has much in common with the colonial colleges. Early American colleges were always closely aligned with the localities whose interests they served, as community colleges are today.[6]

As discussed in previous chapters, many of the early private colleges in Texas began by providing two years of upper-level education along with a strong emphasis on teaching lower-level classes to prepare their students for upper-level work. Thus, the idea of a stand-alone two-year college was not a new one to Texans. Describing these early colleges, Frederick Eby said:

> The early institutions of Texas bore many pretentious names.
> The terms, university, college, academy, institute, seminary, and collegiate institute were rather promiscuously employed. Some of these high titles must be understood to designate their aspirations rather that any standard which they could hope to realize. The people were generally devoid of any sense of educational standards.
> These institutions were practically all organized on the same plan and attempting to do the same kind of work. Few students were of real collegiate standing. Rarely was any protest raised against the bombastic claims. The people in the towns proudly referred to the

"college on the hill," though none of its students could pass the sixth grade of a modern school.[7]

The organization of a junior college as an end goal first occurred in Texas in the town of Decatur in 1898, just over sixty years after the founding of the first four-year college in Texas (Rutersville College) in 1837. That first junior college was Decatur Baptist College, which is today Dallas Baptist University. Its establishment began a significant development in education that has seen many successes.[8]

As with so many things in Texas, the oil business has had a major impact on higher education. One of the most interesting stories of the beginning of a two-year college occurred in Port Arthur. When the famous Spindletop well was discovered in the area in 1901, its prolific production, as well as that of others in the area, led to the building of two oil refineries that then needed qualified workers of all types. One of the founders of the Texas Company (an oilfield owner later known as Texaco), John W. Gates, recognized the need for office workers; he also saw a need for radio operators to provide ship-to-shore communications for the transport ships taking oil to other parts of the world. He approached the Port Arthur City Council with the idea of starting a college—if they would provide the land, he would provide the money. With the council's approval the college opened its doors on October 8, 1909. It changed its name in 1911 to the Port Arthur Collegiate Institute, and today that junior college is known as Lamar State College–Port Arthur.[9]

EARLY ORGANIZATION

Most of the first private junior colleges in Texas were organized by one of several religious denominations; most prominent among them were the Baptist and Methodist churches. Churches had an interest at first in starting colleges primarily to provide religious education and basic education for their members in the communities where the colleges were located.

The importance of these colleges was pointed out by Wayland Moody who served both as president of a church-related junior college and of a public junior college:

> If we had not had the private junior college in Texas, we might never
> have had a public junior college system. Historically, the junior
> college concept grew out of private education. In most instances,
> it was a case where accreditation appeared on the scene that many
> of the private senior colleges could not meet the accreditation
> standards so they cut off the upper two years and became junior
> colleges. The private junior college had a great impact on the
> concept of the public junior college. A large number of people who
> pioneered the public junior college movement started out in the
> private junior college.[10]

The growth of the junior college movement in Texas owes special gratitude to Frederick Eby (1874–1968), who is considered the "Father of the Texas Junior College." Eby was a professor and chair of the Department of History and Philosophy of Education at the University of Texas from 1909 until 1957. In 1927 he made a study of junior colleges in other states where there had been rapid growth in those schools. He initiated a class on the junior college, which he taught for fifteen years. Through this course he taught many of the teachers and administrators who served in junior colleges in Texas and also in other states in the Southwest. Although his service and influence went beyond the junior college field, it is because of his scholarship and service in that area that he is known both as the Father of the Texas Junior College and as the Father of the Junior College Movement.[11]

Eby was honored by the junior college leaders of Texas in June 1949, when the president of Kilgore College, B. E. Masters, acknowledged him as having been the inspiration for many of the public and religious junior colleges established in Texas in the 1920s. He was also credited with the creation of a full professorship in junior college education at the University of Texas, the first of its kind in the United States.[12]

Eby credited Texas with the first system of both a junior college and a four-year college operating under the same board of regents. That first system was established by the Texas Baptist Education Committee in 1897–1898 and included Baylor University and Baylor College at Belton as the senior institutions and three junior institutions: Decatur Baptist, Rusk Baptist, and Howard Payne. Four other junior colleges were added in later years. In 1908, Burleson College at Greenville, which was originally a four-year college, was having financial difficulties and decided to become a junior college and joined the Baylor system. Wayland Baptist College at Plainview and Goodnight Baptist College in the town of Goodnight became members in 1913, and the College of Marshall joined in 1917.[13]

The Methodist church in Texas had for many years an affiliated system among their colleges. By the end of the nineteenth century the only strong Methodist college, both academically and financially, was Southwestern University. The church's other eight colleges were at this time preparatory institutions intended to help students gain entrance into Southwestern, so functioned essentially as feeder schools for the university. The system continued to expand and contract in number and size of schools until finally by 1930 it was no longer being used at all.[14]

One example of a college in the Methodist system was Clarendon College, which opened in 1898 and patterned itself after the traditional colleges of the time with preparatory, academic, and collegiate departments. What made Clarendon College unique was that its primary purpose was to conduct a university training school intended to prepare students to attend a four-year institution. It offered classes through the sophomore year.[15]

The Baptist and the Methodist systems were examples of the early use of a university management system that benefited both senior colleges and two-year colleges in a coordinated system. These systems provided an example of the models that Texas higher education followed.

In 1917, the Thirty-fifth Texas Legislature enacted a law that allowed junior colleges to issue certificates to teachers and gave the State Department of Education in Austin the authority to enforce certain standards for those colleges. In 1918, seventeen were approved as having achieved the highest state standards (see Table 8.1).[16]

Also in 1917, the privately owned John Tarleton College in Stephenville was donated to the state and accepted by the legislature to become a branch of the Texas A&M System. This came about in part because the president of A&M College, W. B. Bizzell, was a former Baylor student familiar with the Baylor system and he advocated for the same structure for A&M. During the same legislative session Grubbs Vocational Institute was also donated to and accepted by the state to become part of the A&M System.[17] The City of El Paso established the first public junior college in Texas in 1920. This was the College of the City of El Paso, and was the first of the Texas public junior colleges to be owned by a local community.[18]

Between 1922 and 1928 seventeen public junior colleges were established in Texas as auxiliaries of local school districts and under the control of the corresponding local school board. For example, in 1923, South Park Junior College was created in Beaumont as a branch of the South Park Independent School District, with the goal of having a junior college of the first class. The district superintendent served as the college's first president, and it opened with 125 students and 14 faculty members. Classes were held on the third floor of the new South Park High School. Years later this college became Lamar University.[19]

The growth of the denominational junior colleges began to slow in the 1920s, with only five private denominational colleges started during this period. Some of the early colleges closed due to lack of both students and funding, and a few of them became four-year institutions.

In 1927 Eby made a study of the junior college movement and prepared a report with recommendations on how to make the institutions that remained strong and valuable to the state. In the report's introduction he examined an important problem in the formation of these institutions: they had all been established based on local needs with little discussion as to what was best for education in the state as a whole. Eby asked a series of pointed questions:

> Shall Texas adopt a definite and intelligent policy looking to the promotion and control of these institutions, or shall we continue our habit of muddling along, always allowing our hopes of harmony and success to triumph over our experience? Is it not time that sectional selfishness should yield to the general welfare, and institutional rivalry to enlightened cooperation? Should it not be the desire, of all citizens that the educational facilities be afforded to every youth just as far as he is capable of deriving benefit from them.[20]

When Eby made his study in 1927 there were about 350 junior colleges in the United States and forty of them were in Texas. He recommended that the Texas Legislature pass a statute giving these colleges legal status and providing state support for their operation.[21]

State recognition of and funding for public junior colleges in Texas finally happened in 1929 when the legislature passed the Texas Junior College Law. There had been seventeen public junior colleges established between 1922 and 1928 and all were auxiliaries of public school districts and under the control of the corresponding local school board. With the Texas Junior College Law, the Legislature validated the public junior colleges already in existence and provided a mechanism by which additional public junior colleges could be established. The law also provided for a specific taxing authority for use by the local school districts. For the first time the legislature allowed local school districts, subject to approval by a district's voters, to use local taxes to support a junior college. This very important legislation enabled the creation of community colleges with local financial support. The law put into place the funding model for community college districts. At that time, supervision of these colleges was given to the Texas Education Agency, but, in 1965 they were placed under the control of the newly formed Texas Higher Education Coordinating Board.[22]

The 1929 law put into place a mechanism that allowed a school district or a city, whichever entity controlled the local schools, to allow voters the choice to establish a junior college district and create a property tax for that district. Under the law, a local board of trustees was given responsibility for governing, managing, and controlling the junior college. In addition, they were given the power to issue bonds and establish a tax rate, all subject to a local vote of the citizens within the district or city's boundaries. There was not yet enough public support for the legislature to provide financial support for these colleges.[23]

The first public junior college established under this law was Amarillo College in 1929. The president of the Amarillo College Board of Trustees is credited with providing support for the passage of the 1929 act that allowed junior college districts to exist separately from public school districts, an idea that was already being used successfully in California. The ability to access a new and dedicated funding source through local taxes was essential to the growth of junior colleges in Texas and around the country.[24]

No additional junior colleges were established in the five years that followed. One new one was established in 1934 (Lee College), and two more—Kilgore Junior College and Corpus Christie Junior College—were established in 1935. No others were founded during the 1930s, primarily because of the negative impacts of the Great Depression on the Texas economy.[25]

By 1939 there were fifteen denominational junior colleges, two state junior colleges, and twenty public colleges. They had a combined enrollment of 10,406, which was 14.8 percent of the total college enrollment in the state. This was a decline from the 1934–35 school year when junior college enrollment had been 19.2 percent of total enrollment. As the number of junior colleges increased, the enrollment numbers decreased. The legislature addressed this issue in 1937 by amending the Texas Junior College Law to provide state aid to the public junior colleges for the first time.[26]

By 1944, in Texas and nationally, it had become generally accepted that there were four major types of educational activity for which junior colleges were responsible:

1. The completion of what is commonly referred to as general or liberal education for a large body of American youth through age nineteen.
2. A program of preprofessional education for those interested in teaching, law, engineering, medicine, and other professions.
3. Provision of a broad base of short-term vocational education for probably as many as 60 percent of the youth in their respective communities who will never go beyond the junior college level or enter a profession or skilled trade.
4. Provision of additional education to an increasing number of adults who realize the necessity for continuous readjustment to conditions of modern life.[27]

While Texas's junior colleges ranked behind those in other states academically, a foundation was being laid for strong support of community colleges that would in time lead to an increase in educational quality. As public support for the role of junior colleges in the overall state higher education system began to increase, the Legislature in 1939 authorized two more public colleges—Cisco Junior College and Blinn Junior College.[28]

The junior colleges in Texas, along with the rest of higher education in the state, did not experience growth during the World War II years because so much of the college-age population was in the military and were stationed in other parts of the world. The Texas Junior College Association became concerned that their colleges needed more well-trained junior college administrators and teachers in order to properly serve the needs of their communities. The association asked the University of Texas to initiate a training program for junior college teachers and administrators as part of its School of Education. The University agreed and in November 1944 chose Clyde Cornelius Colvert, who had been the president of Northeastern Junior College in Louisiana for thirteen years, to head up the new program. He immediately began mailing out a newsletter to all of the junior colleges in Texas, and in 1945 he published a pamphlet for the association entitled "The Junior Colleges of Texas." He hoped that his efforts and the ideas in his publications would help to build support among Texans for the junior college movement. His message was straightforward:

1. The Texas Junior College is Responsive to the Community and Community Needs.
2. The Texas Junior College Raises the Educational Level of the People in the Community by Two years.
3. The Texas Junior College Provides Ample Opportunity for Individual Student Development in His Personality and Aptitudes Through the Student Activity Program.
4. The Texas Junior College Has an Important Function in Offering of Pre-Professional Courses.
5. The Texas Junior College is Obligated to Offer Terminal Courses.
6. The Texas Junior College Offers Adult Education.
7. The Texas Junior College Has Instructors and Administrators Who Specialize in Junior College Students.
8. The Texas Junior College is Economical and Efficient.[29]

In addition to publicizing the idea of junior colleges for Texas, Colvert was involved in the expansion of the junior college program. He served as a consultant to local communities that were considering establishing a junior college.[30] His efforts and those of others encouraged public support for junior colleges, and in 1950 the *Junior College Directory* reported that Texas had a total of fifty-seven junior colleges—thirty-six public and twenty-one private. The public institutions included two state colleges, Tarleton and Arlington, along with thirty-four others under the control of local districts. Ten of the private junior colleges were denominational, three were non-profit, one was supported by the YMCA, and seven were referred to as property schools, which meant they were supported by local property taxes.[31]

From the beginning of the public junior college movement in Texas those institutions were considered part of the public school system, as opposed to part of the state's higher education system. This was because most of the financing for the junior colleges came from local communities that wanted to maintain control.

In 1952, the Texas Education Agency, in a *Public Law Bulletin* noted that:

> An independent school district or a city which has assumed
> control of its schools, having an assessed property value not less
> than $12,000,000, or having an income provided by endowment or
> otherwise that will meet the needs of the proposed junior college
> district, and having an average of not fewer than 400 students in its
> regular four-year high school or high schools may, with the approval
> of the State Board of Education, establish and maintain a junior
> college district.
>
> It is the duty of the State Board of Education to determine
> whether the conditions named have been met and whether,
> considered from the geographical standpoint with reference to
> other colleges in the area, the location is desirable and feasible
> for a junior college. The State Board of Education must order
> an election in the territory proposed for the junior college; if a
> majority of the qualified taxpaying voters of such district approve
> the location of the junior college district, the district is deemed to
> be formed and created.[32]

At first, junior colleges were financed entirely from local school taxes and student fees. In 1941 the state made an appropriation of $325,000 a year, which was an estimated $50 per full-time student. In 1951–52 the per student allotment was raised to $189, and the total annual appropriation for the thirty-three Texas public junior colleges was $2,154,600 (see Table 8.3).[33]

As these institutions became more successful at fulfilling their local missions a movement began in 1949 to make some of the junior colleges into four-year schools. The first to go this route was Lamar College, formerly known as South Park Junior College and founded in Beaumont in 1924. In June 1949 the governor signed a bill making that junior college a four-year, state-supported senior college, with the new name Lamar State College of Technology. A dispute had arisen in the Legislature as to why Lamar College should be the first junior college elevated to a four-year status. Supporters argued successfully that while their area of the state had no four-year college, it had a large concentration of industrial and petrochemical operations and needed the ability to provide more engineering and science graduates to fill the jobs required by those industries.[34]

Lamar's success in gaining senior status spurred attempts by other communities to have their private junior colleges elevated to be state-supported four-year institutions. Another that was successful was Hardin College in Wichita Falls, when in 1959 the Legislature elevated it, then called Midwestern University, to be the nineteenth fully supported institution of higher education in the state.[35] That same year the Legislature also elevated Tarleton and Arlington, while turning down requests from Del Mar College, Odessa Junior College, Laredo Junior College, and San Antonio Junior College. In 1962 the Legislature approved requests from San Angelo College and Pan American College for public senior status.[36]

South Plains Junior College was the only public junior college established during the 1950s. Former Governor Preston Smith, when he was serving as a state representative from the West Texas District that includes the City of Levelland, was able to get legislative approval in 1959 for South Plains.[37] In 1963, Houston Junior College, which had operated as a municipal senior college since 1934, was approved by the Legislature as the University of Houston.[38]

Houston area school districts in Channelview, Deer Park, Galena Park, La Porte, and Pasadena began discussing combining their efforts to establish a junior college that would be supported by taxes from their combined districts. In a local election held May 30, 1960, voters approved the creation of what became San Jacinto College. When it opened it had the largest first-year enrollment of any Texas junior college up to that time.[39] In 1965, a junior college opened in Grayson County where the Grayson County Development Council had organized community support for the school.[40] This is now known as Grayson College.

MEETING STUDENT NEEDS

While the junior college movement in Texas was picking up public support, the schools themselves lagged behind those in the rest of the country in meeting the needs of students. In Texas, transfer curriculum dominated courses offerings, while in other parts of the country the majority of students were enrolled in occupational courses. In an effort to match junior colleges in other states, a movement arose in Texas in 1965 to increase the academic standards and financial support of existing junior colleges, and this led the movement toward statewide coordination. These efforts soon involved then-governor John Connally, who was committed to the idea of long-range planning for the state. He asked for and received permission from the Legislature to appoint a special committee to study education beyond the high school level. The governor's charge to the committee was to recommend steps to achieve a "standard of excellence second to none in the nation."[41]

One of the committee's most far-reaching recommendations was to establish a strong state coordinating board that would determine the number and character of higher education institutions the state should support. The committee also recommended the board formulate new degree programs and abolish others. In addition, the committee recommended an expansion of the junior college program to meet the projected needs of Texas higher education. In 1965, the Legislature (in House Bill 1) enacted nearly all of the committee's recommendations. As a result, the Coordinating Board of the Texas College and University System replaced the Texas Commission of Higher Education, which had been in place since 1955.[42]

The turning point for higher education in both Texas and the United States came in 1965 with the Federal Higher Education Act of 1965, which provided $2.3 billion to be used for scholarships, loans, and work programs. The bill also included federal support for the construction of facilities and the purchase of equipment. President Lyndon Johnson was a strong supporter of higher education and was aware that a lack of facilities and faculty led to a shortage of higher education opportunities. In Texas, the increase in support for junior colleges caused both Dallas County and Tarrant County to develop a strong interest in putting a junior college district in place in their respective counties.[43] That same year voters in Dallas County approved creation of the Dallas County Community College district, while voters in Tarrant County established the Tarrant County Community College District.[44]

DALLAS COUNTY COMMUNITY COLLEGE DISTRICT

The Dallas County Community College District story, including the early efforts to provide a junior college for the area, provides a good example as it closely follows efforts in other communities. There had been attempts in the Dallas area to establish a junior college as early as the late 1800s but those did not come to fruition and the junior college movement did not really begin in Dallas until the 1960s. Even then, it took a decade for the efforts to bear fruit, with the delay hinging on two issues: one, whether the college should serve only the city of Dallas or all of Dallas County, and two, if the new district should be part of the public school district or a separate district.[45]

The first attempt in Dallas to organize a junior college came in 1956 when the Dallas Independent School District (DISD) appointed a Junior College Committee and commissioned University of Texas professor C. C. Colvert to conduct a feasibility study. The study was intended to ascertain the level of interest in a community college on the part of Dallas voters. In 1958, the district superintendent withdrew the idea of a DISD junior college and disregarded the report because there was a concern that a desegregated city college would have an unwelcome impact on Dallas public schools, which were not integrated at the time.[46]

In 1960, the Dallas school board and the County School Superintendent, L. A. Roberts, became interested in establishing a community college district for all of Dallas County. Calvin Colvert's earlier study from 1958 had recommended just such a county-wide district. A DISD survey in the spring of 1964, showed that students and parents in the district were overwhelmingly supportive of the idea. The Dallas Chamber of Commerce became involved and, with support from the business community, in just over one year the voters of Dallas approved by a two-to-one margin a $41.5 million bond program to establish a county-wide community college district. Soon a board was elected that included outstanding business leaders with the clout and the money to make the venture a success. One of those board members, Margaret McDermott, recounted, "There we were: seven people with the money we needed and none of us truly expert in designing a college. We used the best consultants, but from the very first, we wanted the very best."[47]

In 1965, the board hired Bill Jason Priest to head the new college system. Selecting a president was just the first of many tasks facing the newly elected board. A top priority was to secure sites for the seven individual campuses called for by the planning process. At the time, there were fewer than twenty multi-college districts in the United States. By 1968 that number had grown to forty and most were in dense population centers like Dallas. One of the advantages of a multi-college system is leadership by a chancellor. That person has four distinct publics to whom she or he must respond: the Board of Trustees, the individual colleges, the community at large, and the state. The chancellor deals with the requests and needs of the Board of Trustees and the Legislature, thereby freeing the presidents of the individual colleges to deal with their communities and the needs of their particular college. This governing structure is also found in multi-college senior college systems, in Texas and elsewhere.[48]

Despite being behind in other areas, the Texas junior college system was one of the first in the country to emphasize technical and vocational programs as part of the curriculum. This allowed a student to complete a degree or a certificate at a two-year college and be prepared to enter the workforce. This was not common in the United States in 1965, but over the years it has become the standard for community college systems to foster both two-year degree programs and vocational training. The first large community college to do this was Dallas.

The colleges in the Dallas system were to operate with an open-door admission policy, which meant that anyone over the age of eighteen whose high school class had already graduated would be accepted into one of the system's colleges. There was widespread support for teaching remedial courses to improve underprepared students' chances for success. Chancellor Bill Priest also brought to Dallas the concept of non-credit courses, which were at the time called community service courses, for non-degree-seeking students. These were very progressive ideas for the time and they contributed to the fast growth and success of the system.[49]

The Dallas County Community College System has remained successful for several reasons. First, it has always been able to attract top talent to lead the system, beginning with Bill Priest. Second, the Dallas County community has continued to be very supportive of the system and that support has encouraged talented men and women to serve on the Board of Trustees. Two of the most outstanding board chairs over the years were R. L. (Bob) Thornton and Jerry Prater, both of whom served in the position for over a decade and their service provided stability for the system.

The Dallas County Community College System is just one example of how such a system might develop. Another example would be Lamar State College Orange, which offered academic courses in addition to vocational training. It opened in 1969 with the help of the local community, which raised the money to buy the first classroom.[50] Each of the fifty community college systems in Texas has a unique history. For the community college movement to have established such a large and diverse group of institutions in the very short period 1965–1969 was an outstanding achievement (see table 8.2).

The Coordinating Board of the Texas College and University System recommended a plan identifying the community junior college as one of three components, along with universities or colleges, and technical colleges, of Texas higher education. The Board outlined the role and responsibility of the public community junior colleges in three categories:

1. Provide general collegiate education that could lead to either an associate degree or provide preparation for an eventual baccalaureate degree to be earned upon transfer to a four-year institution.
2. Provide education in the technical-occupational area.
3. Offer continuing education along with cultural and public service programs.

In addition, the Board was instructed by the legislature to maintain an "open door" policy to allow access for anyone who could benefit from their instruction.[51]

On September 1, 1969, the James Connally Technical Institute in Waco was removed from the Texas A&M University System and made a stand-alone system with its own board of regents and a new name. The Texas State Technical Institute soon had new campuses in Amarillo and Sweetwater. There was a new awareness of the value of vocational technical education and the business community in the state was especially supportive of these efforts to help train a needed workforce.[52]

The rapid growth of the two-year colleges continued, as evidenced by what occurred in the 1970s. During that decade there was growth in the Dallas County Community College District as it added six additional campuses. San Jacinto College System opened an additional campus in 1974. Tarrant County Junior College District opened its Northwest campus in 1975.[53]

Houston Community College was opened in 1971 and a second junior college district was created in the Houston area in 1972. Three school districts, Aldine, Humble, and Spring, voted to begin the North Harris County College District. The campus opened in May 1976 and it later became the Lone Star Community College System. In Austin a community college was created that would operate under the control of the Austin Independent School District; it opened in 1973. Vernon Regional Junior College District was approved in 1972.[54]

Community/junior colleges in Texas have experienced rapid growth and fulfilled a valuable role in higher education. Because their purpose is broader than that of the liberal arts college or university, its educational programs differ in significant ways. They offer baccalaureate degree credits that are appropriate for the first two years' curriculum at a four-year institution and they provide the opportunity for a two-year associate degree. In addition, these institutions provide types of instruction not found at a senior institution and are noted for responding to local needs in many ways. They provide vocational programs for students who have not been successful in lower schools, and they afford opportunities for continuing education to students who are not interested in pursuing a degree but simply want to increase their knowledge in areas of personal interest.[55]

In *The Two-Year College: A Social Synthesis* written in 1965, the authors note that their "belief that the mission of the public two-year college is to educate all individuals of post-high school age or achievement level to the limits of their abilities is predicated upon the assumption that educational programs appropriate for changing societal needs and a heterogeneous student body can be formulated."[56]

It is likely that the initial statement of the mission of community colleges in the United States came from the report of the President's [Truman] Commission on Higher Education in 1947:

> Whatever form the community college takes, its purpose is educational service to the entire community, and this purpose requires of it a variety of functions and programs. It will provide college education for the youth of the community certainly, so as to remove geographic and economic barriers to educational opportunity and discover and develop individual talents at low cost and easy access. But in addition, the community college will serve as an active center of adult education. It will attempt to meet the total post-high school needs of its community.[57]

Anyone who has ever attended a two-year college, or even visited or read about the impact of one on the local community, has seen proof of the tremendous contribution junior colleges have made to higher education in Texas. The effect these colleges have had in local communities in providing technical training for workers of industry has greatly impacted the economic and population growth of Texas.

Table 8.1 Texas Public Junior Colleges in 1950–51

College Name	Date Established
Alvin Junior College	1949
Amarillo College	1929
Blinn Junior College	1927
Cisco Junior College	1940
Clarendon Junior College	1927
Del Mar Junior College	1935
Edinburg Junior College	1927
Frank Phillips Junior College	1946
Gainesville Junior College	1924
Hardin Junior College	1922
Henderson County Junior College	1946

College Name	Date Established
Hillsboro Junior College	1923
Houston Junior College	1927
Howard Junior College	1946
Kilgore Junior College	1935
Lamar College	1924
Laredo Junior College	1947
Lee Junior College	1934
Navarro County Junior College	1946
Odessa Junior College	1946
Panola County Junior College	1947
Paris Junior College	1924
Ranger Junior College	1926
San Angelo Junior College	1928
San Antonio Junior College	1925
St. Phillips Junior College	1927
Southwest Texas Junior College	1946
Temple Junior College	1926
Texarkana Junior College	1926
Texas Southmost College	1926
Tyler Junior College	1926
Victoria Junior College	1925
Weatherford College	1921
Wharton County Junior College	1946

Table 8.2 New Community Colleges in Texas 1965–1969

School	Date Established
Angelina College	1968
Bee County	1965
Brazosport College	1967
Central Texas College	1965
College of the Mainland	1966
Dallas County Community College District	1965

(Continued)

Table 8.2 Continued

School	Date Established
El Paso Community College	1969
El Centro College	1966
Galveston College	1967
McLennan Community College	1965
Midland College	1969
Tarrant County Junior College District	1965
Tarrant County Junior College District South	1967
Tarrant County Junior College District Northeast	1968
Western Texas College	1969

Table 8.3 Current Schools

Alvin Community College

Amarillo College

Angelina College

Blinn College

Brazosport College

Brookhaven College

Cedar Valley College

Cisco College

Clarendon College

Coastal Bend College

College of the Mainland

Collin College

Del Mar College

Eastfield College

El Centro College

El Paso Community College

Frank Phillips College

Galveston College

Grayson County College

Hill County College

Howard College

Kilgore College

Lamar Institute of Technology

Lamar State College-Orange

Lamar State College-Port Arthur

Laredo Community College

Lee College

Lon Morris College

Lone Star College CyFair

Lone Star College Kingwood

Lone Star College Montgomery

Lone Star College North Harris

Lone Star College Tomball

McLennan Community College

Midland College

Mountain View College

Navarro College

North Central Texas College

North Lake College

Northeast Texas Community

Northwest Vista College

Odessa College

Palo Alto College

Panola College

Paris College

Ranger College

Richland College

San Antonio College

South Plains College

Southwest Texas Junior College

St. Phillip's College

Tarrant County College

Temple College

(Continued)

Table 8.3 Continued

Texarkana College

Texas State Technical College-Harlingen

Texas State Technical College-Marshall

Texas State Technical College-Waco

Texas State Technical College-West Texas

Trinity Valley Community College

Tyler Junior College

Vernon College

Victoria College

Wharton County Junior College

NOTES

1. Stephen Brint and Jerome Karabel, "Community Colleges and the American Social Order," in *ASHE Reader*, 3rd ed., ed. D. D. Bragg and B. K. Townsend (Boston: Pearson Custom Publishing, 2006), 63.

2. Brint and Karabel, "Community Colleges and the American Social Order," 64.

3. Brint and Karabel, "Community Colleges and the American Social Order," 64–65.

4. Thomas J. Kane and Cecilia Rouse, "The Community College: Educating Students at the Margins Between College and Work," in *ASHE Reader on Community Colleges*, 3rd ed., ed. D. D. Bragg and B. K. Townsend (Boston: Pearson Custom Publishing, 2006), 95–112.

5. Clyde E. Blocker, Robert H. Plummer, and Richard C. Richardson, Jr., *The Two-Year College: A Social Synthesis* (Englewood Cliffs, NJ: Prentice-Hall, 1965), 26.

6. Sue Johnson Blair, "The Emergence and Development of the Community/Junior College in Texas" (PhD diss, Texas Tech, 1991), 13–14.

7. Frederick Eby, *The Development of Education in Texas* (New York: Macmillan Co., 1928), 140.

8. H. Stanton Tuttle, "Junior-College Movement," *Handbook of Texas Online*, (http://tshaonline.org/handbook/online/articles/kdj02), accessed August 21, 2016, Uploaded on June 15, 2010. Published by the Texas State Historical Association. There is a disagreement among historians about the first junior-college in America, with some believing that Decatur Baptist College was the first to be established in the U.S. if you count the date of its first opening in 1892 and others believing that the first was Joliet Junior College in Illinois that was established in 1902 (Evans, 1955, 159). It could correctly be said that while Decatur Baptist College was the first private junior college in the country, Joliet Junior College would be the first public junior college.

9. Fernando C. Gomez, *A Texas State of Mind* (College Station: Texas Review Press, 2011), 105–106.

10. Tom S. Sewell, "An Analysis of the Public Junior College Movement in Texas, 1922–1973" (PhD diss., University of Houston, 1975), 53.

11. Franklin Parker, "Dr. Fredrick Eby, 1874–1968: Father of The Texas Junior College Movement," *Journal of Thought* 3, no. 3 (July 1968): 200–203, http://jstor.org/stable/42589970.

12. Ray A. Laird, "Fredrick Eby and the Junior College," *Junior College Journal* 28 (October 1957), 76.

13. Sewell, "An Analysis of the Public Junior College Movement in Texas, 1922–1973," 57–58.

14. The eight colleges that were part of that original affiliation were: Alexander Collegiate Institute in Jacksonville, the University Training School at Blooming Grove, the University Training

School at Granbury, Wall School at Honey Grove, Chappell Hill Female College at Chappell Hill, Clarendon College & University Training School at Clarendon, Coronal Institute at San Marcus, and Hughey and Turner Training School at Weatherford; Sewell, "An Analysis of the Public Junior College Movement in Texas, 1922–1973," 60.

15. Blair, "The Emergence and Development of the Community/Junior College in Texas," 51.

16. C. E. Evans, *The Story of Texas Schools* (Austin: Steck Company, 1955), 161–62.

17. Blair, "The Emergence and Development of the Community/Junior College in Texas," 56–57.

18. Kathleen Bland Smith, "Crossroads in Texas," in *Junior Colleges: 50 States/50 Years*, ed. Roger Yarrington (Washington, DC: American Association of Junior Colleges, 1969), 140.

19. Fernando C. Gomez, *A Texas State of Mind* (College Station: Texas Review Press, 2011), 189.

20. Eby, *The Development of Education in Texas*, 20.

21. Evans, *The Story of Texas Schools*, 159.

22. H. Stanton Tuttle, "Junior-College Movement."

23. Blair, "The Emergence and Development of the Community/Junior College in Texas," 72–73.

24. Joe F. Taylor, *The AC Story: Journal of a College* (Canyon, TX: Staked Plain Press, 1979), 3.

25. Blair, "The Emergence and Development of the Community/Junior College in Texas," 78.

26. Ibid., 79.

27. Ibid., 82.

28. Homer P. Rainey, "Place of Junior Colleges in Texas Education," *Junior College Journal* 15 (December 1944): 167.

29. Blair, "The Emergence and Development of the Community/Junior College in Texas," 80; Clyde C. Colvert, "Colvert Goes to Texas," *Junior College Journal* 15, no. 5 (Jan 1945): 214.

30. Blair, "The Emergence and Development of the Community/Junior College in Texas," 94.

31. Junior College Journal, *Junior College Directory* 20, no. 5 (May 1950): 309–10.

32. Texas Education Agency, Public School Law Bulletin No. 527, 1952, Sections 1, 2, 3.

33. Evans, *The Story of Texas Schools*, 165.

34. Blair, "The Emergence and Development of the Community/Junior College in Texas," 102–103.

35. Everett W. Kindig, "Midwestern State University," Handbook of Texas Online, (http://tshaonline. org/handbook/online/articles/kcm04), accessed June 6, 2016. Uploaded on June 15, 2010. Published by the Texas State Historical Association.

36. Blair, "The Emergence and Development of the Community/Junior College in Texas," 104.

37. Blair, "The Emergence and Development of the Community/Junior College in Texas," 109.

38. Diana J. Kleiner, "San Jacinto College," *Handbook of Texas Online*, (http://tshaonline.org/ handbook/online/articles/kcs07), accessed June 6, 2016. Published by the Texas State Historical Association.

39. Kleiner, "San Jacinto College."

40. Nancy Beck Young, "Grayson County College," *Handbook of Texas Online*, (http://tshaonline. org/handbook/online/articles/kcg05), accessed June 6, 2016, Uploaded on June 15, 2010. Published by the Texas State Historical Association.

41. Daniel C. Morgan, Jr., *Financing Higher Education in Texas*, Public Affairs Series, No. 64. (Austin: Institute of Public Affairs, The University of Texas, 1965), 5.

42. Clifton, McCleskey, Allan K. Butcher, Daniel E. Farlow, and J. Pat Stephens, *The Government and Politics of Texas*, 6th ed. (Boston: Little Brown and Co., 1978), 316.

43. Blair, "The Emergence and Development of the Community/Junior College in Texas," 120.

44. Ibid., 123.

45. Kathleen Krebbs Whitson, *Bill Jason Priest: Community College Pioneer* (Denton: University of North Texas Press, 2004), 30.

46. Whitson, *Bill Jason Priest*, 30–31.

47. Ibid., 34.

48. Ibid., 46.

49. Ibid., 49–50.

50. Gomez, *A Texas State of Mind*, 219.

51. Blair, "The Emergence and Development of the Community/Junior College in Texas," 123, 130.

52. *Handbook of Texas* (tshaonline.org/handbook/online/articles/kct30).

53. The additional campuses were: Mountain View and Eastfield campuses opened in 1970. In 1972 the Dallas District added the Richland Campus; in 1977 were added the campuses at Cedar Valley and North Lake and the final campus was added in 1978, Brookhaven College (Blair, "The Emergence and Development of the Community/Junior College in Texas," 137).

54. Blair, "The Emergence and Development of the Community/Junior College in Texas," 137.

55. James W. Thornton, Jr., *The Community Junior College*, 3rd ed. (New York: John Wiley and Sons, Inc., 1972), 288.

56. Clyde E. Blocker, Robert H. Plummer, and Richard C. Richardson, Jr., *The Two-Year College: A Social Synthesis* (Englewood Cliffs, NJ: Prentice-Hall, 1965), 269.

57. Quentin J. Bogart, "The Community College Mission," in *A Handbook on the Community College in America*, ed. George A. Baker III (Westport, CT. Greenwood Press, 1994), 61–62.

BIBLIOGRAPHY

Baker, George A. III. *A Handbook on the Community College in America: Its History, Mission and Management*. Westport, CT: Greenwood Press, 1994.

Blair, Sue Johnson. "The Emergence and Development of the Community/Junior College in Texas." PhD diss., Texas Tech University. 1991.

Blocker, Clyde E., Robert H. Plummer, and Richard C. Richardson, Jr. *The Two-Year College: A Social Synthesis*. Englewood Cliffs, NJ: Prentice-Hall, 1965.

Bogart, Quentin J. "The Community College Mission." In *A Handbook on the Community College in America*, edited by George A. Baker III, 60–73. Westport, CT. Greenwood Press, 1994.

Brint, Stephen, and Jerome Karabel. "Community Colleges and the American Social Order." In *ASHE Reader on Community Colleges*, 3rd ed., edited by D. D. Bragg and B. K. Townsend, 63–74. Boston: Pearson Custom Publishing, 2006.

Colvert, Clyde C. "Colvert Goes to Texas." *Junior College Journal* 15, no. 5 (Jan 1945): 214–16.

Diener, Thomas. *Growth of an American Invention: A Documentary History of the Junior and Community College Movement*. New York: Greenwood Press, 1986.

Eby, Frederick. *The Development of Education in Texas*. New York: Macmillan Co., 1928.

Evans, C. E. *The Story of Texas Schools*. Austin: Steck Company, 1955.

Gomez, Fernando C. *A Texas State of Mind*. College Station: Texas Review Press, 2011.

Handbook of Texas Online, "Texas State Technical College-Waco," (http://tshaonline.org/handbook/online/articles/kct30), accessed June 7, 2016. Uploaded on June 15, 2010. Published by the Texas State Historical Association.

Henson, Jerry C. *The Person-Centered College: Reminiscences of the First Thirty Years at Eastfield College*. Dallas: Eastfield College, Dallas County Community College District, 2000.

Kane, Thomas J., and Cecilia Rouse. "The Community College: Educating Students at the Margins Between College and Work." In *ASHE Reader on Community Colleges*, 3rd ed., edited by D. D. Bragg and B. K. Townsend, 95–112. Boston: Pearson Custom Publishing, 2006.

Kindig, Everett W. "Midwestern State University," *Handbook of Texas Online*, (http://tshaonline.org/handbook/online/articles/kcm04), accessed June 6, 2016. Uploaded on June 15, 2010. Published by the Texas State Historical Association.

Kleiner, Diana J. "University of Houston-University Park," *Handbook of Texas Online*, (http://tshaonline. org/handbook/online/articles/kcu03), accessed June 6, 2016. Uploaded on June 15, 2010. Published by the Texas State Historical Association.

Kleiner, Diana J. "San Jacinto College," *Handbook of Texas Online*, (http://tshaonline.org/handbook/online/articles/kcs07), accessed June 6, 2016. Published by the Texas State Historical Association.

Junior College Journal. "Junior College Directory." *Junior College Journal* 20, no. 5 (May 1950).

Laird, Ray A. "Frederick Eby and the Junior College." *Junior College Journal* 28 (October 1957): 73–78.

McCleskey, Clifton, Allan K. Butcher, Daniel E. Farlow, and J. Pat Stephens. *The Government and Politics of Texas*. 6th ed. Boston: Little Brown and Co., 1978.

Morgan, Daniel C. Jr. *Financing Higher Education in Texas*. Public Affairs Series, No. 64. Austin: Institute of Public Affairs, The University of Texas, 1965.

Parker, Franklin. "Dr. Fredrick Eby, 1874–1968: Father of The Texas Junior College Movement." *Journal of Thought* 3, no. 3 (July 1968): 200–203, http://jstor.org/stable/42589978.

Rainey, Homer P. "Place of Junior Colleges in Texas Education." *Junior College Journal* 15 (December 1944): 166–69.

Richardson, Rupert Norval. *Texas: The Lone Star State*. New York: Prentice-Hall, Inc., 1950.

Sewell, Tom S. "An Analysis of the Public Junior College Movement in Texas, 1922–1973." PhD diss., University of Houston, 1975.

Smith, Kathleen Bland. "Crossroads in Texas." In *Junior Colleges: 50 States/50 Years*, edited by Roger Yarrington. Washington, DC: American Association of Junior Colleges, 1969.

Taylor, Joe F. *The AC Story: Journal of a College*. Canyon, TX: Staked Plain Press, 1979.

Texas Education Agency. *Public School Law Bulletin*, No. 527, Article 2815h, 1952.

Thornton, James W., Jr. *The Community Junior College*, 3rd ed. New York: John Wiley and Sons, Inc., 1972.

Townsend, Barbara, and Debra Bragg. In *ASHE Reader on Community Colleges*, 3rd ed., edited by D. D. Bragg and B. K. Townsend, 193–200. Boston: Pearson Custom Publishing, 2006.

Tuttle, H. Stanton. "Junior-College Movement," *Handbook of Texas Online*, (http://tshaonline.org/handbook/online/articles/kdj02), accessed August 21, 2016, Uploaded on June 15, 2010. Published by the Texas State Historical Association.

Whitson, Kathleen Krebbs. *Bill Jason Priest: Community College Pioneer*. Denton: University of North Texas Press, 2004.

Young, Nancy Beck. "Grayson County College," *Handbook of Texas Online*, (http://tshaonline.org/handbook/online/articles/kcg05), accessed June 6, 2016, Uploaded on June 15, 2010. Published by the Texas State Historical Association.

PART III:
ACCESS AND EQUITY

9

WOMEN AND HIGHER EDUCATION

The struggle for American women's access to institutions of higher education began in the 1820s and continued to evolve into the early twentieth century, revealing many achievements and new ideas as well as opposition to education for women. American women's struggle for educational opportunities often mirrored their larger social struggle for opportunities and recognition, and were influenced by large-scale social changes, including rapid industrialization, urbanization, and the formalization of educational systems across the country. Educational attainment reinforced the realization for many that their potential lay beyond traditional female roles. Taking on new roles often elicited opposition that sometimes slowed opportunities for women in higher education. As a result, the growth of female enrollment in higher education happened gradually, beginning with female seminaries, then all-women's colleges, coeducation, and finally spreading to all institutions of higher education.[1] Today women make up the majority of students in Texas colleges.

* * * * *

The differing circumstances of life in the North and in the South had an impact on regional approaches to the education of females. In the northeastern part of the United States, cities were compact and in most instances homogeneous in nature. Efforts to increase educational opportunities for females, especially in the minor grades, came sooner, and usually girls were given the opportunity to attend organized schools.[2]

However, in the South, the land was sparsely settled, and even then settlements were usually spread out. In areas dominated by plantations, the distance between families could be great, and the isolation affected education for children. Frequently, a tutor system was employed, which brought teachers to an individual plantation to teach both girls and boys. For the poorer members of Southern society, education, as in England, was left to either the clergy or an apprentice system. In an attempt to educate orphans, Virginia passed a law in 1642 that encouraged guardians to provide education in religion and the fundamentals of reading, writing and arithmetic. Some other Southern states passed laws that required the education or apprenticeship of all children under the age of twenty-one and they called for teaching children to read and write without regard to sex. In North Carolina, there were many settlements of Quaker families in which elementary education for both girls and boys was commonplace. In New Orleans in 1727 the French Ursuline nuns opened a girl's school that offered training in reading, writing, and arithmetic to nearly all girls in the community regardless of ethnicity or social status. These beginning steps would eventually lead to efforts to also provide more advanced learning for girls in the South.[3]

High standards in higher education for women in the United States began with the founding of Vassar College in New York State in 1861. The few women's colleges established before that time, which were all private, had provided an education inferior to that at any of the men's colleges.[4]

The shortage of male students during the Civil War made institutions in the North willing to consider tuition-paying women as students. By 1870, 21 percent of the college students in America were female. By 1880 women constituted 32 percent, by 1910 almost 40 percent, and a decade later in 1920, 47 percent of college enrollment was women. This was roughly equal to the percentage of college age women among all women in the country at the time. At the same time, women constituted 45 percent of the professional work force. It must to be noted that these figures would have included few women of color, as barriers to college access for them at the time were significant. A record 32 percent of college presidents, professors, and instructors were women at the end of the 1930s. Attitudes toward women in higher education and by women about themselves underwent many shifts during the twentieth century, and these shifts were themselves indicators of a general development in America toward a common cultural standard.[5]

EDUCATION FOR WOMEN IN TEXAS

Settlers in early Texas came mainly from other parts of the South, and they brought with them a belief in providing education for women. Trained teachers, both women and men, who moved to Texas took the jobs in educational institutions that were available at the time they arrived. Teachers had an influence on the communities where they resided, and they provided leadership that helped evolve the thinking about education for women.[6] This was a desirable social improvement for many women.

Prior to the Civil War, there were essentially three different types of schools for young women in Texas: independent, unchartered, and denominational. Independent schools, sponsored by either individuals or corporations, obtained a state charter, which in some cases came with free land. Unchartered schools were also controlled by either individuals or corporations of interested citizens, but had no attachment or responsibility to any single group. Denominational schools were each attached to a specific religious group. All three types of schools provided primary as well as advanced schooling.[7]

The first independent schools that provided opportunities for women in Texas were Independence Academy, the University of San Augustine, Nacogdoches University, and Gonzales College.

In the Washington County town of Independence, citizens were interested in starting a school for the education of girls and young women, and worked to establish Independence Academy. On May 23, 1837, town members presented to the Congress of the Republic a petition requesting a charter for an academy that would teach courses to both male and female students, and the charter was granted on June 5. In approving the charter, the congress made clear its views on educational policy in the Republic: "this charter and privilege shall extend to said trustees and their successors in office, as long as they confine the benefits of the same to the advancement of the sciences, and the promotion of useful knowledge to the rising generation, which institution shall be equally to all, without regard to opinion or religion or politics."[8]

The organizing principles for the female department of the Independence Academy, which was operating by May 1839, were discussed in a contemporary newspaper:

> This institution has been commenced under the guidance of Miss M'Guffin in the female department, whose object will be a thorough course of instruction. Attention will be paid to the morals and manners of the children, and the preservation of a friendly feeling towards each other, so necessary to the present happiness and future welfare of those placed here for instruction. Advanced pupils will be required to keep a diary of the manner in which they employ their time, for the inspection of their parents, as are exercises in English grammar and composition.

Independence Academy taught its last classes in 1845. Later that year the property was offered at a sheriff's sale and was purchased by C. W. Taylor who donated it to the newly chartered Baylor University.[9]

In its early years, the town of San Augustine in east central Texas attracted men and women with excellent education levels, often gained at eastern colleges and universities. Their knowledge and abilities gave the community a feeling of intellectualism. Many of the town's citizens referred to it as the "Athens of Texas," so it is not surprising that soon after the Texas revolution of 1836 these citizens began looking into the best way to provide an education for their children.[10] On June 5, 1837, the First Congress of the Republic granted a charter to an independent board of trustees to organize a university in San Augustine. The trustees selected were required to either live in the city or within a ten-mile radius and were to include members who came from various religious denominations and held a wide range of political views. They were empowered to hire teachers, raise money, and do whatever was necessary to open the university.[11]

In 1842, the trustees of the University of San Augustine selected a president, M. A. Montrose, who proposed an aggressive plan to begin the university by providing a liberal arts education as good as any university in the country. To further strengthen the school, an agreement was made with the Presbyterian Church to support the trustees by offering advice, providing aid, and actively soliciting missionaries to come to the eastern part of Texas.[12] The Female Department, whose classes were separate, was provided for: "In one part of the building is a Female Academy, where young ladies will be taught the solid as well as the polite branches of education. A lady of accomplishments will superintend the department of music and drawing for those who wish to pay the extra tuition fees."[13]

The Female Department was as large as all the rest of the university and had two full-time teachers. It had several objectives, the first of which was to teach the scientific and classical courses common at the time. The second objective was to train young ladies in deportment and the refinements of life that would enable them to keep their husbands happy, and thus act as models for their communities. The third objective was to have students participate in activities university leaders considered important in female education, such as spelling bees, speaking contests, and other kinds of training believed to provide intellectual and social edification for women.[14]

One of the most successful of the institutions chartered by an independent board was Nacogdoches University, whose charter was approved by the Congress of the Republic on February 8, 1845.

Upon receiving its charter, the board acquired a two-story building that had been the home of the Mexican commander before the Texas Revolution. The lower floor was designated for male students and the second for the female department. As their first president, the board hired M. A. Montrose from the University of San Augustine, who issued a statement that "ladies attending will be required to practice the same politeness in the schoolroom as they would in the drawing room."[15] Montrose was expressing the thinking at the time on correct deportment for women, and proposals at the university for the training of young women for refined and cultured womanhood were very similar to those at other institutions of the era. President Montrose believed that an ideal education for young women was provided by courses in Latin, French, natural and moral philosophy, and astronomy, along with the ornamental branches, or social graces, that were considered part of female instruction.[16]

The last of the independent colleges of this period was Gonzales College, and its charter was approved on April 17, 1852, specifying that a female department be established. Like the other schools, Gonzales College had separate departments for male and female students. The curriculum for females covered four years and was divided into model, junior, middle, and senior years, with each year divided into two parts. The college's goal was spelled out in its 1859–60 catalogue where it described a president who would give personal instruction and maintain a watchful eye over the students. The college's primary goal was to furnish students with an understanding of the principles of literature and science and provide its students with a quality and a quantity of instruction superior to that provided to most Texas students at the time.[17]

Women at Gonzales College could take any course offered; they just could not take it alongside men. The trustees had been given the power by the congress to confer degrees on any worthy student, and this became an important milestone in the history of college education for women in Texas. The Bachelor of Arts degree was awarded to females at the college as early as 1857, marking the first time this degree was awarded to female graduates in Texas prior to the Civil War. Gonzales College played a significant role in providing superior education to women, and was a forerunner in demonstrating that women were as capable as men in their ability to do college work.[18] The college closed in 1874.

The second type of early educational institution in Texas was the unchartered school, owned and operated by individuals and local in nature. Professors with some level of education who hoped to earn a living were usually the ones starting them, and because the schools were local and mainly short-lived, it is often difficult to find detailed information about them. One of the first was the Washington Female Academy, located in the town of Washington. It was started by three sisters, the eldest of whom had been a tutor for the children of the governor of South Carolina and brought a letter from the governor providing an excellent recommendation for the quality of her teaching. The sisters organized their school, which was exclusively for girls, recruited students, and began immediately. Started in 1842, the school at first served only the lower grades, but two years later added courses in higher-level work.[19]

During the years 1841–1852, the small town of Clarksville located in northeast Texas had three academies for young women. James Sampson, a local minister, allowed girls to attend his academy from 1841 until 1843, when Martha W. Weatherred started the Clarksville Female Academy. In 1847 Eliza Todd began the Clarksville Female Institute. Each school was privately owned, which allowed the proprietors to set their own policies. Weatherred placed her school under a board of trustees and assumed a patronage from the local Methodist Church. Her educational goals were to produce cultured and accomplished women. Todd at Clarksville Female Academy created a privately owned, nonsectarian boarding school for the instruction of girls at the elementary and high school levels. Courses included Latin, music, drawing, painting, and needlework. While the school was nonsectarian, Todd strongly emphasized Christian principles in training her young ladies.[20]

At Bastrop another local minister, B. J. Smith, and his wife opened a third institution, which they named Austin Female Collegiate Institute. As was the case in many of these early schools, classes were conducted in the founders' home. The school had about 150 students, day and boarding, and was designed to provide instruction for elementary, high school, and college students. It did not offer as many of the classical college courses offered to men at the time, but instead substituted music, fine arts, waxwork, and needlework. In explaining this, Smith wrote that he and his wife did not expect their young ladies to be able to discuss politics or solve complex problems and they did not believe Latin and Greek were essential for a young woman's education.[21]

The third type of institution was the denominational college. These were divided between ones exclusively for women and coeducational colleges. The term coeducation has had at least two different meanings in Texas. One is the education of the sexes together in the same college but without having the same courses or degree requirements for women as for men. The other is the identical education of the sexes together.[22]

The first denominational college to accept coeducation was Waco University, previously known as Waco Classical School. Rufus C. Burleson, who had previously been president of Baylor University at Independence, became president of Waco University after resigning from Baylor in 1861. The school was the first coeducational school in the South and the second in the United States. It merged with Baylor University at Waco in 1886.[23]

A denominational college that was exclusively for women was Mary Hardin Baylor in Belton. When the Female Department at Baylor University at Independence was split off from Baylor University in 1876 it was moved to Belton. It never merged with another college and is still operating under its original charter received from the Republic of Texas in 1845. (A more in-depth discussion of denominational colleges can be found in chapter 6.)[24]

All three types of colleges provided an opportunity for women to obtain a college education. However, it was not until Sam Houston Normal Institute opened in 1879 that there was a coeducational public college.

AFTER THE CIVIL WAR

Opportunities for women to attend college began to increase after the Civil War. It had long been true in Texas that the primary grades were coeducational; however, prior to the 1860s, females had been segregated from males in the early academies and colleges, with very few exceptions. The only college to award a bachelor's degree to a female prior to 1860 was Gonzales College, although that degree was not the same as the one awarded to male students. Almost two decades passed before there was coeducation in a public college; this occurred when the University of Texas was opened in 1883. The first religious college to adopt coeducation was Waco University, which did so in 1865 at the recommendation of its president, Rufus C. Burleson. The majority of resistance to coeducation came from Alexander Hogg, who was a professor at Texas Agricultural and Mechanical College. He believed that women should receive a practical education separate from men. He was very effective in carrying his battle to both the Texas Legislature and the federal government, but the battle ended when the University of Texas opened in 1883 as a coeducational institution.[25]

While the battle was still raging, there had been resurgence in the desire for colleges exclusively for women. The earliest was at the end of the Civil War in 1865 at Baylor University, which, since its founding in 1845 at Independence, had had a female department. In 1866, the university's charter was revised, creating Baylor Female College with a separate board of trustees. In 1866, it was decided to move the college to a more central location, mainly in response to the changing population of the state. Several cities bid on the right to host the college, but the City of Belton won, besting its neighbor Temple by only $1,000. The school's name was changed to

Mary Hardin-Baylor College, and it claims to be the only women's college to have operated in Texas since the days of the Republic.[26]

At the beginning of the twentieth century, girls began to make up the majority of the public school enrollment. However, it should be noted that while this was occurring in white schools, there were far fewer opportunities for blacks. In 1900 there were only sixteen black high schools in the entire state (see chapter 10 for a more detailed discussion).[27]

Woman began to appear in professional education classes around 1900, in both education and health care. In education, their numbers in the public schools began to increase rapidly, because after the Civil War there was a shortage of men in the workforce. Men began to leave the teaching profession because of increased pay in other lines of work. This created an opening for women teachers. With a high school diploma, a young woman could easily get a teaching certificate to teach in an elementary school. Over the next several decades, women began to enter college in increasingly larger numbers.[28]

But discrimination in higher education continued to limit women's opportunities. In 1900, women were not admitted to Austin College, the Agricultural and Mechanical College of Texas (now Texas A&M University), St. Mary's, and St. Edwards. However, women did make up one-third of the enrollment at the University of Texas, Southwestern University, and Baylor University. Ten years later at the University of Texas, 40 percent of the enrollment was women. At Southwestern it was 34 percent and at Baylor it was 38 percent. At the time, the average attendance of women in college nationally was 35 percent.[29]

By 1910 the majority of students attending Sam Houston Normal Institute, North Texas State Normal School, and Prairie View State Normal and Industrial College were women. In the normal schools a teaching degree could be obtained at low tuition rates offering women from rural backgrounds a means to enter the middle class. At Prairie View State Normal and Industrial College, the only state college for African Americans, the proportion of enrolled women to men was two to one.[30]

Starting a publicly supported college strictly for women proved to be a difficult task. It was thirty-six years after the Civil War ended before the Texas Legislature passed a bill doing so. The State Grange and Patrons of Husbandry led the campaign, passing a resolution at their annual meeting in 1889 recommending such a college. They pointed to the success at Texas A&M, where the first student had enrolled in 1876.[31] A. J. Rose, head of the Grange, pleaded the case:

> Do [girls] not need an industrial college, too, where they can receive a practical education which will prepare them for some vocation in life, in order that they may not work in the cotton fields from necessity? Certainly the State will not do less for her girls than her boys when appealed to. Let the State Grange stretch forth its strong arm in women's behalf to the next Legislature and ask that an industrial college be provided for girls.[32]

The Grange's request was repeated in 1890 and 1891, and in 1891, a bill was introduced in the legislature to establish a college for women. It passed the senate but failed in the house. Supporters of the bill got a boost in 1893 when women's volunteer organizations, led by the Texas Woman's Christian Temperance Union, and the Texas Federation of Women's Clubs, began to strongly support the legislation. A primary thrust of these groups' interest was to elevate the role of women as managers of the household to that of a respected profession. In the 1890s there was widespread discussion about new scientific approaches to homemaking and child raising. These organizations were discussing the new theory of germs and a scientific approach that could be applied to both public health and private homes. They lobbied legislative leaders on the necessity of creating a vocational college for white women where the curriculum was centered on household economics.[33]

These repeated attempts to get legislation introduced failed, and in 1899 when a bill was finally filed, it was later defeated in both houses. Then, in 1900 the Democratic Party at their annual convention passed a resolution of support for a women's college, and in that same year legislation finally passed, although in both chambers the presiding officer had to break a tie vote. On April 6, 1901, Governor Joseph D. Sayers signed the bill creating the Texas Industrial Institute and College for the Education of the White Girls of the State of Texas in Arts and Science in Denton.[34]

According to the first president of the college, Cree T. Work:

> The Girls Industrial College of Texas will aim to give culture of the highest order, scholarship of the most efficient kind, and domestic and industrial training of the most modern and practical type . . . in short, we want to meet the need of our times in training women who will be competent, intelligent and refined, well fitted for self-support if this should be necessary; thoroughly prepared for woman's work in the industrial and commercial world if they so choose to labor; well trained for companionship with worthy manhood and for motherhood, when this is desired.[35]

The college opened on September 23, 1903, and in the beginning functioned essentially as a junior college. However, it soon offered a three-year degree, and in time, it became the first public senior college for women in Texas. Because it was a single-sex school, students did not experience the marginalization that occurred at many colleges offering coeducation. The college's motto was "We Learn by Doing"; the founders wanted to prepare women for employment in industries, so the school focused on practical education. That focus reflected the influence of the Texas Woman's Christian Temperance Union, which conceived of education as a means of preparing women for an independent life.[36] The college endorsed practicality, while at the same time it stressed the importance of literary work. Electives continued to allow students to shape their programs to their needs, but as time went on, the curriculum moved more toward a traditional liberal arts program. By 1930, the choices contained both traditional liberal arts and practical courses, no doubt reflecting the debate going on at the time, not only in Texas but throughout the country, as to the proper role of women's colleges.[37]

A shift in the college's curriculum from a focus on home economics to the training of teachers to teach home economics also reflected the nationwide demand for female teachers in the early twentieth century. The increasing "feminization" of teaching was reflected in the development of education courses. By 1930, almost all of the fifty graduates of the Texas Industrial Institute who were placed in professional positions went into teaching.[38]

The administration of the college also responded to public demands that it prepare women for other professions besides teaching. In 1914, the school offered classes in hygiene and home nursing, which by 1940 were developed into a Bachelor of Science degree in nursing. In 1930, students could already major in science and medically related fields. The college also responded to the demand to prepare women for jobs in business by expanding its commercial arts courses, and by 1930, students could earn a degree in business administration.[39]

Young women were able to hold offices in organizations after college because of the valuable skills they had gained at the Texas Industrial Institute. The college began providing both vocational and liberal arts education at a time when Texas A&M would not accept female students and the University of Texas, which did accept them, refused to implement a home economics department. Because of its progressive policies, the Texas Industrial Institute provided a good fit for a young woman, regardless of the direction she chose for her education and whether it was to equip her as a homemaker or to work outside the home.[40] The institution had many names; in 1905 its name was changed to Texas College for Industrial Arts, in 1934 to Texas State College for Women, and in 1957 Texas Woman's University.

Opportunities for women in higher education began to increase in the later part of the nineteenth century throughout the United States, but in many institutions the level of instruction for women was not as rigorous as it was for men. This seems to have been especially true in Texas. In the early years, when it was possible for a woman to attend a coeducational college, the opportunity to achieve a high academic level was still not readily available. However, one school—Add-Ran College—did provide for and expect the same academic performance from women as from men.[41]

Two brothers, Addison and Randolph Clark, established Add-Ran College in 1873 at Thorp Spring, southwest of Fort Worth. The brothers were members of the Disciples of Christ, or Christian Church, and their religious training affected their views about educated women. The church granted women a broader social role than did many other Christian denominations at the time. The church's early leaders were well educated, some having graduated from Princeton University or Edinburgh College. The schools they founded were, by the middle of the nineteenth century, providing equal education for male and female students. Add-Ran College's first "catalog" was published in 1873. Under "Male-Female Curriculum" one finds the Department of Ancient Languages, which taught both Greek and Latin. Other courses offered included English, mathematics, physical science, mental and moral science, social and civil history, and primary instruction. Having one set of coursework for both males and females set the college apart from even the coeducational colleges of the time. Add-Ran College eventually became Texas Christian University in 1902.[42]

When women were given an opportunity to compete with men in academics, it quickly became evident that they were at least equal in ability. Another place where this became evident was at Sam Houston Normal Institute, the first Normal school in Texas. The establishment of coeducation at Sam Houston began in the academic year 1879–80 and provided the opportunity to validate the assertion by Texas women of the time that they could compete on an equal level with men. That women were succeeding would have been evident to anyone attending graduation ceremonies at the Institute. During the years 1885–1892 the college awarded the Peabody Medal to the student in the graduating class with the highest scholastic achievement. During those eight years, a female won the award seven times and the winners were also the valedictorians of their respective classes. A silver medal, which was given to the salutatorians of a class, was won by women three times, and a bronze medal, which was given to the best students in a class, went to females thirty-four of the fifty-two times it was awarded. Thus it was evident that young women who were given the opportunity to compete at the college level were bona fide students whose intellects were not inferior to those of men.[43]

Another of the many examples of this may be seen at the University of Texas in their chapter of Phi Beta Kappa, the oldest and best-known honor society in the United States. A review of the graduates of the university's College of Arts shows that from 1884 to 1913, some 153 graduates were elected Phi Beta Kappa and 83 of them were women.[44]

These achievements finally helped put to bed the notion that women did not have the ability to compete academically. More and more Texas colleges began to admit women and to give them the opportunity to take the same courses as men. This success over time caused all the remaining colleges that had been unwilling to admit women on an equal basis to change their positions. It also caused Texas Woman's University to open its doors to men in 1972.[45]

* * * * *

There were always women who took the lead in improving educational opportunities for women. Some are widely known, but others are not. Here we look at four Texas women who suggest the breadth of interest in supporting and increasing educational opportunities for women.

ANNA PENNYBACKER

Anna Pennybacker was born May 7, 1861, in Petersburg, Virginia. Her parents were strong believers in education and their home was full of books. Anna learned to read at age four and was a precocious reader who took full advantage of her father's large library. She attended public school for the first time in West Virginia when her father, a minister, was offered a church there. The family later moved to Kansas where she attended and graduated from high school on May 31, 1878. Although it was her intention to continue her education at the University of Michigan, family finances were not sufficient to cover the tuition. Shortly after she graduated from high school her father accepted a position to pastor a church in Bryan, Texas, which was the home of the recently opened Texas Agricultural and Mechanical College. The college did not admit women but she was allowed to use the school library, which she did to her advantage, and she hired a private tutor in order to learn Latin and Greek. In a small building near her parents' home she briefly opened a private school. Her chance to attend college came when Governor Oran M. Roberts signed the bill creating Sam Houston Normal Institute. The legislation called for competitive exams for tuition-free scholarships to be given to prospective students from each of the state senatorial districts, plus an additional six students to be picked from anywhere in the state. Anna sat for the exam in 1879, the Institute's inaugural. She achieved a perfect score and was awarded a tuition-free scholarship, for which she had to promise to teach in a public school upon graduation.[46]

The purpose of a "normal school" at the time was to train teachers in what was known as the "Normal Method" because it called for the development of subjects and the provision for teaching those subjects to the "natural method of the mind."[47] The method called for a systematic presentation of subjects as opposed to the teaching of isolated or random facts. At the time in Texas, school systems in the small and rural districts did not require teachers to be single-subject teachers. In the larger, city schools a teacher taught only one subject to a class from one period to the next all day long. In the country schools a teacher was required to teach all subjects to a class.[48]

The curriculum at Sam Houston Normal Institute was broadly based on the knowledge teaching demanded at the time. Institute students took classes in elocution, natural philosophy, mental philosophy, and astronomy. The Institute also had a model school where students could practice their teaching skills, Anna was one of a select group who taught at the model school, which proved to be a great help as she began her teaching career. She was a good student and her 99 grade average tied her for first place in her class of fifty students. At the graduation ceremony on June 16, 1880, Anna and another young woman received the Peabody Medal for "superior scholarship and meritorious deportment." Even though she was one of the top students she did not get to speak at the graduation ceremony; that honor was reserved for male students.[49]

Her first teaching position was in Bryan, where her classmate from Sam Houston and husband to be, Percy Pennybacker, was selected principal. After a year she took a position in Carthage, Missouri, while Percy went to Europe for more advanced learning. Upon his return they married and he became superintendent of schools in Tyler and Anna was hired as a principal. In 1888 she wrote *A New History of Texas,* a textbook used for many years in Texas schools to teach Texas history. Her husband died in 1899 and in 1900 she moved to Austin with her three children to be closer to better educational opportunities for them.[50]

Anna Pennybacker's teaching days were over; she continued to help women pursuing college degrees, and with the help of friends set up a scholarship for girls at the University of Texas. During the remainder of her life she spent her time working on issues for women, and she continued to advise teachers and correspond with them about ways to improve classroom teaching. While Anna had a long list of accomplishments and club memberships, she is perhaps best known for her time as president of the State Federation of Women's Clubs in Texas from 1904 until 1908. She died on February 4, 1938, by which time she was known as one of Texas's "first citizens."[51]

Anna Pennybacker was the classic teacher who had the internal driving force to be a good teacher. She worked hard to innovate in the classroom and taught techniques that would work for other teachers in their classrooms. When she retired from teaching she continued to advise teachers on becoming more effective. Her textbook, *A New History of Texas,* provided many years of public school students with the story of Texas. The one year of college she received for free from Sam Houston Normal Institute paid dividends for Texas and for the political leaders who had supported it.[52]

ANNIE WEBB BLANTON

Annie Webb Blanton (1870–1945) was born in Houston on August 19, 1870. Her rise to being the most prominent female educator in the twentieth century in Texas was shaped by the South's reaction to Reconstruction policies forced on it after the Civil War. While the South had been making some progress in education, this was disrupted by reaction to the centralized state school systems the Reconstruction Republicans put in place. In Texas by 1871 that included a common curriculum for all schools, a policy of compulsory attendance, graded class levels, standard teacher certification requirements, and a centralized state board of education made up of the governor, attorney general, and superintendent of public instruction. All of this was contrary to the prior decentralized system of schools in which the counties had played the major role. But, the biggest objection Texans had was to the Republican goal to establish an educational system for all Texans. Long-held racial prejudices meant that the majority of whites did not want their tax dollars used to educate blacks. In 1876, Texans voted the Republicans out of office and rewrote the state constitution. The new constitution called for decentralizing state government and state public education policy. When it became apparent some years later that these new policies resulted in a reduction in the quality of instruction and a decline in the number of students attending school, the school laws were rewritten in 1884. The new laws included a state superintendent to supervise all the public schools and colleges in Texas. It was not until well into the twentieth century that the reformers began to assert themselves so that more progressive educational policies could be put into place. It was at this time that Anna Webb Blanton, a reformer, gained a position of authority.[53]

After the death of Blanton's mother in 1879, the family moved from Houston to La Grange and it was there that Annie graduated from high school in 1887. After graduation she began teaching in the small town of Pine Springs not far from La Grange. After her father's death in 1888 she moved to Austin to stay with her grandfather to more easily pursue her goal of a college education. After teaching for several years at East Austin Elementary, she entered the University of Texas in 1892, and she continued to teach while attending college part time. At the university she concentrated on English, education, and French. In 1899, after going to college for seven years, she graduated with a bachelor of literature degree. Soon after graduation she moved to Denton to teach at North Texas State Normal College (now the University of North Texas), and it was there that she began her career as an educational leader and reformer.[54] In 1916 she was elected president of the Texas State Teacher's Association—the first woman elected to that office.

The suffrage movement in Texas raised public awareness of the injustice of not allowing women to vote. The parallels between legal coverture (the loss of legal identity and rights by a woman after marriage) and disfranchisement were obvious to most observers. In Texas a woman was entitled to control her own property but she was not allowed to vote. Instead, men represented her interests at the polls. The Texas Woman Suffrage Association and its successor the Texas Equal Suffrage Association, created to include male members, began to grow in size and power. After the United States entered World War I in 1917, the suffragists joined other women to do the work that was needed on the home front. They sold Liberty bonds and thrift stamps to raise money for the government, distributed food conservation pledge cards, helped run the canteens for soldiers, and volunteered for the Red Cross. The war gave the suffragists publicity for their good work and patriotic service. It also provided them with a new argument as to why women should be allowed to vote. There was a contradiction inherent in fighting for democracy abroad and living in a country where one-half of the population could not vote. These efforts played a role in the legislature passing a bill in 1918 that authorized women to vote in the primary elections. Because Texas was a one-party state and the winner of the Democratic primary was virtually always elected in the general election, this gave women the power to begin making changes.[55]

After Governor Hobby signed the bill, the suffragists began a major campaign to register women to vote. To increase the turnout of women for the first election in which they were allowed to vote, the head of the Texas Equal Suffrage Movement recruited Annie Webb Blanton. She was asked to run for the office of state superintendent of public instruction. In part because the suffragists also supported Governor Hobby who won by a landslide, Annie Webb Blanton was carried into office, making her the first woman to be elected to a statewide office in Texas. Finally, in 1919 the U.S. Congress passed the Nineteenth Amendment to the Constitution that allowed women to vote. On June 28, 1919, Texas became the ninth state to ratify the Nineteenth Amendment.[56]

Blanton was the first woman to run for the state superintendent's office. As an excellent speaker and former president of the Texas State Teacher's Association, along with the novelty of a woman running for office, she drew large crowds as she traveled the state. The campaign was a hard one with her opponents charging that she was a pawn of others and that she had no chance of winning the election. Much of her support came from the Texas State Teacher's Association and women who were active in the suffragist movement. Her campaign platform was a progressive and ambitious one. She advocated selecting appointees to the department based on merit instead of political connections. Blanton was also a strong supporter of rural schools. She advocated raising the academic and professional standards for teachers and supported an increase in teacher pay.[57]

She won the Democratic primary and was victorious by a large margin in the general election in the fall.[58]

After she was elected she continued to speak out about the need to increase opportunities for women. In the superintendent's office she appointed an equal number of men and women to head divisions in the State Department of Education. She required the Normal schools do the same for their summer examiners and those that did not comply were not allowed to conduct summer sessions. She used her office to encourage local school districts to better utilize women teachers. As a result, the number of women who served on school boards and as superintendents greatly increased during her time in office. It was evident that unless the quality of the public schools was improved, the opportunity for graduates of those schools to receive a meaningful college degree would be lost.[59]

Blanton ran for re-election in 1919 and won easily. Overall her four years in office allowed a continuation of programs begun before she was elected. These included innovative policies that increased teacher pride, and new approaches to the problems of school financing and the need for general educational improvements.[60]

Blanton chose not to run for a third term and returned to the classroom as an education professor at the University of Texas. In 1927 the university created a rural education department within the school of education and she became the department's chair. Later she received a master's degree in education at the University, and in 1926 began working on her doctorate in rural education at Cornell University. After receiving that degree, she returned to the University of Texas in 1927, became a full professor, and was elected to Phi Beta Kappa. Her full-time employment with the University ended in 1940, coinciding with her seventieth birthday.[61]

Annie Blanton, who began as a classroom teacher in a rural school, never lost her passion for the students in the classroom; she had a particular fondness for those in the rural schools that made up such a large part of Texas during her service. She went on to become an excellent professor, first at North Texas and later at the University of Texas. She was well liked by her fellow educators, and it was they whom she mobilized to lead the fight to get her elected as superintendent of public instruction. In that office she had oversight of public education at the lower levels and in the public colleges, and by any measure she performed an excellent service to the state. After leaving office she returned to the classroom at the University of Texas and continued to contribute through her speaking, writing, and teaching.[62]

MARY ELIZABETH BRANCH

Mary Elizabeth Branch (1881–1944) was an important role model for African-American women during the 1930s and 1940s, and her story clearly illustrates the life of an ambitious and successful woman. She was born in Farmville, Virginia, daughter of Tazewell Branch, a former slave whose master had taught him to read and write, something that happened only rarely. Her mother, Harriett, loved education and enrolled their six children in school and encouraged them to read books from their home library.[63]

Tazewell served in the Virginia legislature from 1874–1876, but became disenchanted with the political corruption and quit politics to become a shoemaker. Harriett worked as a domestic to help support the family. A teenage Mary collected laundry from the local state college to bring home for her mother to wash. When Mary obtained a part-time job as a maid at the college, she discovered the school library, and access to its books encouraged her to seek advanced education.[64]

Branch finished high school at the Normal school of Virginia State College in Petersburg. She was interested in making sure that the English language was spoken correctly and she began teaching just that at an elementary school in Blackstone, Virginia. What followed was a twenty-year career at Virginia State College where she worked as the director of dormitories and a student counselor. During the summers she worked on her undergraduate degree at the University of Pennsylvania, Columbia University, and the University of Chicago. In 1922 she received her bachelor's degree in English. Three years later she received her master's degree from the University of Chicago and began working on her doctorate.[65]

In 1925 she began teaching social studies at Sumner Junior College in Kansas City, Missouri. Soon after, she became dean of students at St. Louis Vashon High School. She especially enjoyed that job because she was a role model for the students and enjoyed encouraging them to continue their education.[66]

In 1930 the American Missionary Association asked Branch to become president of Tillotson College in Austin, Texas. When she arrived on campus she found the college had been reduced to a junior college and was suffering from low enrollment because of the Depression.[67] Rising to the challenge, she put into place a five-year plan to improve buildings and attract more students. She was able to expand the library and insisted that all faculty members hold a master's degree. She raised money to establish scholarships to recruit outstanding students to the college.[68]

When Branch began her term at Tillotson the college enrolled just 140 students; by 1944 she had boosted enrollment to 502 and had so improved the college that it became a four-year school once again. The Southern Association of Colleges and Secondary Schools gave the college an "A" rating. In the process, Branch became the first African American woman to be president of such an institution.[69]

Mary Branch died unexpectedly on July 6, 1944. She had been an excellent role model and was well known for encouraging students to finish the work for their degrees, even though she understood the financial constraints that made that goal difficult. Branch believed students should work to help pay their tuition and she took a personal hand in finding them jobs so they had the money to pay their way.[70] Shortly before her death she began working on a merger of Tillotson College and nearby Samuel Huston College that finally occurred in 1952.[71]

JOVITA GONZÁLEZ

Jovita González (1904–1983) was born to a poor family in the border town of Roma, Texas. She began her education in a one-room schoolhouse on the San Roman Ranch. Shortly afterwards, her father moved the family to San Antonio so his children could obtain a better education, one that was taught in English because he felt that would provide his children with greater opportunities.[72]

After graduating from high school, González obtained a teaching certificate in 1918. At the time it was common for high school graduates to be able to teach after taking an exam to receive a teaching certificate. She taught at the cities of Rio Grande City and Encinal, and tutored at Our Lady of the Lake in San Antonio. Because finances were tight, she went to college part time, and in 1927 she obtained her bachelor of arts degree in Spanish at Our Lady of the Lake. Soon after graduation she began teaching full time at St. Mary's Hall in San Antonio while attending the University of Texas to pursue a master's degree.[73] She was one of about thirty students of Mexican descent from the Rio Grande Valley to attend the university and one of about 250 from the entire state.[74]

While a student at the University of Texas, González worked with old family friend Carlos E. Castaneda, and had the opportunity to meet J. Frank Dobie. Both of these men shaped her career as a folklorist, teacher, and writer of historical fiction. It was Dobie, a folklorist, who encouraged her to write about the Texas border lands and its legends.[75] About him, González said: "he made me see their importance and encouraged me to write them, which I did, publishing some in the *Folk-Lore Publications* and *Southwest Review*." As a result, she was awarded the Lapham Scholarship to do advance research along the border and to continue to study for her master's degree. As a result of her 1930 thesis, "Social Life in Webb, Starr and Zapata Counties," she became one of the first Hispanics to receive a master's degree and work as a professor. Based on the content of her thesis and a recommendation from Dobie she was awarded a Rockefeller grant in 1934.[76]

In 1935 she married fellow University of Texas student Edmond E. Mireles. The two began to collaborate on organizing a Spanish program for elementary schools. They moved to Corpus Christi where González taught Spanish and Texas History at W. B. High School for twenty-one years. In 1941 she coauthored *Mi Libro Espanol Libro Uno* with her husband and the superintendent of schools, R. B. Fisher. In 1943 they published *Libro Dos* and *Libro Tres.* These texts included lessons on Alvar Nunez Cabeza de Vaca, Martin De Leon, Lorenzo de Zavala and Father Miguel Hidalgo y Costilla. In 1949 González and her husband wrote *El Espanol Elemental*— six books for six levels used to teach Spanish at the elementary level. These textbooks provided an important teaching tool and helped to establish a Spanish language program at the Corpus Christi school district.[77]

González's own published works include *Folklore of the Texas-Mexican Vaquero* (1927), *America Invades the Border Towns* (1930), *Among My People* (1932), and *With the Coming of the Barbed Wire Came Hunger.* In 1937 she wrote the chapter "Latin Americans" for *Our Racial and National Minorities: Their History, Contributions, and Present Problems,* which was most likely one of the first published discussions of the topic by a person of Mexican descent.[78] A recent discovery of manuscripts for two of her lost novels, *Dew on the Thorn* and *Caballero,* which have now been published, prompted educator and author Leticia M. Garza-Falcón to observe that González remains both "among" her people and removed from "her" people.[79]

Jovita González was a remarkable woman who was not only an outstanding teacher but also a role model for other women of Mexican descent. Her early successes pointed the way for many women, particularly those from the Rio Grande Valley, who often lacked educated and successful role models.

* * * * *

The current structure of higher education stands upon several pillars from the past. These outstanding women along with many other women of their time make up one of the state's strongest pillars of support and success.

Anna Pennybacker, Annie Webb Blanton, Mary Elizabeth Branch, and Jovita Gonzalez—all dynamic and progressive women—exemplify women in education in the late nineteenth and early twentieth centuries in Texas. They were excellent role models and a testament to the abilities and effectiveness of women at all levels of education.

NOTES

1. Snejana Slantcheva, "Women in American Higher Education," http://www.policy.hu/slandtcheva/womeneducation.htac. Accessed June 2016.

2. Thomas Woody, *A History of Women's Education in the United States,* 2 vols. (New York: Science Press, 1929), 1: 178–85.

3. Benson J. Lossing, *Vassar College* (New York: C.A. Alvord Printer, 1867), 169–70.

4. Woody, *A History of Women's Education in the United States*, 2:154.

5. Patricia A. Graham, "Expansion and Exclusion: A History of Women in American Higher Education," *ASHE Reader on the History of Higher Education* (Needham Heights, MA: Ginn Press, 1989), 417–22.

6. C. E. Evans, *The Story of Texas Schools* (Austin: Steck Co., 1955), 33–39.

7. Wreathy Aiken, *Education of Women in Texas* (San Antonio: Naylor Co., 1957), 30.

8. Ibid.

9. Ibid., 31.

10. Evans, *The Story of Texas Schools*, 53.

11. Roberta Scott Ferguson, "The Education of Women and Girls in Texas Before the Civil War" (master's thesis, University of North Texas, 2006), 27.

12. Ibid., 27.

13. Evans, *The Story of Texas Schools*, 24.

14. Aiken, *Education of Women in Texas*, 24.

15. Ibid., 33–34.

16. Ibid., 34.

17. Ibid.

18. Evans, *The Story of Texas Schools*, 38–39.

19. Ibid., 38.

20. Ibid., 38–39.

21. Colby Ann Bosher, "A Rare Combination of Advantages: Women and Higher Education at Add-Ran College, 1873–1910" (master's thesis, Texas Christian University, 2010), 25.

22. Aiken, *Education of Women in Texas*, 61.

23. E. A. Bernhausen, "Development of Education in Waco, Texas" (master's thesis, Baylor University, Waco, Texas, 1937), 15.

24. Evans, *The Story of Texas Schools*, 313.

25. June Rayfield Welch, *The Colleges of Texas* (Dallas: GLA Press, 1981), 10.

26. Joyce Thompson, *Marking a Trail* (Denton: Texas Woman's University Press, 1943), 1. For more background on Baylor's nineteenth-century beginnings and its role in educating women see Rebecca Sharpless, "Sallie McNeill: A Woman's Higher Education in Antebellum Texas," in *Texas Women: Their Histories, Their Lives,* ed. Elizabeth Hayes Turner, Stephanie Cole, and Rebecca Sharpless (Athens: University of Georgia Press, 2015), 82–104.

27. Judith N. McArthur and Harold L. Smith, *Texas Through Women's Eyes: The Twentieth-Century Experience* (Austin: University of Texas Press, 2010), 7.

28. Ibid.

29. Ibid.

30. Ibid.

31. Thompson, *Marking a Trail,* 1.

32. Janice Marie Leone, "The Mission of Women's Colleges in an Era of Cultural Revolution, 1890–1930" (PhD diss., Ohio State University, 1989), 43. ProQuest (AAT 9001986).

33. McArthur and Smith, *Texas Through Women's Eyes,* 9.

34. Thompson, *Marking a Trail,* 4.

35. Leone, "The Mission of Women's Colleges in an Era of Cultural Revolution," 43.

36. Ibid., 113.

37. Ibid., 167.

38. Ibid., 173.

39. David Gold, "Never Mind What Harvard Thinks: Alternative Sites of Rhetorical Instruction in American Colleges, 1873–1947" (PhD diss., University of Texas at Austin, 2003), 145.

40. Bosher, "A Rare Combination of Advantages," 44.

41. Ibid., 55.

42. Aiken, *Education of Women in Texas,* 50.

43. Ibid., 51.

44. Aiken, *Education of Women in Texas,* 25.

45. Joyce Thompson, "TEXAS WOMAN'S UNIVERSITY," *Handbook of Texas Online* (http://tshaonline.org/handbook/online/articles/kct37), accessed January 22, 2016. Uploaded on June 15, 2010. Published by the Texas State Historical Association.

46. Kelly M. King, *Call Her a Citizen: Progressive-Era Activist and Educator Anna Pennybacker* (College Station: Texas A&M Press. 2010), 10.

47. Ibid., 11.

48. Ibid., 11.

49. Ibid., 12–13.

50. Winnie Ouida Davis, "Women Leaders in Texas Since 1860" (master's thesis, University of Texas, 1936), 71–73.

51. King, *Call Her a Citizen,* 196.

52. King, *Call Her a Citizen,* 15.

53. Debbie Mauldin Cottrell, *Pioneer Woman Educator: The Progressive Sprit of Annie Webb Blanton* (College Station: Texas A&M University Press, 1993), 2–4.

54. Ibid., 16–17.

55. Campbell, *Gone to Texas,* 354.

56. McArthur and Smith, *Texas Through Women's Eyes,* 27–31; Elizabeth Hayes Turner, "Part Two: 1880–1925," in *Texas Women: Their Histories, Their Lives,* ed. Elizabeth Hayes Turner, Stephanie Cole, and Rebecca Sharpless (Athens: University of Georgia Press, 2015), 149.

57. Ann Fears Crawford and Crystal Sasse Ragsdale, *Women in Texas: Their Lives Their Experiences Their Accomplishments* (Austin: Eakin Press, 1982), 46.

58. Randolph B. Campbell, *Gone to Texas,* 2nd ed. (New York: Oxford University Press, 2012), 354–55.

59. Evans, *The Story of Texas Schools,* 127.

60. Cottrell, *Pioneer Woman Educator: The Progressive Spirit of Annie Webb Blanton,* 64.

61. Ibid., 77.

62. Evans, *The Story of Texas Schools,* 124.

63. Dorothy C. Salem, *African American Women: A Biographical Dictionary* (New York: Garland Publishing, 1993), 58.

64. Ibid., 58.

65. Olive D. Brown and Michael R. Heintze, "BRANCH, MARY ELIZABETH," *Handbook of Texas Online* (http://tshaonline.org/handbook/online/articles/fbray), accessed January 11, 2016. Uploaded on June 12, 2010. Published by the Texas State Historical Association. Also Salem, *African American Woman: A Biographical Dictionary*, 59.

66. Ibid.

67. Debbie Mauldin Cottrell. "WOMEN AND EDUCATION," *Handbook of Texas Online* (http://www.tshaonline.org/handbook/online/articles/khwku), accessed December 15, 2015. Uploaded on June 15, 2010. Published by the Texas State Historical Association.

68. Brown and Heintz, "BRANCH, MARY ELIZABETH."

69. Nancy Baker Jones, "Mary Elizabeth Branch," Women in Texas History: A Project of the Ruthe Winegarten Memorial Foundation for Texas Women's History, (http://www.womenintexashistory. org/audio/mary-elizabeth-branch/). Retrieved December 15, 2015.

70. Salem, *African American Women*, 58–61.

71. Ibid.

72. Leticia Magda Garza-Falcón, *Gente Decente: A Borderlands Response to the Rhetoric of Dominance* (Austin: University of Texas Press, 1998), 75.

73. Ibid., 75.

74. Cynthia E. Orozco and Teresa Palomo Acosta, "GONZALEZ DE MIRELES, JOVITA," Handbook of Texas Online (http://www.tshaonline.org/handbook/online/articles/fgo34), accessed January 06, 2016. Uploaded on June 15, 2010. Published by the Texas State Historical Association.

75. Garza-Falcon, *Gente Decente*, 77.

76. Donna M. Kabalen de Bichara, *Telling Border Life Stories: Four Mexican American Women Writers* (College Station: Texas A&M University Press, 2013), 50.

77. Orozca and Acosta, "GONZALEZ DE MIRELES, JOVITA," *Handbook of Texas Online* (http://tshaonline.org/handbook/online/articles/fgo34), accessed December 16, 2015. Uploaded on June 15, 2010. Published by the Texas State Historical Association.

78. Orozco and Acosta, "GONZALEZ DE MIRELES, JOVITA." Her chapter appeared in Francis J. Brown and Joseph Slabey Roucek, eds., *Our Racial and National Minorities: Their History, Contributions, and Present Problems* (New York: Prentice Hall, 1937).

79. Garza-Falcón, *Gente Decente*, 77.

BIBLIOGRAPHY

Aiken, Wreathy. *Education of Women in Texas*. San Antonio: Naylor Co., 1957.

Anderson, Bonnie S., and Judith P. Zinsser. *A History of Their Own: Women in Europe from Prehistory to the Present*. Vol. 2. New York: Harper & Row, 1988.

Bernhausen, E. A. "Development of Education in Waco, Texas." Master's thesis, Baylor University, Waco, Texas, 1937.

Blandin, M. E. *History of Higher Education of Women in the South: Prior to 1860*. New York: Neal Publishing Company, 1909.

Boas, Louise Schutz. *Women's Education Begins: The Rise of Women's Colleges*. New York: Arno Press, 1971.

Bosher, Colby Ann. "A Rare Combination of Advantages: Women and Higher Education at Add-Ran College, 1873–1910." Master's thesis, Texas Christian University, 2010.

Brown, Olive D., and Michael R. Heintze, "BRANCH, MARY ELIZABETH," *Handbook of Texas Online* (http://www.tshaonline.org/handbook/online/articles/fbray), accessed January 11, 2016. Uploaded on June 12, 2010. Published by the Texas State Historical Association.

Campbell, Randolph B. *Gone to Texas*. 2nd ed. New York: Oxford University Press, 2012.

Carrington, Evelyn M., ed. *Women in Early Texas*. 2nd ed. Austin: Texas State Historical Association, 1994. With new introduction by Debbie Mauldin Cottrell. Originally published 1975 by Jenkins Publishing Company.

Cochrane, Michelle. "Educational Opportunities Available for Women in Antebellum Texas." Master's diss., University of North Texas, 2006.

Cottrell, Debbie Mauldin. *Pioneer Woman Educator: The Progressive Sprit of Annie Webb Blanton*. College Station: Texas A&M University Press, 1993.

———. "WOMEN AND EDUCATION," *Handbook of Texas Online* (http://www.tshaonline.org/handbook/online/articles/khwku), accessed December 15, 2015. Uploaded on June 15, 2010. Published by the Texas State Historical Association.

Crawford, Ann Fears, and Ragsdale Crystal Sasse. *Women in Texas: Their Lives Their Experiences Their Accomplishments*. Austin: Eakin Press.

Evans, C. E. *The Story of Texas Schools*. Austin: Steck Co., 1955.

Davis, Winnie Ouida. "Women Leaders in Texas Since 1860." Master's thesis, University of Texas, 1936.

Ferguson, Roberta Scott. "The Education of Women and Girls in Texas Before the Civil War." Master's thesis, University of Texas at Austin, 1925.

Garza-Falcón, Leticia Magda. *Gente Decente: A Borderlands Response to the Rhetoric of Dominance*. Austin: University of Texas Press, 1998.

Gold, David. "Never Mind What Harvard Thinks: Alternative Sites of Rhetorical Instruction in American Colleges, 1873–1947." PhD diss., University of Texas at Austin, 2003.

Graham, Patricia A. "Expansion and Exclusion: A History of Women in American Higher Education." *ASHE Reader on the History of Higher Education*. Needham Heights, MA: Ginn Press, 1989.

Humanities Texas. *Texas Originals*. "Jovita González." http://www.humanitiestexas.org/programs/tx-originals/list/jovita-gonzalez.

Jones, Nancy Baker. "Mary Elizabeth Branch." Women in Texas History: A Project of the Ruthe Winegarten Memorial Foundation for Texas Women's History, (http://www.womenintexashistory.org/audio/mary-elizabeth-branch/). Retrieved December 15, 2015.

Kabalen de Bichara, Donna M. *Telling Border Life Stories: Four Mexican American Women Writers*. College Station: Texas A&M University Press, 2013.

Kelly, Diana K. "The Nineteenth Century Experience of Woman College Students: A Profile of Women and Their Motivations." Fullerton College, Fullerton, CA, 1987. ERIC Number: ED292745.

King, Kelley M. *Call Her a Citizen: Progressive-Era Activist and Educator Anna Pennybacker*. College Station: Texas A&M University Press, 2010.

Labalme, Patricia H. *Beyond Their Sex: Learned Women of the European Past*. New York: New York University Press, 1980.

Leone, Janice Marie. "The Mission of Women's Colleges in an Era of Cultural Revolution, 1890–1930." PhD diss., Ohio State University, 1989. ProQuest (AAT 9001986).

Lossing, Benson J. *Vassar College*. New York: C.A. Alvord Printer, 1867.

McArthur, Judith N., and Harold L. Smith. *Texas Through Women's Eyes: The Twentieth-Century Experience*. Austin: University of Texas Press, 2010.

McClelland, Averil Evans. *The Education of Women in the United States: A Guide to Theory, Teaching, and Research*. New York: Garland Publishing, 1992.

Meiners, Fredericka. *A History of Rice University: The Institute Years, 1907–1963*. Houston: Rice University Studies, 1982.

Ogren, Christian. "Education for Women in the United States: The State Normal School Experience 1870–1920." PhD diss., University of Wisconsin-Madison, 1996.

Orozco, Cynthia E., and Teresa Palomo Acosta, "GONZALEZ DE MIRELES, JOVITA," *Handbook of Texas Online* (http://www.tshaonline.org/handbook/online/articles/fgo34), accessed December 16, 2015. Uploaded on June 15, 2010. Published by the Texas State Historical Association.

Palmieri, Patricia A. "From Republican Motherhood to Race Suicide: Arguments on the Higher Education of Women in the United States, 1820–1920." *ASHE Reader on the History of Higher Education*. Needham Heights, MA: Ginn Press, 1989.

Pangle, Thomas L., and Timothy W. Burns. *The Key Texts of Political Philosophy: An Introduction.* New York: Cambridge University Press, 2014.

Perkins, Linda M. "The Impact of the 'Cult of True Womanhood' on the Education of Black Women." *ASHE Reader on the History of Higher Education*. Needham Heights, MA: Ginn Press, 1989.

Salice, Barbara. *Women and Illiteracy in the United States: A Feminist View*. Rev. ed. Washington, DC: U.S. Department of Education Information Analysis (070), 1988.

Salem, Dorothy C. *African American Women: A Biographical Dictionary*. New York: Garland Publishing, 1993.

Slantcheva, Snejana. "Women in American Higher Education." http://www.policy.hu/slandtcheva/womeneducation.htac. Accessed June 2016.

Thompson, Joyce. *Marking a Trail*. Denton, TX: Texas Woman's University Press, 1943.

———. "TEXAS WOMAN'S UNIVERSITY," *Handbook of Texas Online* (http://tshaonline.org/handbook/online/articles/kct37), accessed January 22, 2016. Uploaded on June 15, 2010. Published by the Texas State Historical Association.

Turner, Elizabeth Hayes, Stephanie Cole, and Rebecca Sharpless. *Texas Women: Their Histories, Their Lives*. Athens: University of Georgia Press, 2015.

Welch, June Rayfield. *The Colleges of Texas*. Dallas: GLA Press, 1981.

Wilcox, Kirstin R. "Vindicating Paradoxes: Mary Wollstonecraft's Woman." *Studies in Romanticism* 48, no. 3 (Fall 2009): 447–67.

Woody, Thomas. *A History of Women's Education in the United States*. 2 vols. New York: Science Press, 1929.

10

AFRICAN AMERICANS AND HIGHER EDUCATION IN EARLY TEXAS

INTRODUCTION

The Texas Constitution of 1876 called for the establishment of a branch university for "colored youth," but that turned out to be a nearly insurmountable political obstacle for the state legislature. Finally, in 1947 an act was passed that provided for the establishment of an entirely separate and equivalent university of the first class for black Texans—what is now known as Texas Southern University in Houston. With a long way left to go for educational equality, this legislation can be viewed in the context of a Texas that had been attempting for years to provide separate but equal schools for blacks and whites at all levels. As in many other places, separate was a reality while equal usually was not. But, as events began to unfold after the passage of the 1947 act and coupled with important legal cases that will be discussed below, there began a slow reversal of those earlier policies and a strong push toward a racial equity that no longer focused on "separate but equal" schools, but provided for all citizens, regardless of skin color, the opportunity to attend any school for which they were qualified.

SOCIAL BACKGROUND

The education of slaves had depended upon the attitude of slave owners. Writing in 1919, C. G. Woodson noted in his book *The Education of the Negro Prior to 1861* that Southern planters were more favorably inclined toward the instruction of slaves before 1830. This was primarily because shortly after that date a number of Southern states passed laws that prohibited teaching slaves to read out of fear that it could lead to discontent and revolution. Despite these laws, there were slave owners, clergymen, and even planters' children who taught slaves to read the Bible. At the time Abraham Lincoln issued the Emancipation Proclamation, less than 10 percent of African Americans in the United States had basic reading skills. After the war, especially during Reconstruction, many displayed a hunger for education and looked for ways to pursue some level of learning. Many newly freed slaves flocked to the churches, where on Sundays, and sometimes during the week, they attended impromptu schools.[1]

In Texas, federal troops under the command of General Gordon Granger upon his arrival on June 19, 1865, formally proclaimed the end of slavery. A wave of excitement and joy swept the state and they rejoiced.

> Jubilee, jubilee, Oh! Lord.
> Free at last, free at last!
> Thank God A 'Mighty
> I'm free at last
> Free at last, free at last!
> Thank God A 'Mighty
> I'm free at last![2]

Soon these former slaves discovered that abolition did not come with a guarantee of social, political, or economic equality. Texas lawmakers between 1866 and 1900 put into place segregation laws that limited their rights. It began with the Constitution of 1866 and continued with laws that prohibited blacks from voting, holding public office, and serving on juries. The legislature passed laws that segregated public facilities and made sure that the education system was kept separate from the white schools. The inferior school system made it impossible for blacks to receive a decent education. It is clear that the status of black education in Texas was poor. In 1870, the United States Commissioner of Education said, "In Texas no school legislation has, so far, succeeded, and no public officers are at work for the organization of schools, her entire population being left to grow up in ignorance save as here and there a private enterprise throws a ray of light upon the general darkness."[3]

It fell to the Freedmen's Bureau and missionary and philanthropic groups to fill this lack of educational opportunity.

In the North, education for newly freed slaves was a major concern, and in response the U.S. Congress in 1865 passed a law establishing the U.S. Bureau of Refugees, Freedmen and Abandoned Lands (usually referred to as the Freedmen's Bureau) to promote and supervise the interests of former slaves. The bureau assisted missionary and philanthropic agencies in the organization of schools and also provided funds for school buildings and teacher salaries. The American Missionary Association, a Protestant abolitionist group, furnished teachers for these schools.[4] By 1867, in Texas there were 4,198 students attending 102 of these schools. Ninety-eight teachers served them—some black, some white. In 1868 it was reported that there were 240 students in the "higher branches" of the schools.[5]

The major religious denominations formed philanthropic organizations that directed monetary contributions to blacks in the South, including Texas. Northern denomination boards (governing boards of religious denominations) started four black colleges in Texas between 1873 and 1887. The first was Wylie College in Marshall, begun in 1873 by the Freedmen's Aid Society of the Methodist Episcopal Church. It was located in East Texas where the black population was 50 to 70 percent of the total population. Four years later in 1877, the American Missionary Association of the Congregational Church founded Tillotson College in Austin. Classes began in 1881.

The Presbyterian Board of Missions for Freedmen started the Mary Allen Seminary, a girl's school in Crockett, in 1887. The American Baptist Home Mission Society established Bishop College in Marshall in 1881. These were the earliest schools founded by Northern denomination boards, but others followed in later years, including Samuel Huston College in Austin, which opened in 1900.[6]

In addition to Bishop College the American Baptist Home Mission Society founded Paul Quinn College in Waco and the now-closed Fort Worth Industrial and Mechanical College in Fort Worth in 1881. Following the example of the colleges sponsored by the Northern organizations, Southern church boards of several African-American denominations established additional colleges. These boards understood that they had to help themselves and so they expanded their efforts to provide more education for their communities. Several black Baptist associations founded a group of colleges: Hearne Academy near Hearne in 1881, Guadalupe College in Seguin in 1884, Houston College in Houston in 1885, Central Texas College in Waco in 1901, and Butler College in Tyler in 1905. This activity suggests that black communities were becoming more financially successful and thus more able to support these efforts on their own.[7]

Philanthropic foundations also began to play a role in higher education throughout the South. The first of these was the Peabody Education Fund through which George Peabody, a financier and international merchant, provided $1 million in 1867 and another $2 million in 1869. He gave the money with the stipulation that it was to be used to improve education for the poor classes of the South without regard to skin color. While most of the money went to white colleges, some of the black Normal schools did receive funds. Fund records show that in the period from 1877–1909 they supported 431 Texas students or about 15 percent of the African-American college students. The Peabody Education Fund planted the seed of giving to encourage higher education in the South.[8]

Two large philanthropic donations provided income exclusively for the promotion of black schools in the South. In 1882, John F. Slater of Norwich, Connecticut, created a trust fund of $1 million for the education of emancipated slaves in the South to, as he said, "make them good men and good citizens not only for their sake but for the safety of our common country." The fund was used primarily to assist in preparing teachers and to stimulate industrial training. In order to be eligible for these funds a college had to have either a Normal or industrial department, or both. In the first forty years of this fund's existence, Texas colleges received $96,790. The second of these large donations was $1 million given to the American Missionary Society by Daniel Hand, of Guilford, Connecticut, to support education for blacks. Whether they set up their own funds or contributed to established organizations, many wealthy individuals believed providing such support was the right thing to do, and their generosity had a positive impact.[9]

As noted in the previous chapter in regard to women, changing roles and societal perceptions of a particular group can have both positive and negative effects on education and its accessibility for that group. As the potential roles for women in society changed, educational opportunities changed in response; this was often an attempt to prepare them for these new roles, whether they wanted them or not. For blacks after the Civil War radical social changes and others' perceptions also affected the kind and availability of educational opportunities. Conflicting ideas of how and why blacks should be educated existed even among African Americans themselves. One concept to keep in mind is that of "racial uplift" (or race uplift). This idea grew out of efforts by antebellum blacks to fight slavery and obtain equal rights and continued after slavery was abolished. Many in the African American community felt that blacks who had been able to get ahead, including with education, had a responsibility to provide assistance to other blacks to help lift them up.[10]

For the most part, black higher education institutions believed in providing a classical education for their students, and curriculums were established to support that mission. Southern whites often criticized the efforts of these colleges claiming it was not useful for blacks to study the classics. This controversy extended to the black community where some also wondered if a classical education was in their best interest and thought practical courses were preferable. However, most black leaders believed the better path to achieving the ideals of higher education was the one that provided a classical education. D. O. W. Holmes in his book *The Evolution of the Negro College* wrote: "However mistaken the Northern denominational bodies may have been in their educational theories, without their zeal the Negro race would have been lacking the leadership which the first generation out of slavery furnished, the greater part of which was the product of these schools."[11]

The author W.E.B. DuBois wrote in 1900, *The College Bred Negro*, in which he surveyed the social and economic conditions of black college graduates in the South. In his second book published in 1910, *The College Bred Negro American*, DuBois evaluated the character and the quality of the education offered by black colleges. In both books he concluded that the liberal arts curriculum needed to be strengthened throughout the ranks of black colleges. By this time DuBois had become a focal point within the black community for espousing these views. In an article, "The Talented Tenth" he challenged the views of Booker T. Washington. In this article he said he understood the need for some practical vocational training but he objected to its racial application, saying:

> Education and work are the levers to uplift a people. Work alone
> will not do it unless inspired by the right ideals and guided by
> intelligence. Education must not simply teach work—it must teach life.
> The Talented Tenth of the Negro race must be made leaders of thought
> and missionaries of culture among their people. No others can do this
> work and Negro colleges must train men for it. The Negro race, like all
> other races, is going to be saved by its exceptional men.[17]

Booker T. Washington was the primary leader of the movement that emphasized the teaching of practical courses. Washington had been applying his principles at Tuskegee Institute, which he had founded in 1881 in Tuskegee, Alabama. He believed that "the education of the people of my race be so directed that the greatest proportion of the mental strength of the masses will be brought to bear upon the every-day practical things of life, upon something that is needed to be done, and something which they will be permitted to do in the community in which they reside."[13]

Washington was concerned that students would be able to converse in Latin and have a knowledge of astronomy, but know little about farming, engineering, carpentry, architectural drawings, or other practical skills. At Tuskegee Institute thirty-three different trades and industry skills were taught. Students learned by doing the work, and they were paid for what they produced; so along with learning a skill, they were earning money to pay their college expenses. Washington believed that producing graduates with practical skills would enable them to begin building a foundation of hard work and thrift, and would, in time, allow them to build a bank account. He had in mind that a foundation was being built for all African Americans. About his method he said:

> I would not by any means have it understood that I would limit or circumscribe the mental development of the Negro student. No race can be lifted until its mind is awakened and strengthened. By the side of industrial training should always go mental and more training, but pushing of mere abstract knowledge into the head means little....
>
> I would not confine the race to industrial life, not even to agriculture . . . but I would teach the race that in industry the foundation must be laid—that the very best service which any one can render to what is called the higher education is to teach the present generation to provide a material or industrial foundation. On such a foundation as this will grow habits of thrift, a love of work, economy, ownership of property, bank accounts. Out of it in the future will grow practical education, professional education, positions of public responsibility. Out of it will grow moral and religious strength. Out of it will grow wealth from which alone can come leisure and the opportunity for the enjoyment of literature and the fine arts.[14]

While DuBois and Washington disagreed on the primary mission of black colleges, they did agree that black colleges played a vital part in the advancement of their race.[15]

This debate continued for some years among black leaders, who were slow to recognize that it would take both kinds of education to further the needs of African Americans.[16]

In an effort to acquire empirical data on the quality of education for blacks, the U.S. Bureau of Education (one of the precursors to today's U.S. Department of Education), with the support of the Phelps-Stokes Fund, undertook a study of the period 1914 to 1915 to collect information on both private and public colleges for blacks. The resulting report, published in 1917, demonstrated that education for African Americans in the United States was inadequate at every grade and that no institution was satisfactorily equipped or provided with adequate financial support. They lacked essentials such as decent libraries or laboratories for conducting experiments, and they also lacked good financial and educational leadership from their governing boards. The report was extremely critical of higher education for blacks, revealing that only about 10 percent of those attending the surveyed colleges were doing college-level work, and that 75 percent were doing elementary-level work. Because so many colleges had to provide remedial help for their students, they were hindered in their efforts to teach the basics necessary for a successful college career, and because so few students were doing college-level work, there were not enough of them to justify the development of real college-level programs. In addition, the lack of funds and facilities made it difficult to introduce new college courses. All these problems were exacerbated by the fact that many of the colleges had been created by local church boards that wanted the prestige of having their own college, even when they did not have the financial means or the experience necessary to be successful. Often they continued to push their small colleges to succeed because they wanted the members of their church to attend the church-owned institution.[17] The report also noted that many of these colleges had poor management structures resulting in inadequate financial reports and irresponsible or indifferent boards of trustees.

The Bureau's report also pointed out some of the problems that arose from a focus on a classical education. Educational leaders were attempting to replicate what they thought was being done in white colleges instead of concentrating on the needs of their students and communities.[18]

It was evident from the data in the Bureau's report that the 653 black colleges in the United States lacked adequate financial support. All but twenty-eight of the schools were under private control, and there simply was not enough money in the local communities to maintain them. The report observed that this must be the most impoverished group of educational institutions in the United States, and in writing about those in Texas it said that "the most urgent need of the colored schools in Texas is for trained teachers."[19] The publication of the Bureau of Education's report created concern and dismay in the African-American community, but it also created a new awareness that standards must be increased, along with a new belief in the value of college accreditation.[20]

Not all the organizations and churches that set up colleges for blacks were as thoughtful as they might have been about where they located their schools. Often a sponsored college was established in a local community regardless of whether there was a need for it. Denominational rivalries contributed to this problem, as did the ambitions of various church leaders. This sometimes resulted in clusters of colleges in small communities that could not support them or did not need them, being opened in communities with large black populations. As noted earlier, there were two black colleges operating in each of four relatively small cities at the same time. There were two colleges each in the towns of Marshall, Tyler, Waco, and Austin, and there were five colleges located in close proximity to each other in East Texas. This resulted in reduced growth for all the schools because of limited demand and too much pressure on local financial resources.[21]

One of the most critical issues facing the new black colleges was that most applicants did not have the proper preparation for college work due to the poor quality of elementary and high schools for black children. It was not uncommon to find high school teachers who had no college training and lacked the skills to prepare their students to attend college. This forced the colleges to spend most of their money and faculty time teaching what were really high school, or even lower-level, courses. Colleges were overwhelmed by the task because there was always a shortage of funds, facilities, and qualified faculty, and they were forced to teach lower-level courses at the same time they were trying to provide college-level instruction.[22]

In 1884, the Teachers State Association of Texas was formed with the intent to promote quality education for black students and good working conditions for black teachers. In 1885 it organized as the Colored Teachers State Association of Texas. Its first president was L. C. Anderson, who was also head of Prairie View Normal College. The association's annual meetings were well covered by the press, and meetings were held in most of the major cities and towns in Texas. The meetings were widely attended and the sessions demonstrated the seriousness and integrity of the association's members. This was helpful for both blacks and whites, and the association became a major voice for racial equity in Texas.[23]

In Texas, concern over the quality of higher education for blacks led to reports about ways to change the status quo. In 1915, just before the Bureau of Education issued its report, the Texas State Department of Education had found that coursework in many white colleges was also lacking and it began an effort to standardize all institutions of higher education and bring them to a level where they were requiring genuine college work.[24]

Also in 1915, the State Board of College Examiners, in conjunction with the College Section of the whites-only State Teachers Association, adopted new standards for evaluating colleges and universities. The new standards established minimum requirements for quality of faculty, library and laboratory facilities, and institutional management. As part of the overall effort, any college or university that met the new standards was to be put on an accreditation list and the graduates of these institutions would be granted permanent teaching certificates good anywhere in the state. In addition, a new procedure allowed institutions to obtain recognition as a "first-class" college or university. This was the first serious effort in Texas to provide standards for colleges and universities. The review of black colleges by the federal government had caused Texas officials to begin a closer examination of all colleges and universities in the state.[25]

During the first seventy years of educational efforts in Texas, most classroom teachers at the elementary and high school levels received their teaching certificates by taking a state exam; there was no requirement that they attend college. But it became apparent that this practice was not providing the necessary quality of education. In an effort to deal with this problem, the legislature in 1921 passed a law requiring that all teaching certificates be based on college training; the only exception was when obtaining a temporary certificate. In preparation for enforcing this new law, the State Board of College Examiners adopted new standards for junior colleges, teacher colleges, and colleges for special subjects. If a college received designation as an institution of the first class, then any work done by students at those schools qualified them for teaching certificates. All institutions were to be examined each year to ensure they were meeting the standards. By 1925, there were eight colleges at which blacks could do work on the college level, but only three of them were recognized by the State Department of Education as meeting the state standards. Those three were Prairie View Normal College, Wiley University, and Bishop College.[26]

For the next two decades, this 1921 certification law stimulated the development of the black colleges. Their enrollment increased and their role as the primary training ground for black teachers was strengthened. These new standards spurred significant change in student achievement. In 1921, only 15 percent of the students at black colleges were doing college-level work, but by 1931 this number had increased to 60 percent.[27]

While these schools had made great progress, a second study done by the Bureau of Education on conditions as they existed from 1926 to 1928 produced more evidence of the weakness of the black schools, especially the denominational colleges. These schools were found to be deficient in financial support, administration, pay scale, and the quality of their libraries and laboratory equipment—problems already well known in the black community.[28]

In 1930, the Southern Association of Colleges assumed the role of examining all colleges in Texas. When they began evaluating the black colleges and comparing their standards to those at the white colleges in Texas, they found that only five could be certified. In an effort to clarify the problem, the association issued a statement that both complimented the black colleges and pointed out their problems. In part it said:

> On the other hand there are entirely too many small anemic institutions suffering from lack of support, lack of vision, denominational prejudice, etc. . . . Denominations and boards of control are struggling to maintain many of these schools, and are expending funds out of proportion to the quality of work offered or number of students served. They are not necessarily poor because they are small but too often they are small because they are poor. . . .
>
> There are simply more institutions of this type than are needed or can expect to live and serve on a plane worthy of the church.
>
> The future of these small, struggling colleges is one of the serious problems connected with higher education. Most of them have personal and denominational ties which are of long standing and will be difficult to alter. However, when we consider the purpose back of them is to develop character and leadership for the church and the race, it seems farsighted church leaders would realize these purposes could be attained much better and at equal or less cost, by maintaining fewer but better institutions.[29]

As the Depression of the 1930s gripped the country, financial realities made it impossible for many of these church-sponsored schools to continue and they began to close. On the horizon were constitutional and legal changes that would truly remake the landscape of higher education in Texas.

CONSTITUTIONAL AND LEGAL BACKGROUND

In the first Texas Constitution approved in 1836, there had been no provision for education for African Americans, because most were slaves and did not fall under the scope of the constitution. After the Civil War, the Texas Constitution of 1866 was the first to mention the education of "Africans and their children." It was not a very generous provision in that all it said was the school fund was to be used exclusively for the education of the "white scholastic inhabitants of the State" and that an additional tax might be levied for educational purposes, provided "that all of the sums arising from said tax which may be collected from Africans, or persons of African descent, shall be exclusively appropriated for the maintenance of a system of public schools for Africans and their children."[30] Although the constitution did note that it was "the duty of the Legislature to encourage schools among these people," this was a very weak provision because it was unlikely the taxes collected from poor blacks just coming out of slavery would be sufficient to build adequate schools.[31]

The Constitution of 1869 made some progress by including blacks in the general provisions for education without any reference to skin color. This constitution was called "radical" by many white Texans because it was forced upon Texas by the federal government after the Civil War. When Texas was granted representation in the U.S. Congress as part of the Reconstruction Act of 1870, one of the conditions for the state's readmission was a statute providing that the "Constitution of Texas shall never be so amended or changed as to deprive any citizen or a class of citizens of the United States of the school rights and privileges secured by the Constitution of the State."[32]

While northern states had a more progressive attitude toward the education of African Americans, whites in Texas were afraid they would be forced to raise tax money to support separatist education. In spite of these feelings, there were efforts to open schools. Attendance was mandatory for all children, and many black children did attend school, and for most of them, this was their first time.[33]

Texans at the time understood there was a need to provide an education for blacks, and that was reflected in the Constitution of 1876. Each of the six Texas constitutions shows an increasing understanding of this, but it was a lengthy process that covered just over one hundred years. While Texas was slowly moving toward providing educational opportunities in higher education for blacks, colleges in other states were beginning to admit blacks and encourage their attendance by providing them with tuition money.[34]

The Texas state constitution approved in 1876 specifically required segregation of the races by stating, "Separate schools shall be provided for the white and colored children, and impartial provision shall be made for both." This was the "separate but equal doctrine" the state followed for almost ninety years. While there were still negative feelings about the education of blacks, the majority of whites began to believe they stood to benefit by having a black population with at least some education. Also, for the first time, the state constitution provided a higher education opportunity for blacks because it authorized the establishment and maintenance of a "College or Branch University for the instruction of the colored youth of the State, to be located by a vote of the people."[35]

In 1876, the Texas legislature, using the Morrill Act, which provided public lands to help support establishment of colleges (see chapter 5), authorized an "Agricultural and Mechanical College for the Benefit of Colored Youth," which was to be a part of Texas A&M College. A commission bought the land for the school, near the town of Hempstead (close to Bryan). The school opened on March 11, 1878, as Alta Vista Agricultural College, with eight students. The school closed the next year because of a lack of students.

The legislature then passed a bill establishing a Normal school that would use the closed Alta Vista facilities, and in 1887 the legislature added an agricultural and mechanical department. This college eventually became Prairie View A&M University.[36]

During the late 1800s, while political leaders were waiting for public opinion to change and support efforts to provide better educational opportunities for African Americans, both political parties took strong stands supporting those opportunities. The first occurred in 1883 when the Republican Party at its annual convention in Dallas called for the completion of the University of Texas and for a "colored branch" at the university. In the election year of 1886 the Republican Party again spoke out on the issue, and because of its stand, the subject was widely discussed and this public discussion, which was extensively covered by the press, began to build support for the idea of a "colored branch." Then in 1892 Republicans, by a convention resolution, demanded that the legislature comply with the constitutional provision and establish a branch of the state university for "colored people." In 1894 while meeting in Dallas, the party platform called for equal school provisions for all citizens and urged the state as soon as was practical to take steps to institute the "colored branch" of the university.[37]

Democrats at their state convention in Fort Worth in 1896 included in their platform a pledge for equal protection for the enjoyment of life, liberty, and the pursuit of happiness for "all races and classes." They also proposed adding additional buildings to the campus at Prairie View Normal School and supported the legislature setting aside 50,000 acres of unappropriated land to pay for improvements for the school.[38]

One of the most vocal groups in Texas to call for a separate branch for African Americans was the Colored Teachers State Association of Texas. Beginning in spring 1896, its members organized a campaign for a black college. In an address before the association, their president called for directors of Texas A&M College, the overseers of Prairie View Normal School, to add additional branches or courses that would allow the school to become a university.[39] At the same time, many of the state's white educational and political leaders were advocating for the expansion of Prairie View as the best solution to providing a black university. In 1899 and 1901 the state legislature passed laws that called for an expansion plan at Prairie View that would make the college a "classical college." Prior to this, the college taught only rudimentary agricultural and mechanical courses; this was an attempt to make it more like what is referred to today as a liberal arts college. In the end it became a combination of the two.[40]

Also during the late nineteenth century and the early twentieth century there were several futile attempts by the legislature to authorize the establishment of a Negro branch of the University of Texas, in accordance with the constitutional provision that one be established. In 1897, the legislature authorized 100,000 acres be set aside as part of a permanent endowment for a branch at the University of Texas for "the colored race," only to discover that there was none to set aside because all the public land had already been given away or sold.[41]

In 1899 the legislature approved a bill that said in part:

> Resolved, further, that as soon as the commission appointed to investigate and ascertain the exact status of the public domain and the public free school lands of Texas shall make a report to the Governor the amount of land still belonging to the State, that steps be taken to establish said University for the colored race, either by appropriating public domain, if there is any domain, or by appropriating land retained to the State from railway corporations that have refused to comply with their charter grants or to obey the laws of Texas.[42]

When the state was unable to identify any available land, the 1915 legislature called for a constitutional amendment to take 600,000 acres from the Permanent University Fund and allocate it to Texas A&M College and require 150,000 acres from that be allocated to Prairie View College. The amendment was placed on a state ballot and was defeated by the voters on July 24, 1915, by a vote of 81,658 to 50,398.[43]

In 1919 the legislature passed another bill requiring an amendment to the constitution that would divide the Permanent University Fund between the University of Texas and Texas A&M College on a two-to-one basis, and called for the College to appropriate from their land an interest that it determined to be equitable, to go to Prairie View College. The voters—76,422 to 36,560— also defeated that amendment.[44]

There was a growing concern in the state and among members of the legislature over the lack of opportunities in Texas for blacks to obtain advanced and professional degrees. All efforts to start such schools had failed. The legislature decided to set aside a small amount of money to provide scholarships for qualified African-American applicants who wanted to obtain an advanced degree and were willing to attend an out-of-state college. This practice began in 1939. Students in programs in law, medicine, social work, dentistry, pharmacy, library science, physical education, home economics, agriculture, music, business, engineering, architecture, and education were eligible to apply. These scholarships enabled many blacks to further their education, and these graduates provided the foundation of a black professional class in Texas. The scholarship program ended in 1954 when the U.S. Supreme Court decision in *Brown v. Board of Education of Topeka* [347 U.S. 483 (1954)] made such programs illegal.[45]

In another effort to improve higher education opportunities for blacks, the legislature in 1945 passed a bill that changed the status, function, and name of the Normal school at Prairie View.

The school was now to be called Prairie View A&M College and the bill provided that it:

> be authorized, in addition to the courses of study then authorized,
> to conduct courses in law, medicine, engineering, pharmacy,
> journalism, and any other generally recognized college course taught
> at the University of Texas, such course to be substantially equivalent
> to those offered at the University of Texas. . . . [and] remove the
> obligation to teach in the Negro public free schools for one year

in the cases of students of law, medicine, engineering, pharmacy, journalism, and any other generally recognized college course taught at the University of Texas.[46]

As the members of the legislature wrestled with a constitutional provision for a branch for blacks at the University of Texas, it had become evident that it was not politically possible to make such an amendment happen. A new idea was proposed to establish an entirely new and separate university for blacks. In 1947, the legislature passed a bill that established such a university. This bill was especially significant and its passage had a bearing on subsequent legal cases. Section 2 identified the bill's purpose:

> To provide instruction, training and higher education for colored people, there is hereby established a University of the first class in two divisions: The first, styled, "The Texas State University for Negroes," to be located in Houston . . .; the second, to be styled "The Prairie View Agricultural and Mechanical College of Texas," at Prairie View. . . . At the Prairie View Agricultural and Mechanical College shall be offered courses in agriculture, the mechanical arts, engineering, and the natural sciences connected therewith, together with any other courses authorized at Prairie View at the time of passage of this Act, all of which shall be equivalent to those offered at the Agricultural and Mechanical College of Texas. The Texas State University for Negroes shall offer all other courses of higher learning . . . all of which shall be equivalent to those offered at the University of Texas. Upon demand being made by any qualified applicant for any present or future course of instruction offered at the University of Texas, or its branches, such courses shall be established in order that the separate Universities for Negroes shall at all times offer equal educational opportunities and training as that available to other persons of this State.[47]

Another section of the act called for the formation of and appropriation of money for an interim School of Law at the Texas State University for Negroes.[48]

Later in this same 1947 legislative session a bill was passed establishing Texas Southern University at Houston. With this legislation the legislature was finally acting upon the requirement of the constitution ratified in 1876 to provide for a university for African Americans.[49]

IN THE COURTS

There was a succession of legal cases that had critical impacts on the education of blacks in Texas. In a report to the legislature in April 1951, the Texas Legislative Council noted that:

> Although the quality of Negro education is improving remarkably, it is a generally recognized fact that in many places and in many educational areas it is still greatly inferior to white education. This is true to a marked degree on the higher education level. This disparity between the legal educational rights and privileges of the Negro and the actual educational benefits afforded him has given rise to interesting court cases in Texas and other segregation states.[50]

The first Texas court case to address the reality of educational opportunities for blacks, as opposed to their stated legal rights, was *Givens v. Woodward* [145 Tex. 150 (Tex. 1946)]. Dr. Everett H. Givens, the plaintiff, was an African-American dentist from Austin who filed a suit on September 30, 1946, in Travis County District Court against Dudley K. Woodward, Jr., chairman of the University of Texas Board of Regents, and all the other members of the board. The suit cited the provision of the 1876 state constitution that established a branch of the University of Texas for "Negro youths," the 1882 election that had provided for the branch to be located in Austin, and the fact that the legislature had never appropriated the money for the branch. Givens was requesting that the branch be established as called for in the Constitution of 1876, but the case was denied. Givens then appealed the ruling to the Texas Court of Appeals, which denied his petition on the grounds that the constitution authorized the location of the school and not its establishment, arguing that the problem was not with the regents but with the legislature, which had not authorized the branch. Givens then appealed his case to the Texas Supreme Court, which dismissed the case on February 18, 1948. Even though Givens lost his case, his suit motivated the legal community to begin rethinking the issue of education for African Americans.[51]

A more significant case regarding state policy was *Sweatt v. Painter* [339 U.S. 629 (1950)]. In February 1946, Heman Marion Sweatt applied for admission to the school of law at the University of Texas. At the time there was only one Texas public law school. The president of the University of Texas, T. S. Painter, denied Sweatt's application pending an opinion from the state attorney general regarding the application. The attorney general issued a ruling saying that Sweatt was not entitled to be admitted at that time, but if the State of Texas did not offer him equal education, then the university must admit him. The case was then filed with a Travis County District Court, and there Sweatt obtained an interlocutory writ, or temporary order, to enter the University of Texas School of Law, with a suspension for six months to give the state the opportunity to establish a school of law for blacks, as contemplated in the 1945 act that created Prairie View University. In December 1946, Sweatt was denied a writ of mandamus, which asked the court to allow him to enter the University of Texas School of Law. The denial was contingent upon the state opening a school of law for blacks at Houston, a branch of Prairie View University, in time for the second semester. The judgment also said that such a school had to make available to Sweatt legal training substantially equal to that offered at the University of Texas School of Law.[52]

Sweatt's lawyers filed an appeal with the Texas Court of Civil Appeals. In response to this the legislature on March 3, 1947, passed a bill establishing the State University for Negroes at Houston. The attorney general then asked the Court of Civil Appeals to remand the case to the district court in Travis County. The attorney general in his pleadings said that the University of Texas had established an interim school of law for Negroes until the newly authorized school could begin operating. On April 28, 1947, the appeals court remanded the case to the district court for a new trial.[53]

In the new trial, Sweatt's attorneys changed their strategy, putting more emphasis on the segregation aspects of the case instead of the discrimination aspects. This turned out to be a very effective strategy. The case developed by Sweatt's attorneys turned on the issue of the constitutionality of the Texas segregation laws under the Fourteenth Amendment of the U.S. Constitution. The district court at the end of the trial denied Sweatt admission to the University of Texas law school on the grounds that a substantially equal opportunity was offered at the separate school for blacks. This decision put the case on a path to the United States Supreme Court as a segregation case.[54]

However, the next step was the Third Court of Civil Appeals in Austin on January 29, 1948, where Sweatt's attorneys continued to make the case about segregation. A month later on February 28, the appeals court agreed with the district court and sustained its judgment denying Sweatt's admission to the University of Texas School of Law. Sweatt's attorneys filed a motion for rehearing arguing that they had presented arguments about segregation but the judge had rendered his opinion based on equal opportunity. The appeals court denied the motion for rehearing, which meant the State of Texas was on record as saying that Texas was providing equal facilities for blacks and that segregation was legal.[55]

Toward the end of 1948, the case was accepted by the United States Supreme Court, and on June 5, 1950, Chief Justice Fred M. Vinson delivered the opinion of the Court: "We hold that the Equal Protection Clause of the Fourteenth Amendment requires the petitioner to be admitted to the University of Texas School of Law. The judgment is reversed and the cause is remanded for proceedings not inconsistent with this opinion."[56]

Most of the Supreme Court's decision discussed the quality of the educational differences between the University of Texas School of Law and Prairie View University, the new State University for

Negroes at Houston, and the interim law school at Austin. The court believed that the differences in quality and opportunity were significant and it made that clear in its opinion:

> Whether the University of Texas Law School is compared with the original or the new law school for Negroes, we cannot find substantial equality in the educational opportunities offered white and Negro law students by the State. In terms of number of the faculty, variety of courses and opportunity for specialization, size of the student body, scope of the library, availability of law review and similar activities, the University of Texas Law School is superior. What is more important, the University of Texas Law School possesses to a far greater degree those qualities which are incapable of objective measurement but which make for greatness in a law school. Such qualities, to name but a few, include reputation of the faculty, experience of the administration, position and influence of the alumni, standing in the community, traditions and prestige. It is difficult to believe that one who had a free choice between these law schools would consider the question close.[57]

The Supreme Court's ruling in *Sweatt v. Painter* played an important role in how Texas began dealing with education for blacks. It had an immediate effect on enrollment at the University of Texas. A number of blacks were admitted shortly after the ruling. The attorney general of Texas advised the Board of Regents that the decision meant the opening of the doors of the University to blacks in most cases.[58]

* * * *

This chapter has shown that the church-related black colleges in Texas were the primary sources of education and advancement for black people in Texas and the South. Both white and black religious denominations began to establish these colleges soon after the ending of the Civil War in an effort to provide religious education for the newly freed slaves. The religious colleges during the late nineteenth and early twentieth centuries took upon themselves the role as the primary educators of the black race. Without these colleges and the northern missionary societies the majority of the blacks in Texas would have remained completely illiterate. As an example, even though the Texas legislature established two black colleges, the black church-related colleges produced a majority of the state's black college graduates. Between 1930 and 1954 an average of 43 percent of Texas black college students attended either Prairie View or Texas Southern, while 57 percent attend black denominational colleges such as Bishop, Wylie, Tillison, Samuel Huston, and Paul Quinn. One of the main criticisms of the denominational colleges was that they were unable to establish strong financial bases. This criticism is a little harsh when one realizes that the colleges drew most of their financial support from the most impoverished segments of Texas. Most whites were either hostile or apathetic to black education. It was by skillful management and countless sacrifices by their supporters and strong determination in what they thought must be done that these colleges were able to offer their students meaningful educational opportunities.[59]

Conflicts over higher education for black Texans did not, of course, end here, but these were important beginnings. This chapter, like others on the experience of women and Hispanics, has by default looked at a discrete element of higher education in Texas that really cannot be fully examined in a vacuum. It is important to remember that the experience of higher education for African Americans, has been, and often still is, complex, and is frequently complicated by two important additional variables— socioeconomic resources and gender.

NOTES

1. Carter Godwin Woodson, *The Education of the Negro Prior to 1861: A History of the Education of the Colored People of the United States from the Beginning of Slavery to the Civil War* (Washington, DC: Associated Publishers, 1919), 264.

2. Heintze, *Private Black Colleges in Texas, 1865–1954* (College Station: Texas A&M University Press, 1985) 16.

3. Heintze, *Private Black Colleges in Texas, 1865–1954*, 19.

4. Shaun R. Harper, Lori D. Patton, and Ontario S. Wooden, "Access and Equity for African American Students in Higher Education: A Critical Race Historical Analysis of Policy Efforts," *Journal of Higher Education* 80, no. 4 (Jul/Aug 2009): 389–414.

5. Anna Victoria Wilson, "EDUCATION FOR AFRICAN AMERICANS," *Handbook of Texas Online* (http://www.tshaonline.org/handbook/online/articles/kde02), accessed September 25, 2013. Uploaded on June 12, 2010. Published by the Texas State Historical Association. See also Amilcar Shabazz, *Advancing Democracy: African Americans and the Struggle for Access and Equity in Higher Education in Texas* (Chapel Hill: University of North Carolina Press, 2004), 14–15 for discussion of the role of the Bureau and direction to additional sources.

6. David A. Williams, *Bricks Without Straw: A Comprehensive History of African Americans in Texas* (Austin: Eakin Press, 1997), 228.

7. William E. Montgomery, "HEARNE ACADEMY," Handbook of Texas Online (http://www.tshaonline.org/handbook/online/articles/kbh16), accessed November 01, 2014. Uploaded on June 15, 2010. Published by the Texas State Historical Association; Williams, *Bricks without Straw*, 234, 248–49; Frederick Eby, *The Development of Education in Texas* (New York: Macmillan Co., 1925), 264.

8. Williams, *Bricks Without Straw*, 19; George Dillingham, *The Foundation of the Peabody Tradition* (New York: University Press of America, 1989), 180.

9. Eby, *The Development of Education in Texas*, 268–69.

10. Linda M. Perkins, "The Impact of the 'Cult of True Womanhood' on the Education of Black Women," in *ASHE Reader on the History of Higher Education* (Needham Heights, MA: Ginn Press, 1989). 154–55.

11. Dwight Oliver Wendell Holmes, *The Evolution of the Negro College* (New York: AMS Press, 1970), 70.

12. Heintze, *Private Black Colleges in Texas, 1865–1954*, 4.

13. Booker T. Washington, *Tuskegee and Its People: Their Ideas and Achievements* (New York: D. Appleton & Co., 1905), 19.

14. Washington, *Tuskegee and Its People*, 20–21.

15. Heintze, *Black Colleges in Texas, 1865–1954*, 5.

16. Eby, *The Development of Education in Texas*, 270–71. See also Shabazz, *Advancing Democracy*, 18–19.

17. Williams, *Bricks Without Straw*, 22.

18. U.S. Department of the Interior, Bureau of Education, *Negro Education: A Study of the Private and Higher Schools for Colored People in the United States.* 2 vols. Bulletin, 1916, No. 38, Bulletin 1916, No. 39 (Washington, DC: Government Printing Office, 1917), 2:247–48.

19. Bureau of Education, *Negro Education*, 2:615.

20. Bureau of Education, *Negro Education*, 1:248.

21. Anne Brawner, *Guadalupe College: A Case History of Negro Higher Education 1884–1936* (master's thesis, Southwest Texas State University, 1980), 9–10; E. Franklin Frazier, *The Negro Church in America* (New York: Schocken Books, 1963), 46.

22. Brawner, "Guadalupe College," 46.

23. Vernon McDaniel, *History of the Teachers State Association of Texas* (Washington DC: National Education Association, 1977), 13–14. See also Shabazz, *Advancing Democracy*, 17–19 for a discussion of the Association's development and role.

24. Bureau of Education, *Negro Education*, 1:55–56.

25. Brawner, "Guadalupe College," 29; Eby, *The Development of Education in Texas*, 298.

26. Brawner, "Guadalupe College," 21–23; Eby, *The Development of Education in Texas*, 272.

27. Brawner, "Guadalupe College," 23.

28. Ibid., 22–24

29. Ibid., 24.

30. Texas Constitution of 1866; http://tarlton.law.utexas.edu/constitutions/texas1866.

31. Williams, *Bricks Without Straw*, 217.

32. Ibid.

33. Ibid., 218.

34. Ibid., 217–218.

35. Staff of the [Texas] Legislative Council, "Higher Education for Negroes in Texas," Staff Monograph No. 51-1 (Austin: Staff of the Texas Legislative Council, 1951), 2–5.

36. Texas Constitution of 1876, http://tarlton.law.utexas.edu/constitutions/texas1866; J. J. Lane, "History of Education in Texas," Washington, DC: Government Printing Office, 1903. [US Bur of Educ Circ 1903 2:1–234. *Contributions to American Educational History*, no. 35, circular of information 2, 1903.]

37. Williams, *Bricks Without Straw*, 9.

38. Ibid., 10.

39. Ibid., 9.

40. Eby, *The Development of Education in Texas*, 274. See also Shabazz, *Advancing Democracy*, 17–19 for a discussion of the Association's activities.

41. Staff of the [Texas] Legislative Council, "Higher Education for Negroes in Texas," 7.

42. HCR 26, Staff of the [Texas] Legislative Council, "Higher Education for Negroes in Texas," 8.

43. HJR 34.

44. Staff of the [Texas] Legislative Council, "Higher Education for Negroes in Texas," House Joint Resolution 29, passed March 18, 1919.

45. C. E. Evans, *The Story of Texas Schools* (Austin: Steck Company, 1955), 221–23.

46. Williams, *Bricks Without Straw*, 208.

47. Act of March 3, 1947, Ch. 29.

48. Staff of the [Texas] Legislative Council, "Higher Education for Negroes in Texas," 10.

49. Williams, *Bricks Without Straw*, 85–86.

50. Staff of the [Texas] Legislative Council, "Higher Education for Negroes in Texas," 11.

51. Ibid., 11–12.

52. Ibid., 12.

53. Ibid., 13.

54. Ibid., 13.

55. Ibid.,14.

56. Ibid., 14.

57. *Sweatt v. Painter*, 339 U.S. 629 (1950).

58. Staff of the [Texas] Legislative Council (1951), 16. See also Shabazz, *Advancing Democracy*, esp. chapters 3 and 4; and Gary M. Lavergne, *Before Brown: Heman Marion Sweatt, Thurgood Marshall, and the Long Road to Justice* (Austin: University of Texas Press, 2010) for additional discussion.

59. Heintze, *Private Black Colleges in Texas, 1865-1954*, 180.

BIBLIOGRAPHY

Allen, Walter R., Joseph O. Jewell, Kimberly A. Griffin, De'Sha S. Wolf. "Historically Black Colleges and Universities: Honoring the Past, Engaging the Present, Touching the Future." *Journal of Negro Education* 76, no. 3 (Summer 2007): 263–80.

Barr, Alwyn, *Black Texans: A History of African Americans in Texas, 1528–1995*. 2nd ed. Norman: University of Oklahoma Press, 1973.

Barr, Alwyn, Calvert, Robert A. *Black Leaders: Texans for their Times*. Austin: Texas State Historical Association, 1981.

Behnken, Brian D. *Fighting Their Own Battles, Mexican Americans, African Americans, and the Struggle for Civil Rights in Texas*. Chapel Hill: University of North Carolina Press, 2011.

Boxill, Bernard R. *The Negro Problem*. New York: Humanity Books, 2003.

Brawner, Anne. "Guadalupe College: A Case History in Negro Higher Education 1884–1936." Master's thesis, Southwest Texas State University, 1980.

Briscoe Center for American History, The University of Texas at Austin. "African American History Resources: Education," 2014. https://www.cah.utexas.edu/research/subject guides/ africanam_edu.php.

Dillingham, George. *The Foundation of the Peabody Tradition*. New York: University Press of America, 1989.

DuBois, W. E. B. *W. E. B Dubois Speaks: Speeches and Addresses 1920-1963*. New York: Pathfinder Press, 1970.

Eby, Frederick. *The Development of Education in Texas*. New York: Macmillan Co., 1925.

Evans, C. E. *The Story of Texas Schools*. Austin, TX: Steck Company, 1955.

Frazier, E. Franklin. *The Negro Church in America*. New York: Schocken Books, 1963.

Harper, Shaun R., Lori D. Patton, and Ontario S. Wooden. "Access and Equity for African American Students in Higher Education: A Critical Race Historical Analysis of Policy Efforts." *Journal of Higher Education* 80, no. 4 (Jul/Aug 2009): 389–414.

Heintze, Michael R. "A History of the Black Private Colleges in Texas, 1865–1954." PhD diss., Texas Tech University, 1981.

Holmes, Dwight Oliver Wendell. *The Evolution of the Negro College*. New York: AMS Press, 1970. First printed 1934 by Bureau of Publications, Teachers College, Columbia University, New York.

Kirk, W. Astor, and John Q. Taylor King. "Desegregation of Higher Education in Texas." *Journal of Negro Education* 27, no. 3, Desegregation and the Negro College (Summer, 1958): 318–23.

Lane, J. J. "History of Education in Texas," Washington, DC: Government Printing Office, 1903. [US Bur of Educ Circ 1903 2:1-234. *Contributions to American Educational History*, no. 35, circular of information 2, 1903: whole no. 293]

Lavergne, Gary M. *Before Brown: Heman Marion Sweatt, Thurgood Marshall, and the Long Road to Justice*. Austin: University of Texas Press, 2010.

Leak, Halima N., and Chera D. Reid. "'Making Something of Themselves': Black Self-Determination, the Church and Higher Education Philanthropy." *International Journal of Education Advancement* 10, no. 3 (2010): 235–44.

McCuistion, Fred B. *Graduate Instruction for Negroes in the United States*. Nashville, TN: George Peabody College for Teachers, 1939.

McDaniel, Vernon. *History of the Teachers State Association of Texas*. Washington DC: National Education Association, 1977.

Miller, Kelly. "The Education of the Negro" in *Report of the United States Commissioner of Education for 1900-1901*. Vol. 1. Washington, DC: Government Printing Office, 1902, 121–27.

Perkins, Linda M. "The Impact of the 'Cult of True Womanhood' on the Education of Black Women." In *ASHE Reader on the History of Higher Education*, edited by Lester F. Goodchild and Harold S. Wechsler, 154–159. Needham Heights, MA: Glnn Press, 1989.

Shabazz, Amilcar. *Advancing Democracy: African Americans and the Struggle for Access and Equity in Higher Education in Texas*. Chapel Hill: University of North Carolina Press, 2004.

Taylor, Clifford H. "Jarvis Christian College: Its History and Present Standing in Relationship to the Standards of the Texas State Department of Education and the Southern Association of Colleges and Secondary Schools." Research paper in lieu of a thesis, Bachelor of Divinity, Brite College of the Bible of Texas Christian University, 1948.

Texas Department of Education. Minutes of the State Board of Examiners, 1915–1931.

Texas. Legislative Council. Staff of the. "Higher Education for Negroes in Texas." Staff Monograph No. 51-1. Austin: Staff of the Texas Legislative Council, 1951.

Tillman, Linda C. *The Sage Handbook of African American Education*. Thousand Oaks, CA: Sage Publications, 2009.

U.S. Department of Education (Henry Barnard). "Special Report of the Commissioner of Education on the Condition and Improvement of Public Schools in the District of Columbia," requested by Congress 1867 GPO 1871. New York: Arno Press, 1969.

U.S. Department of the Interior, Bureau of Education Bulletin. *Negro Education: A Study of the Private and Higher Schools for Colored People in the United States.* 2 vols. *Bulletin,* 1916, No. 38, *Bulletin* 1916, No. 39. Washington, DC: Government Printing Office, 1917.

U.S. Department of the Interior, Bureau of Education Bulletin. *Statistics of Education of the Negro Race 1925–1926.* Bulletin, 1928, No. 19. Washington, DC: Government Printing Office, 1928.

Washington, Booker T. *The Negro Problem, Industrial Education for the Negro.* New York: James Patt & Co, 1903.

———. *Tuskegee and Its People: Their Ideas and Achievements.* New York: D. Appleton & Co., 1905.

Williams, David A. *Bricks Without Straw: A Comprehensive History of African Americans in Texas.* Austin: Eakin Press, 1997.

———. "The History of Higher Education for Black Texans, 1872–1977." EdD diss, Baylor University, 1978.

Wilson, Anna Victoria. "EDUCATION FOR AFRICAN AMERICANS," *Handbook of Texas Online* (http://www.tshaonline.org/handbook/online/articles/kde02), accessed September 25, 2013. Uploaded on June 12, 2010. Published by the Texas State Historical Association.

Woodson, Carter Godwin. *The Education of the Negro Prior to 1861: A History of the Education of the Colored People of the United States from the Beginning of Slavery to the Civil War.* Washington, DC: Associated Publishers, 1919.

Woolfolk, George Ruble. "PRAIRIE VIEW A&M UNIVERSITY," *Handbook of Texas Online* (http://www.tshaonline.org/handbook/online/articles/kcp06), accessed May 27, 2014. Uploaded on June 15, 2010. Modified on June 14, 2013. Published by the Texas State Historical Association.

11

HISPANICS AND HIGHER EDUCATION

INTRODUCTION

As with the preceding discussions of higher education for women and African Americans, we are pulling out a topic that has in reality a complex involvement with historical, legal, and social factors. While Hispanics in Texas will have had some experiences in common with other students of higher education, their experiences will most likely also have been affected by their ethnic background, whether they were male or female, and by a variety of interwoven socioeconomic factors that should be kept in mind while considering this chapter's historical review.

THE ROLE OF TERMINOLOGY

How people refer to themselves and others has received much attention in recent years. Ethnic designations can be especially problematic, and misunderstandings often stem from a lack of historical knowledge and differing personal experiences. Texas's complex history makes it especially important to clarify some of this terminology.

In Texas during the Spanish and Mexican periods it was relatively easy to identify the human population. In the Spanish period, people were often described by their racial and ethnic backgrounds. "Spanish" meant "white," but it did not always mean that the person had been born in Spain. In this chapter, Spanish settlers include a wide variety of both ethnic and multiracial people. This is illustrated by *mestizos*, who were of Spanish and Indian descent. After Mexican independence in 1821, the people of the Rio Grande border region used the term *Mexican* to describe themselves.[1]

After Texas became a state in 1848, Mexicans in Texas called themselves *mejicanos*, or Mexicans, and by the late nineteenth century, Mexicans had begun using the term *Tejanos*. Among *Tejanos* there were three other terms—*ricos, pobres,* and *peones. Ricos* were rich *Tejanos*, and *pobres* were poor *Tejanos,* while *peones* were unskilled laborers. A small part of the mixed-race population was referred to as *mulattoes,* and they were grouped with the black population.[2]

In today's Texas, many people of Spanish or Mexican origin refer to themselves as Hispanic, and that is generally what is used here. However, especially in periods of social transition, terminology can vary widely in its usage and acceptance. While Hispanic may be preferable or accepted among certain groups, others may favor Latino or Latina, Tejano, or Mexican American. Understanding an institution's particular history and constituency is critical for administrators in higher education.

HISPANICS IN TEXAS HISTORY

The history of Texas contains many episodes of discrimination against Hispanics in regard to education, particularly with efforts to block their ability to access higher education. It is a complex history, and parts of it are just now being brought to light. For many years, historians either ignored or were unaware of the contributions made by the earliest Texas settlers—the Tejanos who dominated the politics of Texas under Spanish and Mexican rule. The colonization of Spanish Texas began in 1716, while the Mexican period began after Mexico broke away from Spain in 1821. During those years, Tejanos—Spanish for "Texan male"—held the major local political offices in Texas. These leaders were, for the most part, very supportive of the empresarios' efforts to bring in Anglo-Americans to settle Texas lands, and they paved the way with the Mexican government to make this settlement possible.[3]

During the Texas Revolution in 1836 some Tejanos participated on the Texas side, and three Tejanos were among the fifty-six signers of the Texas Declaration of Independence. Tejanos like Juan Seguin took part in the battles that led to the success of the revolution. In the battle of the Alamo it was the Tejano merchants of San Antonio who furnished much of the materiel needed by the fort, mostly on credit.[4]

It is important to understand how much this early era was dominated by Tejanos in order to grasp the significance of later treatment of this important group of Texans by the Anglo majority in regard to educational opportunities. While Tejanos were considered "white" under the various state constitutions, education was not the only area in which they were treated differently than the more numerous Anglo-Americans.[5]

In the late eighteenth and early nineteenth centuries, the majority of Tejano Texans lived in southern and central Texas, where most made their living as farm laborers. There were a fairly large number of Tejano Texans living in three of the cities that had been founded in the early eighteenth century: San Antonio, Nacogdoches, and Goliad. A population estimate made in 1834 reported that in San Antonio and the surrounding area there were about 2,400 Hispanic Texans, in Nacogdoches about 500, and in Goliad about 700. In the newer town of Victoria, founded in 1824 by Martin De Leon, there were 300 Hispanic Texans by 1834, and in Laredo on the Rio Grande there were 2,000 in 1835.[6] In 1834, Juan N. Almonte, after visiting Texas, estimated the total population of Texas at 24,700, including slaves. In 1836 it was estimated that there were 5,000 blacks; 30,000 Anglo-Americans; 3,470 Hispanics; and 14,200 American Indians.[7] It is obvious that the rapid increase in Anglo-American population was overpowering the smaller number of Hispanics.

The Tejano population was socially stratified. *Ricos* made up the highest level, and they held the government positions, owned most of the business, and owned and ran large ranches. At the lowest level of society were the *peones* and the day laborers; among them were Hispanicized Indians and people of mixed blood.[8]

Even as the population of Anglo settlers began to increase and dominate the population of Tejanos, the relationship between the Tejano elites and the Anglos was for the most part cordial. There were, however, settlers who were not friendly or sympathetic toward Tejanos. With the differences in language, religion, and political culture, discord between the two groups was not surprising. Tejanos were considered Mexican and the Mexicans were seen by many as the enemy, even though most Tejanos had come to Texas from the Canary Islands or Spain.[9] This history is currently being examined by writers such as Jesus F. de la Teja, Paul A. Ramos, Andres Tijerina, David Weber, as well as others. Most of the history of this period is outside the scope of this text, but readers are encouraged to explore this important and often overlooked era of Texas history.[10]

In the early period of colonization of the American continent there was competition for economic and political power between English-speaking peoples and those who spoke Spanish. In Texas in 1716 at the beginning of the settlement period, Spanish speakers dominated politics and the economy. With considerable help from the policies of both the Spanish and Mexican governments that were intended to increase the population of Texas, the influx of Anglo-Americans caused their numbers to overwhelm the Tejano population and this changed the power relationships in politics and the economy.[11]

The end of the Mexican period in 1836 brought major changes for Texas. Anglos set up a new constitution for the Republic of Texas based on a republican form of government rooted in U.S. laws, not Mexican laws. Anglos were generally not Catholic, but Protestant, and they brought with them a social order that subjugated minorities. These qualities and beliefs were the ones that characterized the new Republic of Texas. A society that had been about assimilating English speakers into a Spanish culture became one that was trying to do the reverse. Almost two centuries have passed, and Texas still struggles with these issues. Cultural differences and disagreements from the past have tended to keep the two groups apart.[12]

The lack of cooperation in regard to education is partially explained, although not justified, by this history. The struggle of Hispanics to gain access to higher education in Texas has been a long and difficult one. Understanding is not facilitated by a reading of the various constitutions of both the republic and the state, because they contain no segments calling for discrimination against Hispanics. While most of those early constitutions, unsurprisingly, contained references to African Americans, who until 1865 and the Emancipation Proclamation were mostly slaves, there were no specific references to Hispanics because they were considered white.[13]

PUBLIC SCHOOLS

It is widely accepted that without a good basic educational foundation it is not possible to enter a higher education institution and be successful, so it is critical to understand what was occurring in the lower grades in education for Hispanic Texans. This will help us begin to understand why it took so long for Hispanics to be accepted into higher education institutions in Texas.

One of the more difficult challenges was how to provide an education for Spanish-speaking children, especially those from families at lower economic levels. Generally speaking, it is more difficult for Spanish-speaking children to deal with an English-speaking school at the beginning because they have more to learn. Before they can begin to take in the subjects being taught, they have to learn English, and coming from a different cultural heritage they often lack the general knowledge of historical and cultural events common to their English-speaking counterparts. Many of these children came from homes with parents who had not had good educational opportunities themselves, so children often did not have the home educational support more likely to have existed in English-speaking homes. This meant that Spanish-speaking children usually began school already behind their fellow students, and each year it became more and more difficult to not fall further behind. In addition, families many times found themselves in difficult economic circumstances and required their children's help to support the family, so children were often taken out of school for part of the year to work in the fields. These challenges could completely overshadow the desire to get an education, and many children dropped out of school before they finished high school. In the nineteenth century, there were a relatively small number of Spanish-speakers who were prepared for college.[14]

In the nineteenth century, most Tejano families worked on farms and ranches, and parents sent their children to school, if there was one, when school hours did not conflict with harvesting responsibilities. This was, and still can be, a common scenario in agrarian societies. Poverty and the disorganized manner in which early Texas began its public school system put up additional barriers. Demonstrated school attendance in the days before mandatory attendance spoke to a strong desire to be educated.[15]

Educational opportunities for Tejanos grew as communities began to provide public schools and Catholics, Presbyterians, and Methodists opened the first religious schools. One of these was the John McCullough Presbyterian Day School, which opened in San Antonio in the 1840s. This school educated both Anglos and Tejanos.[16] In the nineteenth century the Tejano community in general relied heavily on the Catholic schools to educate their children; between 1848 and 1900, dozens of Catholic schools for girls and boys were established. During the first half of the twentieth century Tejano children still attended these schools in some numbers, but the majority attended public schools.[17]

In counties such as Nueces and Duval, there were large enrollments of Tejano children. In Corpus Christi (Nueces County) there were 110 Tejano children in 1896. In Duval County, the City of San Diego had a significant number of Tejano children in the mid-1880s, and the school system was headed by Luis Puebla, a Mexican immigrant who had been educated in Washington, DC, and provided an early role model for Tejano advancement in academia.[18] In all of Texas in 1900, fewer than 18 percent of Mexican-American children between the ages of five and seventeen were enrolled in public schools.[19]

Children from wealthy Tejano families were sent to excellent schools where they received a quality education. Their success in school was on a par with their Anglo counterparts, and demonstrated their ability to succeed.[20] But, the story was different for children from poor families. While there were no laws that called for the separation of Mexican or Tejano children from Anglo children, the reality was that they were not treated fairly or equally. In areas of the state where there was a high density of Mexican children, especially if those children were sons and daughters of agricultural workers, they were put into separate schools. For example, in Corpus Christi, from the very beginning of public schools there were separate schools, reflecting Anglo sentiment in the county where a German farmer was quoted as saying: "We draw the line pretty strong. They don't mix at all in school. They don't go to high school; if they want to go, they go to Tex-Mex school below Kingsville."[21]

Mexican children began to enroll in schools in 1891. In 1896, the Mexican grammar school in Corpus Christi had 110 students, and by 1929 it had an enrollment of 1,320. Despite having children in all six grades when the school opened in 1891, it was not until 1901 that the first student graduated from this school, reflecting the difficulties students encountered. However, a local American teacher noted about this student that "Her example had an influence." In addition to the other challenges, a significant factor in students' lack of success was the poor quality of their teachers; only the most inexperienced teachers were assigned to these Mexican schools, which added greatly to student learning problems.[22]

It is interesting to note that the separation of students usually ended at high school. There were so few Mexican children who attended high school that there was little reason for school districts to provide separate high schools. In 1905 Texas passed the school compulsory attendance law. It applied to children age eight to fourteen who lived within two and one-half miles of the schoolhouse, unless the district made available transportation to a more distant school. The law also required a minimum of one hundred days of school attendance per year.[23]

In rural Texas—and in the early years that included a large part of the state, particularly in South Texas—cotton needed to be picked at what was the traditional start of the school year, and many Mexican children were required by their parents to help with the crop. This meant that when they did begin school it was later in the school year and they were usually hopelessly behind their Anglo counterparts.[24]

The makeup of elected local school boards had a significant effect on the quality of schools for Mexican children. In many cases, the large Anglo farm families had a member on the local school board. These farmers did not want Mexican children to be educated because they knew that with education came other work opportunities and those workers would leave the area for the larger cities, thereby diminishing the local labor supply.[25]

The table below from Arnoldo De Leon's *Mexican Texas*, provides a telling comparison of the experience of education for Mexican-Americans and Anglo-Americans in Texas.

Table 11.1

	Mexican-Americans		Anglo-Americans	
Year	1850 (1860)	1900	1850 (1860)	1900
Percentage of the Population	69.7%	51.5%	19.9%	40.4%
Number in the Population	13,907	74,005	3,975	58,039
Percent of Children	46.3%	51.9%	24.1%	43.5%
Percent of Children Attending School	16.7%	17.3%	33.9%	38.9%
Percentage of Literate Population over age 20	25.1%	12.4%	97.0%	92.8%

Note: This table combines sample data from Bexar County and the Lower Rio Grande Valley in 1850 with data from El Paso County in 1860. The 1900 estimates are based on combined data from Bexar, Cameron, El Paso, Starr, and Webb Counties.
Source: De Leon, p. 188

For his 1934 study *An American-Mexican Frontier: Nueces County, Texas,* Paul Taylor's charge was to study Mexican schools wherever they were concentrated. One place he observed conditions was in Dimmit County, which lies in the agricultural Winter Garden district of South Texas. He found that no more than 25 percent of school-age Mexican children attended school at any one time throughout the school year. The 1920 census reported that only about 55 percent of all school-age children in Dimmit County attended school, and Taylor attributed this to low attendance by Mexican children. He points out that, while the law mandated school attendance, there was no enforcement of the law in regard to Mexican children. He also found that local attitudes reflected a belief that these children should not be educated for a variety of reasons including the need of the local economy for a large pool of unskilled labor and beliefs that Mexicans in general were inferior to Anglos and that the Mexican community as a whole lacked ambition regarding education. Taylor's research also showed that many Mexicans believed that sending their children to local Catholic schools offered the best route for their children's education.[26] Roberto Trevino in his 2003 article entitled "Jim Crow: Catholic Sisters and the 'Mexican Problem' in Texas," more clearly stated the problem, noting that the majority of the local population did not want these children in their schools. It was the Catholic nuns who provided a more hospitable atmosphere for them, even to the point of providing meals when they were needed. Because of the advocacy of these women, it is not surprising that many Mexican families placed their children in the Catholic schools, but even there the numbers were small in comparison with the number of Anglo-American children in the public schools.[27]

In 1930, the estimated enrollment of Mexican children in public schools was probably about 50 percent of the total number of children enrolled in public schools. Their attendance record was so poor, however, that when their numbers are included in the overall numbers they only represent about one-third of the children actually attending school. A breakdown of the numbers shows that almost half of all school-age Mexican children were enrolled in the first grade and that nearly three-fourths were enrolled in the first three grades. However, the percentage declined to almost nothing after sixth grade because there was a large drop in attendance when children reached age thirteen. These low numbers reflect several issues. The low incomes of most Mexican families meant they needed the children to work in the fields to help support the family. In addition, as noted earlier, Mexican children who had been taken out of school during harvest time, which included most of the first semester of school, were so hopelessly behind in their schoolwork that they often became discouraged at the prospect of further education. The population of Mexican children in high school was only 3 to 4 percent of all children in attendance, and in colleges and universities the number was less than one-fifth of one percent.[28]

The children of more privileged Tejano families, including those who owned rancheros, were sent to the better schools in South Texas and to schools in other parts of the United States. Some girls attended the school at the Incarnate Word Convent in Corpus Christi. In 1884, there were sixty Tejano students from Duval County who attended schools outside the area. Fourteen of them attended Columbia College in Rolla, Missouri. Some Mexican Americans went to Goliad College in Goliad, Texas, and some distinguished themselves, like A. de la Garza who received the gold medal for declamation in 1884. Others attended Lagarto College in Lagarto, Texas, and a number went to St. Joseph's College in Victoria, Texas. When Tejano children were able to attend good schools, they clearly demonstrated academic abilities equivalent to those of Anglo students.[29]

In their 2003 essay "Historical Perspectives on Latino Access to Higher Education, 1848–1900," Victoria-María MacDonald and Teresa García point out how rare it was for anyone, regardless of race or ethnicity, to obtain a college education in the mid-nineteenth century. Tejanos who did were primarily from privileged backgrounds. Other than Manuel Garcia, who graduated from the University of

Texas in 1894, there is very little known about Tejanos in the Texas higher education system. MacDonald and García cite a 1928 survey that found only 57 undergraduates at the University of Texas who had a Hispanic surname, and they represented only 1.1 percent of the total enrollment of 5,390 students that year. In that same year, only one person with a Hispanic name was a member of the graduating class of 465 students.[30]

Herschel Thurman Manuel (1897–1976), who was a professor of educational psychology at the University of Texas at Austin, was an advocate for the education of Spanish-speaking children. In 1926 he received a grant to conduct research on the subject, which resulted in his book *The Education of Mexican and Spanish-speaking Children in Texas* (1930).[31] The data he published from his survey (completed shortly before 1930) about Hispanic attendance at colleges and universities provides insight into higher education attainment at the time. It must be remembered that in the early years of higher education, Texas had many college institutions teaching courses that would today be considered high school courses. When Manuel was determining what responses to use in his survey he wanted to include only data from institutions that had a reputation for teaching college-level courses. Thus his information is not entirely accurate, but it is representative of what was occurring in Texas in 1930. The colleges that responded to his survey included the twenty-three senior level colleges, the eight state teacher colleges, the thirty junior colleges, and all the colleges controlled by the Texas A&M University system. He also included surveys from one theological seminary, two medical schools, and eight schools he classified as miscellaneous. In total he received seventy-six surveys.[32]

His survey captured 38,538 students of which only 188 could be classified as Mexican. Of these, thirty-four students were residents of Mexico. The 188 students represented one-half of one percent of the total enrollment in the surveyed institutions. Because not all institutions responded to his survey, Manuel believed the true total enrollment of all colleges in Texas ranged between 40,000 and

45,000, and the total of all Mexican students was probably fewer than 250 students. It should be noted that the same survey showed that there were 2,000 African American students in attendance at the time—six times as many African Americans as Hispanics attending colleges.[33]

One reason for the increased participation by African Americans might have been that the Texas Legislature had by then made many attempts to increase higher education opportunities for African Americans, with a long history of support for both Prairie View College and Texas Southern University being the most notable. However, the record reflects no similar debate over or support for colleges for Mexican Americans.

Between 1880 and 1970 there were four private institutions founded in Texas specifically to provide higher education for Mexican Americans. They were: Holding Institute, founded in 1880 by the Methodist Church, primarily for the lower grades; Colegio Jacinto Trevino (1969); Houston International College (1970); and Juarez-Lincoln University (1970). All these institutions were short lived, and none are still operational today.[34]

A LEGAL APPROACH

A system that had one school system for Anglo-Americans and one system for Mexican Americans finally began to wear thin on the latter community. It was obvious to the majority of Mexican Americans in Texas that they were not getting a fair shake when it came to public education and they began to seek out attorneys willing to file discrimination suits. The structure of these first cases was shaped by the Jim Crow laws, even though under the Texas Constitution there were only two racial categories: white or black. Judges involved in these early cases considered Mexican Americans to be members of one of the "other white races." The early cases were based on a law passed in 1893 by the state legislature that called for separate but equal schools for white and "colored" children. The definition of colored under that law was "all persons of mixed blood descended from Negro ancestry," but the law was silent on the definition of "white." In the beginning, lawyers representing Mexican Americans filed their discrimination lawsuits using the premise that a client had been denied rights because their "whiteness" had not been recognized or respected. But, using this strategy made it very difficult to bring class action suits on behalf of large numbers of Mexican Americans.[35]

Finally, in Texas in 1929 national Mexican American business leaders organized the League of United Latin American Citizens (LULAC), which aimed to integrate citizens of Mexican descent into the U.S. mainstream. When their protest demonstrations did not change things for the better, they too resorted to litigation. While Texas laws were silent regarding the segregation of Mexican children, the state legislature had passed a law in 1905 that negatively impacted these children. It stated: "it shall be the duty of every teacher in the public free schools ... to use the English language exclusively, and to conduct all recitations and all school exercises exclusively in the English language." Lawyers believed that this had led to the separate classrooms or "Mexican schools." At the time LULAC was organized, about 90 percent of public schools in South Texas were segregated by Anglo or Mexican enrollment. In 1930, LULAC filed its first lawsuit. In that case, [Del Rio] *Independent School District v. Salvatierra* [33 S.W.2d 790 (Tex. Civ. App. 1930)], the Texas Court of Appeals held that public school officials could not arbitrarily segregate Mexican students solely based on ethnic background. However, most school districts simply ignored the ruling.[36]

Success finally came in 1948 when lawyers representing Mexican-Americans were able to convince a federal court to declare segregation of Mexican Americans unconstitutional in *Delgado v. Bastrop Independent School District*.[37]

In 1954, LULAC lawyers in conjunction with lawyers from the American G.I. Forum of Texas, another group organized to advance the rights of Mexican Americans, were successful in arguments before the United States Supreme Court in *Hernández v. State of Texas*. In that case, the court decided that Mexican Americans, although technically classified as Caucasian, suffered discrimination as a class and were entitled to protection under the Fourteenth Amendment. In 1957, the American G.I. Forum filed a lawsuit in federal court and the court agreed that the segregation of Mexican American children in Texas schools was unjustified.[38]

Legal efforts by Mexican American litigants, along with changing social, political, and legal conditions beginning in the 1940s, paid off, and the playing field began to level in terms of Mexican American students gaining access to good primary education, and more opportunities for a college education.

While it had been difficult for Hispanics to receive a college education in the nineteenth century because of the poor quality of the public schools many of them attended and the prejudice they experienced, there was a change in the twentieth century. In addition to all of the legal efforts, an increasing number of middle-class Hispanics gained in influence. Many had served in the U.S. military and these veterans used the funds provided by the G.I. Bill to pay for tuition and living expenses thus making it possible for them to attend college.

* * * * *

In the early twenty-first century, considerable effort has been made by Texas senior public colleges to increase enrollment of Hispanic students. It would be difficult today to find a college or university in Texas that does not have a significant population of Hispanic students. Colleges and universities that can prove at least 25 percent of their student body is Hispanic can receive a federal designation as a "Hispanic Serving Institution" (HSI). Those institutions are receiving significant federal funds to support their efforts to facilitate the success of Hispanic students. In 2015, these Hispanic Serving Institutions included twenty-nine senior colleges and thirty-two junior colleges. Those institutions are responding to the work of the Texas Higher Education Coordinating Board as represented in their 2000 report "Closing the Gaps," and to the Board's call for fair play in treating students of all races and ethnicities equally when it comes to educational opportunities.[39]

NOTES

1. David J. Weber, *The Mexican Frontier, 1821–1846: The American Southwest under Mexico* (Albuquerque: University of New Mexico Press, 1982), 214; Matt S. Meir and Feliciano Rivera, *Dictionary of Mexican American History* (Westport, CT: Greenwood Press, 1981), 220.

2. Weber, *The Mexican Frontier*, 214; Meir and Rivera, *Dictionary of Mexican American History*, 338

3. Raul A. Ramos, *Beyond the Alamo* (Chapel Hill: University of North Carolina Press, 2008), 83.

4. Ibid., 157.

5. Herschel Thurman Manuel, *The Education of Mexican and Spanish-Speaking Children in Texas* (Austin: Fund for Research in the Social Sciences, University of Texas, 1930), 187.

6. Andrés Tijerina, *Tejanos and Texas under the Mexican Flag, 1821–1836* (College Station: Texas A&M University Press, 1994), 13–15.

7. "CENSUS AND CENSUS RECORDS," *Handbook of Texas Online* (http://www.tshaonline.org/handbook/online/articles/ulc01), accessed April 15, 2015. Uploaded on June 12, 2010. Published by the Texas State Historical Association.

8. Arnoldo De León, "MEXICAN TEXAS," *Handbook of Texas Online* (http://www.tshaonline.org/handbook/online/articles/npm01), accessed April 11, 2014. Uploaded on June 15, 2010. Published by the Texas State Historical Association.

9. Tijerina, *Tejanos and Texas under the Mexican Flag*, 9.

10. Jesus F. de la Teja, ed., *A Revolution Remembered: The Memoirs and Selected Correspondence of Juan N. Seguin* (Austin: Texas State Historical Association, 2002), vii–xii, "Discovering the Tejano Community in 'Early' Texas," *Journal of the Early Republic* 18, no. 1 (Spring, 1998): 73–98, *Tejano Leadership in Mexican and Revolutionary Texas* (College Station: Texas A&M University Press, 2010); Alberto Prago, *Strangers in Their Own Land: A History of Mexican-Americans* (New York: Four Winds Press, 1973); Andrés Tijerina, *Tejanos and Texas under the Mexican Flag* (College Station: Texas A&M University Press, 1994); Andrés Tijerina, "Tejanos and Texas: The Native Mexicans of Texas 1820–1850" (PhD diss., University of Texas at Austin, 1977); David J. Weber, *The Mexican Frontier, 1821–1846: The American Southwest under Mexico* (Albuquerque: University of New Mexico Press, 1982), "The Spanish Legacy in North America and the Historical Imagination" *Western Historical Quarterly* 23, no. 1 (Feb. 1992), 4–24. http://jstor.org/stable/970249, "The Spanish Borderlands, Historiography Redux" *History Teacher* 39, no. 2 (Nov 2005): 43–56, and *Foreigners in their Native Land: Historical Roots of the Mexican Americans*, Rev. ed. (Albuquerque: University of New Mexico Press, 2004).

11. Roberto R. Calderón, "TEJANO POLITICS," *Handbook of Texas Online* (http://www.tshaonline.org/handbook/online/articles/wmtkn), accessed April 11, 2014. Uploaded on June 15, 2010. Published by the Texas State Historical Association; de la Teja, *Tejano Leadership*, 8.

12. Arnoldo De León, *The Tejano Community* (Albuquerque: University of New Mexico Press, 1982), 10.

13. Steven H. Wilson, "*Brown* over 'Other White': Mexican Americans' Legal Arguments and Litigation Strategy in School Desegregation Lawsuits," *Law and History Review* 21, no. 1 (Spring, 2003): 145–94.

14. Victoria-María MacDonald, and Teresa García, "Historical Perspectives on Latino Access to Higher Education, 1848–1900," In *The Majority in the Minority: Expanding the Representation of Latina/o Faculty, Administrators and Students in Higher Education*, ed. Jeanett Castellanos and Lee Jones (Sterling, VA: Stylus Publishing, 2003), 22.

15. Manuel, *The Education of Mexican and Spanish-Speaking Children in Texas*, 118.

16. De León, "MEXICAN TEXAS."
17. De León, *The Tejano Community*, 187.
18. Paul Schuster Taylor, *An American-Mexican Frontier: Nueces County, Texas* (Chapel Hill: University of North Carolina Press, 1934), 194.
19. Guadalupe San Miguel, Jr., "MEXICAN AMERICANS AND EDUCATION," Handbook of Texas Online (http://www.tshaonline.org/handbook/online/articles/khmmx). Uploaded on June 15, 2010. Published by the Texas State Historical Association.
20. De León, *The Tejano Community*, 190–91.
21. Taylor, *An American-Mexican Frontier*, 217.
22. Ibid., 191.
23. Ibid., 194.
24. Ibid., 194, 387.
25. Ibid., 217–18.
26. Ibid., 338–96.
27. Ibid., 338–96.
28. Manuel, *The Education of Mexican and Spanish-Speaking Children in Texas*, 95, 103.
29. De León, *The Tejano Community*, 190.
30. MacDonald and García, "Historical Perspectives on Latino Access to Higher Education," 15–45.
31. Teresa Palomo Acosta, "MANUEL, HERSCHEL THURMAN," Handbook of Texas Online.
32. Manuel, *The Education of Mexican and Spanish-Speaking Children in Texas*, 104–105.
33. Manuel, *The Education of Mexican and Spanish-Speaking Children in Texas*, 106.
34. John H. McNeely, "HOLDING INSTITUTE," *Handbook of Texas Online*, (http://tshaonline.org/handbook/online/articles/kbh07). Uploaded on June 15, 2010. Published by the Texas State Historical Association; Aurelia M. Montemayor, "COLEGIO JACINTO TREVIÑO," *Handbook of Texas Online* (http://tshaonline.org/handbook/online/articles/kbc51). Uploaded on June 12, 2010. Published by the Texas State Historical Association; Teresa Palomo Acosta, "HOUSTON INTERNATIONAL UNIVERSITY," *Handbook of Texas Online* (http://www.tshaonline.org/handbook/online/articles/kch18), accessed June 26, 2015. Uploaded on June 15, 2010. Published by the Texas State Historical Association.aria-Cristina Garcia, "JUARAZ-LINCOLN UNIVERSITY," *Handbook of Texas Online* (http://tshaonline.org/handbook/online/articles/kcj03). Uploaded on June 15, 2010. Published by the Texas State Historical Association.
35. Ariela J. Gross, "Texas Mexicans and the Politics of Whiteness," *Law and History Review* 21, no. 1 (Spring, 2003): 195–205.
36. Wilson, *"Brown* over 'Other White,'" 7.
37. Ibid., 9.
38. Ibid., 11–13; V. Carl Allsup, "AMERICAN G.I. FORUM OF TEXAS," *Handbook of Texas Online* (http://www.tshaonline.org/handbook/online/articles/voa01), accessed April 16, 2014. Uploaded on June 9, 2010. Published by the Texas State Historical Association.
39. Texas Higher Education Coordinating Board, http://www.txhighereddata.org.

BIBLIOGRAPHY

Acosta, Teresa Palomo. "MANUEL, HERSCHEL THURMAN," *Handbook of Texas Online* (http://tshaonline.org/handbook/online/articles/fmadp), accessed November 10, 2010. Uploaded on June 15, 2010. Published by the Texas State Historical Association.
———. "HOUSTON INTERNATIONAL UNIVERSITY," Handbook of Texas Online (http://www.tshaonline.org/handbook/online/articles/kch18). Uploaded on June 15, 2010. Published by the Texas State Historical Association.

Alonzo, Armando C. *Tejano Legacy: Rancheros and Settlers in South Texas 1734–1900*. Albuquerque: University of New Mexico Press, 1998.

Allsup, V. Carl. "AMERICAN G.I. FORUM OF TEXAS," *Handbook of Texas Online* (http://www.tshaonline.org/handbook/online/articles/voa01), accessed April 16, 2014. Uploaded on June 9, 2010. Published by the Texas State Historical Association.

Barrera, Aida. "The 'Little Schools' in Texas, 1897–1965: Educating Mexican American Children." *American Educational History Journal* 33, no. 2 (2006): 35–45.

Blanton, Carlos Kevin. *The Strange Career of Bilingual Education in Texas, 1836–1981*. College Station: Texas A&M University Press, 2004.

Calderón, Roberto R. "TEJANO POLITICS," *Handbook of Texas Online* (http://www.tshaonline.org/handbook/online/articles/wmtkn), accessed April 11, 2014. Uploaded on June 15, 2010. Published by the Texas State Historical Association.

de la Teja, Jesus F. "Discovering the Tejano Community in 'Early' Texas." *Journal of the Early Republic* 18, no. 1 (Spring, 1998): 73–98. (jstor.org/stable/3124734) Accessed December 23, 2013.

———. *Tejano Leadership in Mexican and Revolutionary Texas*. College Station: Texas A&M University Press, 2010.

———, ed. *A Revolution Remembered: The Memoirs and Selected Correspondence of Juan N. Seguin*. Austin: Texas State Historical Association, 2002.

De León, Arnoldo. "MEXICAN TEXAS," *Handbook of Texas Online* (http://www.tshaonline.org/handbook/online/articles/npm01), accessed April 11, 2014. Uploaded on June 15, 2010. Published by the Texas State Historical Association.

———. *The Tejano Community*. Albuquerque: University of New Mexico Press, 1982.

———, and Robert A. Calvert, "CIVIL RIGHTS," *Handbook of Texas Online* (http://www.tshaonline.org/handbook/online/articles/pkcfl). Uploaded on June 12, 2010. Modified on August 27, 2013. Published by the Texas State Historical Association.

Eby, Frederick, ed. "Education in Texas," Source Materials: Education Series No. 1, *The University of Texas Bulletin* No. 1824. Austin: University of Texas Press, 1918.

Fehrenbach, T. R. *Seven Keys to Texas*. El Paso: Texas Western Press, 1983.

Garcia, Maria-Cristina, "JUARAZ-LINCOLN UNIVERSITY," *Handbook of Texas Online*, (http://tshaonline.org/handbook/online/articles/kcj03). Uploaded on June 15, 2010. Published by the Texas State Historical Association.

Gross, Ariela J. "Texas Mexicans and the Politics of Whiteness." *Law and History Review* 21, no. 1 (Spring, 2003): 195–205.

MacDonald, Victoria-María, and Teresa García. "Historical Perspectives on Latino Access to Higher Education, 1848–1900." In *The Majority in the Minority: Expanding the Representation of Latina/o Faculty, Administrators and Students in Higher Education*, edited by Jeanett Castellanos and Lee Jones, 15–43. Sterling, VA: Stylus Publishing, 2003.

Manuel, Herschel Thurman. *The Education of Mexican and Spanish-Speaking Children in Texas*. Austin: Fund for Research in the Social Sciences, University of Texas, 1930.

McNeely, John H. "HOLDING INSTITUTE," *Handbook of Texas Online,* (http://tshaonline.org/handbook/online/articles/kbh07). Uploaded on June 15, 2010. Published by the Texas State Historical Association.

Meir, Matt S., and Feliciano Rivera. *Dictionary of Mexican American History*. Westport, CT: Greenwood Press, 1981.

Montemayor, Aurelia M., "COLEGIO JACINTO TREVIÑO," *Handbook of Texas Online,* (http://tshaonline.org/handbook/online/articles/kbc51). Uploaded on June 12, 2010. Published by the Texas State Historical Association.

Prago, Alberto. *Strangers in Their Own Land: A History of Mexican-Americans*. New York: Four Winds Press, 1973.

Ramos, Raul A. *Beyond the Alamo*. Chapel Hill: University of North Carolina Press, 2008.

San Miguel Jr., Guadalupe. *Chicana/o Struggles for Education: Activism in the Community*. College Station: Texas A&M University Press, 2013.

———. *"Let All of Them Take Heed": Mexican Americans and the Campaign for Educational Equity in Texas, 1910–1981*. Austin: University of Texas Press, 1987.

———. "MEXICAN AMERICANS AND EDUCATION," *Handbook of Texas Online* (http://www.tshaonline.org/handbook/online/articles/khmmx). Uploaded on June 15, 2010. Published by the Texas State Historical Association.

Scott, Robert J. *After the Alamo*. Plano, TX: Wordware Publishing, Inc., 2000.

Taylor, Paul Schuster. *An American-Mexican Frontier: Nueces County, Texas*. Chapel Hill: University of North Carolina Press, 1934.

———. "Education and School Separation," in *Mexican Labor in the United States: Dimmit County, Winter Garden District, South Texas*. University of California Publications in Economics, vol. 6, no. 5. Berkeley: University of California Press, 1930, 372–96.

Trevino, Roberto R. "Facing Jim Crow: Catholic Sisters and the 'Mexican Problem' in Texas." *Western Historical Quarterly* 34, no. 2 (Summer, 2003), 139–64. http://jstor.org/stable/25047254.

Tijerina, Andrés. *Tejanos and Texas under the Mexican Flag, 1821–1836*. College Station: Texas A&M University Press, 1994.

Weber, David J. *The Mexican Frontier, 1821–1846: The American Southwest under Mexico*. Albuquerque: University of New Mexico Press, 1982.

———. "The Spanish Borderlands, Historiography Redux." *History Teacher* 39, no. 2 (Nov 2005): 43–56.

———. "The Spanish Legacy in North America and the Historical Imagination." *Western Historical Quarterly* 23, no. 1 (Feb. 1992), 4–24. http://jstor.org/stable/970249.

Wheat, John, comp. "Mexican American History Resources at the Briscoe Center for American History: A Bibliography," Education, 83–90. https://www.cah.utexas.edu/documents/subject_guides/mexican_american_2010.pdf.

Wilson, Steven H. "*Brown* over 'Other White': Mexican Americans' Legal Arguments and Litigation Strategy in School Desegregation Lawsuits." *Law and History Review* 21, no. 1 (Spring, 2003), 145–94.

Wortham, Louis J. *A History of Texas: From Wilderness to Commonwealth*. Ft. Worth, TX: Wortham-Molyneaux Co., 1924.

PART IV:
STRUCTURE

12

HIGHER EDUCATION ORGANIZATION AND LEADERSHIP

THE HISTORY OF EDUCATIONAL ORGANIZATION

In the ancient world higher education began in the urban centers of the Nile River Valley, Mesopotamia, Crete, and the river valleys of India and China along with lesser development in Central and South America. The growth of large population centers led to an abandonment of agriculture as the sole means of earning a living. This led to the development of different skills, arts, and crafts that began to serve a more complex culture. Increased specialization helped create a class of learned professionals in a wide variety of fields. The maintenance and transmission of these skills necessitated the establishment of schools to pass the knowledge from one generation to the next. In a modern setting these schools would not be called colleges, but they were providing a form of a higher education to those societies. The intellectual, artistic, and technological advancement of these ancient cultures could not have existed without them.[1]

* * * * *

Colleges and universities almost always become large and complex organizations, and ever since these institutions came into being there have been discussions about how to make them work better for the societies in which they operate. The history of higher education organization in the West can be traced back to the medieval beginnings of universities in Paris, Oxford, Cambridge, Toulouse,

Orleans, and Bologna. Not only did issues among the universities, political rulers, and the church have to be worked out, but often conflicts arose between the universities and the localities in which they were situated.

Within the institutions themselves, ideas about purpose, organization, and management came under discussion. In the early days, the management of universities could be chaotic. Issues were discussed and dissected and then processes were put in place to deal with them. Some of the first concerns included how to manage a group of scholars interested in teaching as a profession, how to pay those scholars and how much work to demand of them, who should be responsible for ensuring students were properly prepared, and what was the most efficient way to provide services. These issues and many others had to be worked out over time and some continue to be reexamined and refined even today.[2]

In the United States, the English model for universities was evident in the founding of the first two colonial colleges—Harvard in 1636 and William and Mary in 1693. The language in Harvard's charter was very much like the language in the English charters for Oxford and Cambridge. Early American colleges all had governing boards consisting of the president of the institution and members of the faculty, but it was not many years before this all changed to boards made up of external members instead of academics. This form of lay governing board came to America from colleges and universities in Holland, Scotland, and Ireland.[3]

During the colonial period from 1607 to 1776, nine colleges were established by royal or colonial charter. Seven of these became private, independent institutions and two became public colleges. The first state university was provided for in North Carolina's state constitution in 1776 and it opened in 1789. Georgia, Tennessee, and Vermont had all established state colleges by 1800.[4]

The Northwest Ordinance of 1787 enacted by the U.S. Congress under the Articles of Confederation authorized land grants for colleges, and as a result, the following were opened: Ohio University

(1804), Miami University in Ohio (1809), the University of Michigan (1817), Indiana University (1820), and the University of Wisconsin (1849). All of this activity reflected the beginning of an American style of higher education—the clear influence of Western Europe combined with American traditions that modified and affected the development of colleges in the United States. In their book *Higher Education in Transition*, Brubacher and Rudy observe that the interaction between these two cultures combined with the growth of democracy in every aspect of American life, spurred the development of a truly unique system of higher education.[5]

The Morrill Act of 1862, which awarded land grants to the states to establish colleges of agriculture and mechanical arts, offered a stimulus to state governments to create more colleges. In time, twenty-two states established colleges because of the Act.[6] The growth of different types of higher education institutions and the complexities that arose from their formation put pressure on state legislatures to come up with ways to manage these institutions.

From the outset, Texas followed the model of outside lay boards as evidenced by the early charters granted at the beginning of the nineteenth century, first by the Republic and then by the state. Those early colleges were, for the most part, sponsored by religious institutions (see chapter 6). As Texas began to discuss how public colleges were to operate, it incorporated the first idea of "coordination" into the state Constitution of 1876 where it called for Texas A&M College to be a branch of the University of Texas. Even though this early idea did not work, because both institutions had their own boards and found it difficult to work together, this did not stop Texas from continuing to examine methods of coordination.[7]

Early on in an effort to coordinate the oversight of both public schools and higher education in one place, Texas designed a system to put the state treasurer in charge of education. However, that job was soon given to the state comptroller. In both cases the person held the title of ex officio state superintendent of instruction, "ex officio" because school oversight was not their primary constitutional duty.

Because the legislature wanted the person holding the job to have an understanding of the finances and performance of these public institutions, it was decided the job was best held by the comptroller rather than the treasurer. The comptroller was required to make an annual report that was sent first to the governor for review and then to the legislature.[8]

The comptroller remained the ex officio state superintendent until after the Civil War when in 1866 the state constitution was rewritten and called for creation of a new statewide office of superintendent of public instruction. It included provisions setting the term of office at four years and establishing an annual salary. The constitution also called for a board of education consisting of the governor, comptroller, and superintendent. The first formal attempts to oversee not only public education but also public higher education began with this board of education.[9]

The state board of education exercised only advisory authority over the state college boards. The various college and university boards made their budget recommendations to the legislature, along with recommendations on courses of study, with particular emphasis on not duplicating fields of study offered by other institutions, so as to eliminate waste.[10]

These first state superintendents helped put in place many of the early rules and customs of higher education management in Texas. Although at the start of this process the governor appointed the superintendent, by 1918 the superintendent was elected by a statewide vote. There were many successful superintendents in the period from 1918 until 1955 during which the position had oversight of both colleges and public schools. A closer look at two of the more outstanding superintendents provides an overview of the work done by them and their counterparts during this time.[11]

Annie Webb Blanton was the third person to hold the job of superintendent during this era and she served two terms from 1919 until 1923. Her two predecessors had been appointed to the job, so she was the first to be elected. Blanton completed her secondary education in the Houston and La Grange schools, and received both bachelor's and master's degrees from the University of Texas and a PhD from Cornell University. She had been an associate professor of English at North Texas State College from 1901 to 1918. After her tenure as superintendent, she was a professor of education administration at the University of Texas and head of the Rural Education Department from 1923 to 1946.[12]

In Blanton's first primary election in July 1918—in which women voted for the first time—she defeated two opponents by a wide margin. Her victory in the general election that same year made her the first woman in Texas history to be elected to a statewide office. During her tenure a system of free textbooks was established, teacher certification laws were revised, and teachers' salaries were increased. She also made efforts to upgrade the quality of schools in the state's rural areas.[13]

One of the longest-serving state superintendents was Starlin Lebanon Marion Newberry Marrs. Marrs served from 1923 until his death in 1932. Born in West Virginia in 1862 he obtained a bachelor of science degree from the National Normal School in Lebanon, Ohio, and moved to Texas in the early 1880s. Prior to his election as state superintendent he served as superintendent of public schools in the towns of Stephenville, Hamilton, Cleburne, and Terrell. Marrs had worked in the state department of education as a chief clerk and head supervisor of the high school division. He was elected to his first term as state superintendent in 1922 and was re-elected to four additional terms. He was serving the last year of his fifth term when he died of a heart attack at College Station on April 18, 1932.[14]

Marrs was well known for advocating a nonpolitical state board of education to replace the ex officio state board of education composed only of elected officials—the governor, secretary of state, comptroller—and the state superintendent. Ultimately he was successful in his effort to get that changed.[15] In 1928, a constitutional amendment was passed authorizing a state board of education, and in 1929 the legislature passed a bill establishing a nine-member board with overlapping six-year terms. This new board assumed all of the duties of the previous ex officio board.[16]

In the early years of higher education in Texas, only a very small portion of the population attended colleges or universities, and those institutions had low enrollments. As a larger percentage of the population began to seek higher education, colleges and universities began to grow in size and become more complex and duplicative in their academic offerings. Legislators worried about the rising costs of higher education and how to control them. This led to discussions about the consolidation of colleges and universities as a means to that end. The thinking was to put independent colleges and universities into a "system"—an organization where one appointed board and staff would oversee and regulate the performance of all the schools in its system. Local communities and colleges that wanted to remain independent fought this effort.[17]

The idea of central management and control went back to the state Constitution of 1876, which had called for a single college system in which Texas A&M College was to become a branch of the University of Texas. Ironically, when the constitution was being written, Texas A&M existed, but the University of Texas did not; however, the constitution's authors were very clear that they wanted the University of Texas to be the lead university and A&M to be a branch. Thus even early on, the writers of the constitution felt strongly about central control of higher education.[18]

As time went by, a number of other colleges were attached to the University of Texas. Although several colleges and specific agencies that had a role in supporting agriculture were assigned by the legislature to Texas A&M College, they were not formally recognized as institutions in a system.[19]

The state was on its way to consolidating the independent colleges, but there was push back from local communities and their elected representatives to make those institutions stand-alone colleges. These disputes, along with an effort to improve efficiency and control costs, encouraged efforts to create a state organization to oversee public higher education and to deal with issues that were becoming increasingly difficult for the legislature to handle, such as duplication of course offerings in many of the colleges.[20]

Soldiers returning home after World War II and the availability of the GI Bill were for Texas, as for the rest of the country, watershed events. Texas colleges experienced a rapid growth in enrollment, which caused a shortage of faculty and facilities and a demand for the legislature to increase funding. The competition between colleges put pressure on legislators and fostered another series of discussions about coordinating the efforts of these public institutions. This finally led Texas in 1955 to become one of the first states in the country to establish a state coordinating agency for higher education. This agency, the Texas Commission of Higher Education, had a stormy existence and was reorganized by the legislature after ten years of service. A new reconstructed agency—the Texas Commission on Higher Education, Texas Colleges and University Systems—was an attempt to make the commission work better, but it too had difficulties.[21]

The third attempt by the legislature to deal with coordination came in 1965 with the creation of the Texas College and University System Coordinating Board, which was intended to provide unified planning and development of a comprehensive system of higher education. In 1967, the legislature simplified the board's name to the Texas Higher Education Coordinating Board. The board continues to provide leadership statewide for achieving excellence in college education through the efficient use of resources guided by the goal of eliminating duplication of facilities and program offerings.[22]

Today, most public colleges and universities in Texas belong to one of the six university systems. In addition, there are four public universities that are stand-alone institutions in that they have their own board of regents and are not part of any of the six systems.

TEXAS STATE UNIVERSITY SYSTEM

The first college system for which the legislature granted authority in 1911 was under the Board of Regents of State Teachers Colleges, which consisted of the state superintendent of public instruction as ex officio chairman and four members appointed by the governor. The legislature in 1913 increased the board to six members, and the name was changed to State Normal School Board of Regents. Now known as the Texas State University System, this system was created to oversee the Normal schools—colleges dedicated to educating teachers. Interestingly enough, in their first years those schools offered a two-year teaching degree as it was thought that two years of education was sufficient for a teacher.[23]

Initially the legislature transferred into the new system Sam Houston Normal Institute, North Texas State Normal School, Southwest Texas Normal School, and West Texas State Normal School, all of which had previously been administered by the State Department of Education. Later, other normal schools were added: Sul Ross Normal School in 1923; Stephen F. Austin Normal College in 1975; Angelo State College in 1995; and later, Lamar University, Lamar Institute of Technology, Lamar State College-Orange, and Lamar State College-Port Arthur.[24] Over the years, some institutions have been taken out of the system by the legislature and are now either independent or have become part of one of the other university systems.

TEXAS A&M UNIVERSITY SYSTEM

On July 8, 1948, the Board of Directors of Texas A&M College adopted a rule effective September 1, putting into place a Texas A&M System and at the same time appointing, as its first chancellor, Gibb Gilchrist. Originally the system was made up of the Agricultural and Mechanical College of Texas, North Texas Agricultural College (later called Arlington State College), John Tarleton State Agricultural College, Prairie View Agricultural College, the Texas Agricultural Experiment Station, the Texas Agricultural Extension Service, the Texas Engineering Experiment Station, the Texas Engineering Extension Service, the Texas Forest Service, the Fireman's Training School, and the Rodent Control Service. The chancellor, as chief executive officer, was put in place to insure that there would be a united administration.[25] It appears that the A&M board was following the example of other states in creating the office of chancellor as the chief executive officer. Montana had been the first state to place a system chancellor as chief executive officer of all state institutions in 1915. It was followed by Oregon in 1934 and Oklahoma in 1940.[26]

In the organization still used today, the chancellor of the Texas A&M System administers the colleges and agencies through an executive officer at each institution—a president at a college and a director at an agency. Each of these presidents and directors reports directly to the chancellor. The current members of the A&M System are: Texas A&M University, Prairie View University, Texas A&M-Commerce, Tarleton State University, West Texas A&M University, Texas A&M University-Kingsville, Texas A&M University-Corpus Christi, Texas A&M International University, Texas A&M University-Texarkana, Texas A&M University-Central Texas, Texas A&M University-San Antonio, and Texas A&M Health Science Center.[27]

UNIVERSITY OF TEXAS SYSTEM

The Board of Regents of the University of Texas created the office of the chancellor in 1950 and elected U.S. Supreme Court Justice James P. Hart as their first chancellor. The chancellor coordinated the following units in the system: University of Texas at Austin, University of Texas Medical Branch at Galveston, University of Texas School of Dentistry at Houston, University of Texas M.D. Anderson Hospital for Cancer Research at Houston, University of Texas Postgraduate School of Medicine at Houston, Southwestern Medical School of the University of Texas at Dallas, Texas Western College of the University of Texas at El Paso, W. J. McDonald Observatory at Fort Davis, and the Institute of Marine Sciences at Port Aransas. In the intervening years, the legislature has added the following: University of Texas at Brownsville, University of Texas at Dallas, University of Texas-Pan American, University of Texas of the Permian Basin, University of Texas at San Antonio, and University of Texas at Tyler. In addition to the University of Texas Southwestern Medical Center and the University of Texas Medical Branch at Galveston have been added the University of Texas Health Science Center at San Antonio and the University of Texas Health Science Center at Tyler along with the renamed University of Texas Health Science Center at Houston.[28]

UNIVERSITY OF HOUSTON SYSTEM

The University of Houston System was established by the legislature in 1977. It is governed by a nine-member board of regents appointed by the governor. In 1995, William P. Hobby, a former, long-time lieutenant governor serving as chancellor, led an organizational review of the system that recommended a change, which was approved by the board of regents. The new structure provided that the chancellor of the system would also serve as the president of the University of Houston. This is the only Texas university system with this leadership structure. The current members of the University of Houston System are: University of Houston, University of Houston-Clear Lake, University of Houston-Downtown, and University of Houston-Victoria.[29]

UNIVERSITY OF NORTH TEXAS SYSTEM

In 1980 the University of North Texas Board of Regents created a system to help with the management of the Texas College of Osteopathic Medicine, which five years earlier had been made part of the University of North Texas. The legislature formalized that arrangement in 2003. The current members of the system are: University of North Texas, University of North Texas Health Science Center, and University of North Texas Dallas, including the College of Law.[30]

TEXAS TECH UNIVERSITY SYSTEM

After several legislative attempts to establish a college in western Texas, the legislature in 1923 established the Texas Technological

College. Governance of the college was by a nine-member board of regents appointed by the governor, approved by the state senate, and serving six-year terms. In 1996 the legislature granted Texas Tech University the ability to establish a university system and its first chancellor was John T. Montford. The present members of the system are Texas Tech University, Texas Tech University Health Science Center, and Angelo State University.[31]

There are currently four public universities in Texas that have their own board of regents and are not part of any university system. Each has its own particular history. They are Texas Woman's University, Stephen F. Austin State University, Midwestern State University, and Texas Southern University.

The Texas State College for Women, the first public college for women in Texas, was established by the legislature in 1901 and opened in 1903. It also holds the distinction of being the first college of arts and industry in the state. The legislative act called for the establishment of the "Texas Industrial Institute and College for the Education of White Girls of the State of Texas in the Arts and Sciences." That same statute put into place a board of regents appointed by the governor to oversee the institution. From 1903 to 1913, the board consisted of seven regents, but from 1913 to 1927, it was reduced to six. In 1927 the board was increased to its present size of nine members and today this college is Texas Woman's University. More about the university's history is discussed in chapter 8.[32]

Stephen F. Austin State University, located in Nacogdoches, was founded in 1923 as a Normal school for teachers, and named after Texas founder Stephen F. Austin. Originally the college was governed by the State Normal School Board of Regents; however, later the legislature removed it from the system and provided for a separate nine-member board of regents appointed by the governor. Local interests in East Texas felt it was in the best interests of the college and the region to have an independent college.[33]

Midwestern State University located in Wichita Falls was originally founded in 1922 as the Wichita Falls Junior College. It was the second municipal junior college in Texas, and was operated by the Wichita Falls Independent School District. In 1937, it was renamed Hardin Junior College. In 1941 the legislature separated the college from the school district, and in 1950, changed its name to Midwestern University.[34]

Texas Southern University began as the Houston Colored Junior College in 1927. In 1947 the legislature designated it as Texas State University for Negroes. In 1951 it became Texas Southern University. It is governed by a nine-member board of regents appointed by the governor.[35] More about the university's history is discussed in chapter 10.

These four independent public universities have been the subject of much discussion over the years whenever the legislature looks at ways to reduce the cost of higher education. The argument against the independent schools has been that having them as part of a system would lower their costs of operation, as most systems use their immense buying power to lower the prices charged by their various suppliers and those savings are passed on to member institutions. The argument for the independent colleges has always been that local control is important and that the independent colleges also work on methods to reduce their costs.

There is one system that no longer exists independently. In 1951 the legislature established the Lamar University System, which consisted of Lamar University, Lamar Institute of Technology, Lamar College-Port Arthur, and Lamar College-Orange. In 1995 the legislature decided to move that system into the Texas State University System.[36]

* * * * *

Discussions about how to structure higher education in Texas have included ideas about reorganizing all of higher education, including the membership of the individual systems. It has been argued that all institutions with a common purpose, for example general academic institutions, should be put together to make them more manageable for a board of regents. There has been discussion about putting all of the research universities into one system, so that its governance board could concentrate on producing the best research and teaching results and be able to attract high-quality research professors to a system where they could work with more than one institution. Other conversations have revolved around putting all of the medical schools in one system to foster cross-pollination of ideas and better health care.

These discussions have occupied many legislative committee meetings over the last fifty years during which a very strong tendency to protect the status quo has prevailed. However, at some point in the future when the costs of higher education reach an intolerable level, public opinion will perhaps force these issues to be addressed once more. Administrators who are armed with an understanding of the history of higher education in Texas in general and at their institution specifically may find it easier to navigate the discussions and debates that will surely arise.

NOTES

1. Leslie S. Domokos, "History of Higher Education," in *ASHE Reader on the History of Higher Education,* edited by Lester F. Goodchild and Harold S. Wechsler (Needham Heights, MA: Ginn Press, 1989), 1–22.

2. Charles Homer Haskins, *The Rise of Universities* (Ithaca, NY: Great Seal Books, 1957), 22–23; Herman Weimer, *Concise History of Education from Solon to Pestalozzi* (New York: Philosophical Library, 1962), 21–26.

3. E. B. Duryea, "Evolution of University Organization," in *Organization and Governance in Higher Education*, edited by M. Christopher Brown II, 3–15. 5th ed. ASHE Reader Series. (Boston: Pearson Custom Publishing, 2000), 6.

4. Elwood Cubberly, *Public Education in the United States* (New York: Houghton Mifflin Company, 1919), 67.

5. John S. Brubacher and Willis Rudy, *Higher Education in Transition: An American History, 1636–1956* (New York: Harper & Row, 1958), 3.

6. C. E. Evans, *The Story of Texas Schools* (Austin: Steck Co, 1955), 257–58.

7. Texas Constitution of 1876, Article VII, http://tarlton.law.utexas.edu/constitutions/texas1876.

8. Fredrick J. Waddell, "A Historical Review of Coordination of Higher Education in Texas" (PhD diss., North Texas State University, Denton, 1972), 38–44.

9. Texas Constitution of 1876, Article VII, http://tarlton.law.utexas.edu/constitutions/texas1876.

10. Evans, *The Story of Texas Schools*, 252.

11. Ibid., 110.

12. Debbie Mauldin Cottrell, "BLANTON, ANNIE WEBB." *Handbook of Texas Online* (http://www.tshaonline.org/handbook/online/articles/fbl16), accessed February 6, 2014. Uploaded on June 12, 2010. Published by the Texas State Historical Association.

13. Evans, *The Story of Texas Schools,* 124.

14. Ibid., 128–30.

15. Ibid., 128–29.

16. Ibid., 128.

17. Arthur J. Klein and Franklin V. Thomas, "Cooperation and Coordination in Higher Education" *American Council of Education Studies,* Series 1, Vol. 2, No. 5, April 1938; Evans, *The Story of Texas Schools,* 228–231.

18. Texas Constitution of 1876, Article VII, http://tarlton.law.utexas.edu/constitutions/texas1876.

19. Frederick Eby, *The Development of Education in Texas* (New York: Macmillan Co., 1925), 290–91.

20. Harry N. Graves, Texas Legislature Joint Legislative Committee on Organization and Economy, and Griffenhagen and Associates, *The Government of the State of Texas: report of the Joint Legislative Committee on Organization and Economy and Griffenhagen and Associates, specialists in public administration and finance,* Vols. 11, 12, 13 (Austin: A. C. Baldwin & Sons, 1932–33).

21. Waddell, "A Historical Review of Coordination of Higher Education in Texas," 53.

22. Ibid., 58.

23. Leticia M. Garza-Falcon, "The Foundation of Public Education: Development of the Normal School Movement," in Gomez, *A Texas State of Mind,* 30–31.

24. Evans, *The Story of Texas Schools,* 119–20.

25. "TEXAS A&M UNIVERSITY SYSTEM," *Handbook of Texas Online* (http://www.tshaonline.org/handbook/online/articles/kct09) accessed February 11, 2014. Uploaded June 15, 2010. Published by the Texas State Historical Association.

26. Susan R. Richardson, "Oil, Power and Universities: Political Struggle and Academic Advancement at the University of Texas and Texas A&M, 1876–1965" (PhD diss., Pennsylvania State University, 2005), 304–305.

27. Henry C. Dethloff, "TEXAS A&M UNIVERSITY," *Handbook of Texas Online* (http://www.tshaonline.org/handbook/online/articles/kct08), accessed January 11, 2016 Uploaded on June 15, 2010. Modified on December 2, 2015. Published by the Texas State Historical Association.

28. "UNIVERSITY OF TEXAS SYSTEM," *Handbook of Texas Online* (http://tshaonline.org./handbook/online/articles/kcu40). Accessed March 26, 2015. Uploaded on June 15, 2010, Published by the Texas State Historical Association.

29. Diana J. Kleiner, "UNIVERSITY OF HOUSTON SYSTEM," *Handbook of Texas Online* (http://tshaonline.org/handbook/online/articles/kcunr). Accessed March 26, 2015. Uploaded on June 15, 2010. Modified on February 10, 2011. Published by the Texas State Historical Association.

30. University of North Texas System; http://untsystem.edu, accessed March 26, 2015.

31. Texas Tech University System; http://texastech.edu, accessed March 26, 2015.

32. Joyce Thompson, "TEXAS WOMAN'S UNIVERSITY," *Handbook of Texas Online* (http://tshaonline.org/handbook/online/articles/ket37). Accessed March 26, 2015. Uploaded on June 15, 2010. Published by the Texas State Historical Association.

33. C. K. Chamberlain, "STEPHEN F. AUSTIN STATE UNIVERSITY," *Handbook of Texas Online* (http://tshaonline.org/handbook/online/articles/kcs19). Accessed on March 26, 2015. Uploaded on June 5, 2009. Published by the Texas State Historical Association.

34. Evertt Kinding, "Midwestern State University," *Handbook of Texas Online* (http://tshaonline.org/handbook/online/articles/kcm04). Accessed March 26, 2015. Uploaded on June 15, 2010. Published by the Texas State Historical Association.

35. Cary D. Wintz, "TEXAS SOUTHERN UNIVERSITY," *Handbook of Texas Online* (http://tshaonline.org/handbook/online/articles/kct27), accessed March 26, 2015. Uploaded on June 15, 2010. Modified on June 14, 2013. Published by the Texas State Historical Association.

36. Fernando C. Gomez, *A Texas State of Mind: The Texas State University System Story Still Going Strong After 100 Years* (Austin: Texas Review Press, 2011), 194.

BIBLIOGRAPHY

Berdahl, Robert O. *Statewide Coordination of Higher Education.* Washington, DC: American Council of Education, 1971.

Brubacher, John S., and Willis Rudy. *Higher Education in Transition: An American History, 1636-1956.* New York: Harper & Row, 1958.

Chamberlain, C. K. "STEPHEN F. AUSTIN STATE UNIVERSITY," *Handbook of Texas Online.* (http://tshaonline.org/handbook/online/articles/kcs19). Accessed on March 26, 2015. Uploaded on June 5, 2009. Published by the Texas State Historical Association.

Clark, Burton R., and Guy R. Neave, eds. *The Encyclopedia of Higher Education.* 4 vols. National System of Higher Education. New York: Pergamon Press, 1992.

Cottrell, Debbie Mauldin, "BLANTON, ANNIE WEBB." *Handbook of Texas Online* (http://www.tshaonline.org/handbook/online/articles/fbl16), accessed February 6, 2014. Uploaded on June 12, 2010. Published by the Texas State Historical Association.

Cubberly, Elwood. *Public Education in the United States,* New York: Houghton Mifflin Company, 1919.

Dethloff, Henry C. "TEXAS A&M UNIVERSITY," *Handbook of Texas Online* (http://www.tshaonline.org/handbook/online/articles/kct08), accessed January 11, 2016 Uploaded on June 15, 2010. Modified on December 2, 2015. Published by the Texas State Historical Association.

Duryea, E. B. "Evolution of University Organization." In *Organization and Governance in Higher Education,* edited by M. Christopher Brown II, 3-15. 5th ed. ASHE Reader Series. Boston: Pearson Custom Publishing, 2000.

Domonkos, Leslie S. "History of Higher Education." In *ASHE Reader on the History of Higher Education,* edited by Lester F. Goodchild and Harold S. Wechsler, 1-22. Needham Heights, MA: Ginn Press, 1989.

"TEXAS A&M UNIVERSITY SYSTEM," *Handbook of Texas Online* (http://www.tshaonline.org/handbook/online/articles/kct09) accessed February 11, 2014. Uploaded June 15, 2010. Published by the Texas State Historical Association.

Eby, Fredrick. *The Development of Education in Texas.* New York: Macmillan Co., 1925.

Evans, C. E. *The Story of Texas Schools.* Austin: Steck Co., 1955.

Garza-Falcon, Leticia M. "The Foundation of Public Education: Development of the Normal School Movement." In Gomez, *A Texas State of Mind,* 28-31.

Gomez, Fernando C. *A Texas State of Mind: The Texas State University System Story Still Going Strong After 100 Years.* Austin: Texas Review Press, 2011.

Graves, Harry N., Texas Legislature Joint Legislative Committee on Organization and Economy, and Griffenhagen and Associates. *The Government of the State of Texas: report of the Joint Legislative Committee on Organization and Economy and Griffenhagen and Associates, specialists in public administration and finance.* Vols. 11, 12, 13. Austin: A.C. Baldwin & Sons, 1932-33.

Haskins, Charles Homer. *The Rise of Universities.* Ithaca, NY: Great Seal Books, 1957.

Hobbs, Walter C. *Government Regulation of Higher Education.* Cambridge, MA: Ballinger Publishing Co., 1978.

Kinding, Evertt, "MIDWESTERN STATE UNIVERSITY," *Handbook of Texas Online.* (http://tshaonline.org/handbook/online/articles/kcm04). Accessed March 26, 2015. Uploaded on June 15, 2010. Published by the Texas State Historical Association.

Klein, Arthur J., and Franklin V. Thomas. "Cooperation and Coordination in Higher Education." In *American Council of Education Studies,* Series 1, Vol. 2, No. 5, April 1938.

Kleiner, Diana J. "UNIVERSITY OF HOUSTON SYSTEM," *Handbook of Texas Online.* (http://tshaonline.org/handbook/online/articles/kcunr). Accessed March 26, 2015. Uploaded on June 15, 2010. Modified on February 10, 2011. Published by the Texas State Historical Association.

Richardson, Richard C., Kathy Reeves Bracco, Patrick M. Callan, and Joni E. Finney. *Designing State Higher Education Systems for a New Century.* Phoenix, AZ: Oryx Press, 1999.

Richardson, Susan R. "Oil, Power and Universities: Political Struggle and Academic Advancement at the University of Texas and Texas A&M, 1876–1965." PhD diss., Pennsylvania State University, 2005.

Texas, *The Laws of Texas, 1822–1897.* Compiled and arranged by H. P. N. Gammel. 10 vols. Austin: Gammel Book Company, 1898.

Thompson, Joyce. "TEXAS WOMAN'S UNIVERSITY," *Handbook of Texas Online* (http://tshaonline.org/handbook/online/articles/ket37). Accessed March 26, 2015. Uploaded on June 15, 2010. Published by the Texas State Historical Association.

"UNIVERSITY OF TEXAS SYSTEM," *Handbook of Texas Online* (http://tshaonline.org./handbook/online/articles/kcu40). Accessed March 26, 2015. Uploaded on June 15, 2010, Published by the Texas State Historical Association.

Waddell, Fredrick J. "A Historical Review of Coordination of Higher Education in Texas." PhD diss., North Texas State University, Denton, 1972.

Weimer, Herman. *Concise History of Education from Solon to Pestalozzi.* New York: Philosophical Library, 1962.

Wintz, Cary D. "TEXAS SOUTHERN UNIVERSITY," *Handbook of Texas Online* (http://tshaonline.org/handbook/online/articles/kct27), accessed March 26, 2015. Uploaded on June 15, 2010. Modified on June 14, 2013. Published by the Texas State Historical Association.

Wooten, Dudley G. *The History of Texas: 1685 to 1897.* Dallas: William G. Scharff, 1898.

★ 13 ★

TEXAS COLLEGES PAST AND PRESENT

As this book demonstrates Texas has had a long and storied history of institutions in higher education. This chapter provides a listing of all of the institutions in Texas, colleges and universities that are currently in operation followed by a second section that lists institutions of the past. This is not an attempt to describe each institution in depth as that information is readily available from many sources but to provide basic information about dates of openings and any name changes that might have occurred.

CURRENT COLLEGES AND UNIVERSITIES

Abilene Christian University

Abilene Christian College was chartered as Childers Classical Institute and opened in 1906. The college was accredited as a junior college in 1916 and as a senior college in 1920. It began a graduate program in 1953. At one time Abilene Christian College had the distinction of being the largest senior college in the world, with a faculty made up entirely of Church of Christ members. It became Abilene Christian University in 1976.[1]

Amberton University

Amberton University began as a branch of Abilene Christian College in 1971 and was called ACC Metrocenter. Before it opened its own campus, most of its classes were held at the campus of the defunct Christian College of the Southwest. In 1974 when it moved to its new campus in Garland, its name was changed to Abilene Christian College at Dallas. On June 1, 1981, it became a separate institution named Amber University. In 2001, its name changed to Amberton University.[2]

Angelo State University

Angelo State University was founded in San Angelo in 1928 as San Angelo College, a junior college. It became a full four-year college in 1963, and the Texas Higher Education Coordinating Board approved graduate studies in 1971. The university became a member of the Texas State University System in 1975, and in 2007 the legislature transferred it to the Texas Tech University System.[3]

Arlington Baptist College

Arlington Baptist College was started in 1939 as the Fundamental Bible Baptist Institute. The first classes were held at the First Baptist Church in Ft. Worth. In 1956 the college moved to its new home in Arlington. In 1945 the college was re-chartered and named Bible Baptist Seminary. It name was changed again in 1965 to Arlington Baptist Junior College. In 1972 the college became a four-year institution and was renamed Arlington Baptist College.[4]

Austin College

The Presbytery of Brazos at Huntsville founded Austin College in 1849 after Dr. Daniel Baker secured almost $100,000 for the college's support. The college remained open at that location until 1871 with Sam Houston State College ultimately receiving the building. In 1876, Austin College moved to Sherman, where its first building was completed in 1878, and sixty-three students enrolled that year. In 1930, when the Texas Synod of the Presbyterian Church ordered its three senior colleges to consolidate as Austin College, one of the colleges, Daniel Baker at Brownwood, did not, but Texas Presbyterian College at Milford did join with Austin College.[5]

Baylor University

The Union Baptist Association of Travis County created the Texas Education Society in 1841 in order to establish a Baptist university in Texas. The Ninth Congress of the Republic of Texas granted a charter for Baylor University in 1845. The school opened in Independence in 1846. In 1886, the Baptist General Association of Texas and the State Convention, under whose control Baylor had been operating since 1848, merged and, as a result, Baylor and Waco University were combined under the name of Baylor University. Baylor was established on the Waco campus in 1887.[6]

Concordia Lutheran College

In the late nineteenth century, Texas Lutherans were determined to build a school to prepare their young men for the ministry. There were three short-lived attempts—at New Orleans in 1883, in Giddings in 1894, and at Clifton in the early twentieth century. After World War I, they were finally successful in founding the Lutheran College of Texas at Austin. The school kept that name until 1965, when it was changed to Concordia Lutheran College. A junior college was started in 1951, and by 1955 women were matriculating. High school classes were discontinued in 1967. The Southern Association of Colleges and Schools accredited the college in 1968. In 1979, the synod authorized Concordia to become a four-year institution. The first bachelor's degrees were awarded in 1982.[7]

Dallas Baptist University

Dallas Baptist University is the successor to Decatur Baptist College, a junior college operating in Decatur from 1861 till 1965. In 1965, the college moved to Dallas and changed its name to Dallas Baptist College. By 1968 the college had become a four-year institution. The name was changed in 1985 to Dallas Baptist University when it began offering graduate degrees in education, religion, and business administration.[8]

East Texas Baptist University

Founded in 1912 as the College of Marshall, the school opened in 1917 as a two-year junior college and academy. The board of trustees changed the name to East Texas Baptist College in 1944 when it was reorganized as a four-year college; and then in 1984, it became East Texas Baptist University.[9]

Hardin-Simmons University

Hardin-Simmons University was founded as Abilene Baptist College in 1891 by the Sweetwater Baptist Association and a group of cattle-men and pastors who sought to bring Christian higher education to the Southwest. The purpose of the school would be to "lead students to Christ, teach them of Christ, and train them for Christ." The origi-nal land was donated to the university by rancher C.W. Merchant. It was the first school of higher education established west of Fort Worth. The school was renamed Simmons College in 1892 in honor of an early contributor, James B. Simmons. By 1907 it claimed an enrollment of 524 and a staff of 49. In 1925, it became Simmons University. It was renamed Hardin-Simmons University in 1934 in honor of Mary and John G. Hardin, who were also major contri-butors. The University has been associated with the Baptist General Convention of Texas since 1941.[10]

Houston Baptist University

Originally begun as Houston Baptist College, the school opened its doors in 1963. It grew rapidly during the 1960s and 1970s with new buildings, a large enrollment, and an expanded curriculum reflective of its growth. In 1973, the school changed its name to Houston Baptist University to reflect its new status. Gradually, master's degrees were offered in education, psychology, pastoral counseling, and health administration.[11]

Howard Payne University

Howard Payne College was founded at Brownwood in 1889 by Dr. John D. Robnett and the Pecos Valley Baptist Association. The college opened in 1890 with 10 teachers and 247 pupils. Its motto was "Economy, more and more for less and less; patriotism in the heart of Texas and in the heart of Texans; democracy, the college where everybody is somebody." Howard Payne College merged with the Daniel Baker College, which had also opened in 1889 at Brownwood, with seven teachers and 111 students.[12]

Huston-Tillotson College

Located in Austin, Huston-Tillotson College is a coeducational liberal arts and sciences college. It is operated jointly by the American Missionary Association of the United Church of Christ and the board of education of the United Methodist Church. The school was formed by the merger of Samuel Huston College and Tillotson College on October 24, 1952. Huston-Tillotson College has remained primarily a black college, although there were no restrictions as to race. The college is fully accredited and awards baccalaureate degrees in three divisions: liberal studies, professional studies, and science and technology with major concentrations in nineteen areas. It became Huston-Tillotson University on February 28, 2005.[13]

Incarnate Word College

The Congregation of the Sisters of Charity of the Incarnate Word started Incarnate Word College in 1881. In 1897, the order purchased George W. Brackenridge's 280-acre estate and in 1900 opened the academy at the Motherhouse of the Brackenridge Villa. From 1910 to 1920, the collegiate division of Incarnate Word grew as the college's recognition as a senior college grew. During this time, the college offered bachelor's degrees in arts, science, mathematics, and home economics. The university also operates an all-girls school, Incarnate Word High School, as well as a coeducational high school, St. Anthony Catholic High School.

In addition, it operates two elementary schools, St. Anthony's and St. Peter Prince of the Apostles. [14]

Independent Baptist College

Independent Baptist College began as Independent Baptist School of the Bible and was unique in that it was a Baptist institution not sponsored by an association or a convention but by a single Baptist church—Trinity Temple Baptist Church of Dallas. The college opened in 1964 and for the first five years offered only Bible instruction. In 1969 it achieved senior college status when it began to offer a Bachelor of Arts degree in Bible. It changed its name in 1969.[15]

Jacksonville Baptist College

Jacksonville Baptist College began in 1899 as a senior college with an enrollment of eighty-two students. However, from 1919 to 1930, it operated as a junior college. It was accredited by the State Department of Education from 1923 to 1939. Since 1939, it has operated as a senior college.[16]

Jarvis Christian College

Beginning as Jarvis Christian Institute in 1912, the school offered high school level education to black Texans in Hawkins. In 1927, the school became a junior college and in 1937 a senior college. It was chartered in 1939. In 1950, Jarvis Christian College received the honor of being the only black college with accreditation in the region when the Southern Association of Colleges and Schools put the school on the "Approved List of Colleges and Universities for Negro Youth." The school remained financially viable during the twentieth century due to the discovery of oil wells on the school's property in the 1940s.[17]

Lamar University

The South Park Independent School District at Beaumont operated the South Park Junior College from 1923 until 1932. In 1932, the independent district provided plant and equipment for the school and changed its name to Lamar College. In 1951, the name was changed again to Lamar State College of Technology. Because the school was designated as a technological college, it was "required to offer, develop, and especially stress courses in chemical engineering, industrial engineering, industrial chemistry, plastics, and other phases of engineering and technology." The college did not confer bachelor's degrees until 1953. In 1952–1953, the college enrolled 2,560 students and had a faculty of 125. It became a four-year college in 1949, and in 1969 it opened its first extension center in Orange. It became Lamar University in 1971. Also in 1971, Port Arthur College merged with Lamar University and began operating as Lamar University-Port Arthur.[18]

LeTourneau College

LeTourneau College began as LeTourneau Technical Institute of Texas. Built in Longview in 1946 by Robert Gilmour LeTourneau, the school originally served as a junior college. It became a four-year coeducational college in 1961 and changed its name to LeTourneau College. In the 1980s and 1990s, the college expanded its scope by changing its name to LeTourneau University and adding a research division, a teacher certification program, a master of business administration program, and an adult education program. The university currently operates sites in Longview, Austin, Bedford, Dallas, Houston, and Tyler.[19]

Lubbock Christian University

Lubbock Christian College opened in 1957 as a junior college. It became a four-year institution in 1972. With continued growth in 1987 it became Lubbock Christian University.[20]

McMurry University

McMurry College began as Stamford College opened in 1907 and closed in 1918 after a fire destroyed the administration building. In 1920, the institution moved to Abilene and was renamed

McMurry College. It reopened there in 1923. The alumni of the former Seth Ward College were considered alumni of McMurry College. The institution became McMurry University in 1990.[21]

Midwestern State University

Midwestern State University was founded in 1922 as Wichita Falls Junior College. It was the second municipal junior college in Texas. In 1937 it acquired a new campus and changed its name to Hardin Junior College. In 1946 the school added a senior college division and became Hardin College. Four years later it became Midwestern University, retaining Hardin Junior College as the junior division. Later graduate studies were added, the school became part of the state university system, and the junior college was dissolved. In 1975 it was renamed Midwestern State University.[22]

University of North Texas

Texas Normal College operated as a private teachers college in Denton from 1890 to 1901. In 1899, the Texas legislature passed an act to establish North Texas Normal College and locate it in Denton. The legislature gave control of the college to the State Board of Education, which modeled its administration of the college and its finances, as well as the college's admission requirements and student discipline, after the way the board governed Sam Houston State Teachers College. In 1911, the legislature turned governance of the college over to the State Board of Education. In 1923 it was renamed North Texas State Teachers College. In 1949 the legislature changed the college's name to North Texas State College. At that time it became an independent college with its own board of regents. The institution continued to change its name; in 1961 it became North Texas State University and in 1988 it was renamed University of North Texas.[23]

Our Lady of the Lake

The Sisters of Divine Providence established Our Lady of the Lake College in Castroville in 1868. The college moved to San Antonio in 1896. From 1912 to 1919, it operated as a junior college, and in 1919, it became a senior college. The graduate Wordon School of Social Service was established in 1942.[24]

Paul Quinn College

Paul Quinn College was founded in Austin in 1872 by the African Methodist Episcopal Church. In 1877 the college moved into new buildings in Waco. Steady growth in the early twentieth century lasted until the 1930s. In 1932 the Great Depression, coupled with the college's outstanding debt, caused the president to call upon fellow small colleges, alumni, and community leaders to restore the college. By 1936 those efforts had paid off. With the debt repaid, and the school's prospects looking up, it received accreditation in 1938. By the mid-1980s the school was struggling to compete with larger colleges, and in 1990, it was moved to Dallas to take over the newly closed campus of Bishop College.[25]

Prairie View A&M University

In 1876, the legislature passed a law to establish a black agricultural and mechanical college. The act appropriated money to build buildings for the college, but, instead, Ashbel Smith, J. H. Raymond, and J. D. Giddings purchased buildings and land near Hempstead. Prairie View has functioned as a training school for teachers of black children and as an agricultural and mechanical school for black students. Since Texas did not establish a black state university, Prairie View has also functioned as a black state college. After its establishment, the college enrolled a few students, but had none at all in 1879, the year the legislature authorized the establishment and support of a Normal school to train black teachers at the school. Graduates of the Normal course and those who passed an entrance examination were allowed into the teacher-training course. Graduates of that course were entitled to teach at any free black school in Texas.

In 1899, the legislature changed the school's name to Prairie View State Normal and Industrial College and added an agricultural and mechanical department for male students and an industrial department for female students. In 1901, the college adopted a four-year classical and scientific course of study with the legislature's authorization. In the 1931–1932 school year, out of 145 students there were 74 education majors, 40 industrial arts majors, 16 agricultural majors, and 15 other majors. In 1945, the legislature changed the school's name to Prairie View University and authorized its board of directors to expand the school's course of study to include courses in law, medicine, engineering, pharmacy, journalism, and other general courses taught at the University of Texas. In 1976 the legislature changed its name to Prairie View A&M University.[26]

Rice University

Rice University, which opened in 1912, is a private, independent, coeducational university in Houston, first established as the William Marsh Rice Institute. It had been chartered in 1891 by a former Houston merchant, William Marsh Rice, with a $200,000 interest-bearing note payable to Rice Institute upon his death. After his death and legal wrangling, additional money went to the school, and when it opened the endowment was about $9 million. Because of this, until 1965 students were admitted without the need to pay tuition. Rice University maintains a variety of research facilities and laboratories, and its library houses 1.3 million volumes and 1.6 million microforms. Rice University's goal has been to combine the teaching emphasis of a liberal arts college with the scholarship of a research university.[27]

Sam Houston State University

Sam Houston State University first opened in 1879 as Sam Houston Normal Institute. The Peabody Educational Board gave a $6,000 subsidy to establish the school and continued subsidizing it in smaller amounts for several years. The institute was the first training school for white teachers established in Texas. When it opened in 1879 it had 100 students, seven of whom earned diplomas by the end of the year.

The law establishing the Sam Houston Normal Institute had specified that the State Board of Education controlled the institute. In 1911, the legislature provided the school with its own board of regents, and the course of study was extended to four years with the last two years being at the college level. It was a junior college until 1915 when a bachelor's degree was added. The legislature changed the name of the institute to Sam Houston State Teachers College in 1923, and the offering of master's degrees was authorized in 1936. In recognition of the broadened scope of the college, the legislature changed the name to Sam Houston State College in 1965 and Sam Houston State University in 1969. Today it is part of the Texas State University System.[28]

Schreiner University
Schreiner University was founded in 1917 as the Schreiner Institute by Charles A. Schreiner who placed in trust to the Presbyterian Synod of Texas $250,000 and 140 acres of land in Kerrville. The school began as a preparatory school and junior college. In 1982 it became a four-year college. The name was changed to Schreiner University in 2001. The school has retained its ties to the Presbyterian Church.[29]

Southern Methodist University
In 1910, the five annual conferences of the Methodist Church appointed an Educational Commission, which located Southern Methodist University in Dallas. The university was designated as the "connectional institution" for Methodist Church conferences west of the Mississippi River, and a board of trustees was chosen to govern the university. The school's first session in 1915 had an enrollment of 706 students.[30]

Southwestern Adventist College
In 1894 Southwestern Adventist College opened as Keene Industrial Academy, then Southwestern Junior College, then Southwestern

Union College, and finally Southwestern Adventist College. The school grew steadily and in 1977 became a four-year institution and in 1989 a university. It continues to place an emphasis on finding work experience for students.[31]

Southwestern Bible Institute

Southwestern Bible Institute, which is operated by the Assembly of God, was established in Enid, Oklahoma, in 1927, and moved to Fort Worth in 1941. The institute was moved to Waxahachie in 1943. At one time it included a three-year high school, a two-year liberal arts junior college, and a four-year Bible college with a fifth year of postgraduate work. Completion of the four-year Bible college course culminated with a bachelor's degree, and a bachelor of theology degree upon completion of the fifth year of theological work.[32]

Southwestern University

Southwestern University at Georgetown is said by some to be the oldest college in Texas because the university considers itself the continuation of, or successor to, Rutersville College, which was chartered in 1840 by the congress of the Republic. Southwestern is also considered the successor of Wesleyan College founded in 1844, McKenzie College founded in 1848, and Soule University founded in 1856.

Southwestern University opened in 1873. It was first called Texas University, but in a charter revision on February 6, 1875, it gave up that name to the state in order to avoid conflict with the future state university, and took the name Southwestern University. As the school grew it became the cornerstone of Texas Methodism. A major crisis occurred when Southern Methodist University (SMU) was opened in 1915 and it became the central Methodist college in Texas. As a result, Southwestern began experiencing financial problems. However, those difficulties were resolved and Southwestern became the fifth largest of all the Methodist colleges and continues to be a well-regarded liberal arts college.[33]

Southwestern Assemblies of God College

Southwestern Assemblies of God College is a coeducational, liberal arts institution owned and operated by the North Texas, South Texas, West Texas, New Mexico, Arkansas, Louisiana, and Oklahoma districts of the Assemblies of God Church. The school developed from the merger of three previously independent church-related institutions—Southwestern Bible Institute, Shield of Faith Bible School established at Amarillo in 1931, and the Southern Bible College—which by 1941 had moved to Fort Worth, where they were united under the name of Southern Bible Institute. In 1943 the school relocated to Waxahachie. During the 1944–1945 school year it added a junior college. In 1946 it became a four-year school. It later dropped the elementary and high school courses, and in 1994 assumed its present name.[34]

Stephen F. Austin State University

In 1917, the legislature provided for the establishment of Stephen F. Austin Normal College. The locating committee chose the town of Nacogdoches partly as a result of the city offering two hundred acres for the campus. Establishment of the college was delayed when, during a special legislative session, the legislature repealed appropriations for the buildings and maintenance for the college. Consequently, the school did not open until September 18, 1923. It had 158 students and used the facilities of the Nacogdoches public schools for the first school year. In 1949, by an act of the legislature, the school's name was changed from Stephen F. Austin State Teachers College to Stephen F. Austin State College. During the 1960s it was one of the fastest growing colleges in Texas. It became Stephen F. Austin State University in 1969.[35]

St. Edward's University

Five priests of the Congregation of the Holy Cross from Notre Dame established St. Edward's College outside the Austin city limits in 1878. The school's name was changed to St. Edward's University in

1925. St. Edward's University is a private Roman Catholic institution that offers a liberal arts coeducational environment with a wide variety of courses and programs.[36]

St. Mary's University

St. Mary's University was opened as St. Mary's Institute by four brethren of the San Antonio mission of the Society of Mary. They were sent to the mission from Europe by the Reverend J. M. Odin after a trip to Texas. The school opened in 1852 in an old shop on the corner of Military Plaza. It adopted the word "college" in its name and then became St. Louis College. In 1923, the entire college department was transferred to the Woodlawn area of San Antonio. There, the name was changed to St. Mary's College and later to St. Mary's University when the school expanded. The college continues to grow and prosper.[37]

Sul Ross State University

The thirty-fifth legislature approved the establishment of Sul Ross Normal College at Alpine in 1917. The establishment of the school required the residents of Brewster County to deed at least one hundred acres of land for the college. The college's opening was delayed until construction of the buildings was completed in 1920. In 1923 the legislature changed the name of the school to Sul Ross State Teachers College, in 1949 to Sul Ross State College, and in 1969 to Sul Ross State University in recognition of its increased academic standing.[38]

Sul Ross State University Rio Grande College

Sul Ross State University Rio Grande College was established in 1972 by Sul Ross State University on the campus of Southwest Texas Junior College in Uvalde, Del Rio, and Eagle Pass to provide upper-level and graduate work in teacher education and business administration.[39]

Tarleton State University

Located in Stephenville, Tarleton State University began as Stephenville College, established in 1893 under Marshall McIlhaney of

Marble Falls. In its first year, Stephenville College, which offered courses from primary to college level, enrolled about one hundred students, ranging in age from ten to fifty years old. In conjunction with crop failures in the town, debts on the college's buildings forced Stephenville College to close in its third year (1895–1896). The building sat unused until 1917 when John Tarleton, a wealthy rancher from Palo Pinto County left approximately $85,000 for the establishment of a college for Erath County boys and girls. The college opened in 1899 under the presidency of W. H. Bruce of Athens and with three assistant teachers. Bruce later served as president of North Texas State College. In 1917, Stephenville residents donated the entire school plant of the college, valued at about $175,000, and $75,000 for a student loan endowment. The institution was placed under control of the A&M Board of Directors. In the 1917–1918 school year, the school enrolled 261 students. It is currently the second largest college by enrollment in the Texas A&M System.[40]

Texas A&M University-College Station

This is the oldest public institution of higher education in Texas. The Eleventh Texas Legislature approved a joint resolution on November 1, 1866, accepting the terms of the federal government's Morrill Land-Grant College Act of July 1, 1862. (See chapter 5 for more on the Morrill Act and the founding of the university.) The state's Constitution of 1876 specified that Texas A&M College would be a branch of the proposed University of Texas. Texas A&M opened on October 4, 1876, with 106 students and a faculty of six. It began as an all-male military institution with required participation in the Corps of Cadets, and it commissioned more officers than did any other institution. On August 23, 1963, the college became a university. In 2016 Texas A&M University is the largest university in Texas, is world renowned for its quality research, and is one of two public universities in Texas to be considered a major research center.[41]

Texas A&M University-Corpus Christi

Texas A&M University-Corpus Christi was chartered in 1947 as Arts and Technological College, a four-year liberal arts college affiliated with the Baptist General Convention of Texas. The name was changed in 1947 to the University of Corpus Christi, and in 1973 the school became part of the Texas A&M University System.[42]

Texas A&M University-Commerce

Texas A&M University-Commerce was originally established by William L. Mayo at Cooper, in Delta County, in 1889 as Mayo or Mayo's College. The school grew for the next five years but when a fire burned its building in 1894, the school began to look for a new location. It moved to Commerce and was re-chartered as East Texas Normal School in 1894. Between 1889 and 1917 more than 30,000 students received their basic educational training at this school; records show that it prepared more teachers for the public schools that any other college in Texas during this period of time. In 1923 the name was changed to East Texas State Teachers College. In 1957 the school dropped the word "teachers" from its name and added a doctoral program. In 1995 the school was made a part of the Texas A&M University System.[43]

Texas A&M University-Galveston

Texas A&M University-Galveston is the maritime and marine branch of the Texas A&M System, and is unique among state universities in the United States. The school offers specialized educational programs in marine curricula leading to an accredited Bachelor of Science degree. The Galveston Marine Laboratory, founded in the late 1950s, and the Texas Maritime Academy, established shortly after, provided the foundation for this university.[44]

Texas A&M-Kingsville

Texas A&M University-Kingsville was projected to be a state teacher training school when it was first proposed in 1913. It opened in

1929 as the South Texas State Teachers College, but that same year it was changed from a teachers college to a technical school and the name was changed to Texas College of Arts and Industries. In 1967 it became Texas A&I University, and in 1993 the Legislature changed its name to Texas A&M University-Kingsville and it became part of the Texas A&M University System.[45]

Texas A&M University-Texarkana

Texas A&M University-Texarkana opened in 1971 as the East Texas Center at Texarkana. The school was on the campus of Texarkana College, a community college. It was established to offer upper level courses. In 1995 the school was renamed Texas A&M University-Texarkana and transferred to the A&M System. It was not until 2004 that the university acquired a gift from the city of 375 acres along with an additional 75 acres from the Truman Arnold Foundation for a new campus. Construction began on the new campus after a legislative appropriation in 2006.[46]

Texas Bible College

Texas Bible College was opened and operated by the United Pentecostal Church in 1961. Its purpose was to establish a doctrinally sound, spiritually strong Bible college for the church in Texas. The college is located in Houston and offers diplomas in theology and religious education.[47]

Texas Christian University

Texas Christian University had its beginnings in Add-Ran Christian University. Add-Ran began when, on a visit to Fort Worth in 1873, Randolph Clark bought property to establish a school at Thorp Spring. The school, then called Add-Ran Christian College, opened later that year with thirteen students. The following year enrollment was 117, and in the school's tenth year, it was 435, with students coming from fifty-four counties. The school's name became Add-Ran Christian University in 1890 when the Christian

Churches of Texas took over the property, and in 1895 the school moved to Waco.

The university experienced considerable economic hardship from 1895 to 1902. In 1902, Add-Ran became Texas Christian University with the Department of Arts and Sciences named Add-Ran College of Arts and Sciences as a nod to the university's former name. In 1919 major fire destroyed much of the campus. In 1911 the institution moved to Ft. Worth. Texas Christian University holds to the view that religion is an indispensable part of education.[48]

Texas Southern University

The Texas Constitution adopted in 1882 contains a provision for a branch university for blacks. That same year, the legislature passed a law to put the location of this branch university up for a vote by the people. The majority of voters voted to locate the new university at Palestine. However, the 1883 legislature took no action to enact the constitutional amendment establishing the university. The Bi-Racial Commission, appointed by Governor Cole in 1946, recommended that the state establish a black university in Houston or the Dallas-Fort Worth area. The commission suggested that the university be an agricultural and mechanical college with standards, faculty, course offerings, buildings, and equipment comparable to those of the University of Texas and Texas A&M. The legislature accepted this recommendation and established the Texas State University for Negroes at Houston in 1947. In 1951, the legislature changed the school's name to Texas Southern University.[49]

Texas State University

Texas State University began as Southwest Texas State Normal School, established by the state legislature in 1899. From 1899 to 1911, the ex-officio State Board of Education controlled the school until the four Normal schools at Huntsville, Denton, San Marcos, and Canyon came under control of the State Normal School Board of Regents in 1911. In 1918, Southwest Texas State Normal School became a senior college. In 1923 the name was changed to Southwest Texas State Teachers College and the same year it was admitted to the American Association of Teacher Colleges. The legislature changed its name again in 1959 to Southwest Texas State College, and in 1969 to Southwest Texas State University in recognition of its strong graduate program. During the 1960s the school received much national attention as the alma mater of the sitting president Lyndon Baines Johnson. In the 1970s and 1980s the university increased its landholdings when it purchased the former San Marcos Baptist Academy, and then received the bequest of a 3,485-acre ranch. A new library opened in 1990, which houses the Southwestern Writers Collection and the Wittliff Gallery of Southwest. The university also operates a campus at Round Rock.[50]

Texas Tech University

Texas Technological College was founded on February 10, 1923, when Governor Pat M. Neff signed the bill to establish a college in West Texas to "give instruction in technological, manufacturing, and agricultural pursuits and to elevate the ideas, enrich the lives, and increase the capacity of the people for democratic self-government." The college was governed by a nine-member board of directors appointed by the governor. A steering committee made up of Lubbock citizens purchased 2,008 acres of land for the college and the state later purchased that land. The college opened September 30, 1925. The legislature changed its name in 1969 to Texas Tech University. The university has the distinction of being the largest comprehensive higher education institution in the western two-thirds of the state of Texas. It is known as the "Mother of the Plains" because of its impact on West Texas.[51]

Texas Wesleyan University

Texas Wesleyan University is a private liberal arts institution four miles southeast of downtown Ft. Worth. Its origins can be traced back to 1890 as Polytechnic College. In 1914 the name was changed to Texas Woman's College. In 1934 the college became coeducational and changed its name to Texas Wesleyan College. It became Texas Wesleyan University in 1989.[52]

Texas Woman's University

In 1901, the Legislature authorized the establishment of a college called the Texas Industrial Institute and College for the Education of White Girls of the State of Texas in the Arts and Sciences, but called the Girls Industrial College by the board of regents. The college opened in 1903 in Denton, and in 1905, was renamed the College of Industrial Arts. In 1934, the college's name was changed to Texas State College for Women. However, this name change was not legalized until 1945.

The Texas State College for Women was an "academic pioneer" for several reasons. First, it contained the first home economics labs in Texas. The college was also the first state institution to award degrees in home economics, public school music, health and physical education, library science, kindergarten through primary education, and home demonstration for county agents. Additionally, the college was the first in Texas to use grade books and photo static transcripts in order to improve record keeping and student registration, and the first in Texas to develop an "academic advisory system" for students and to set a requirement of fifteen admission units in order to attend. In 1957, after it became a doctorate-granting institution, the name was changed to Texas Woman's University.[53]

Trinity University

The Cumberland Presbyterian Church established three colleges in Texas prior to 1866. These colleges were Chapel Hill College, which opened in Daingerfield in 1859, Ewing College, which opened in La Grange in 1852, and Larissa College, which opened in Larissa in 1855. At the time, Larissa College offered the best available science courses of any college in Texas. In 1866, the Brazos,

Colorado, and Texas Synods started accepting bids for a location for a central Presbyterian institution. The town of Tehuacana offered to donate 130 acres in the Tehuacana Hills and 1,500 acres in the prairie below the hills for the institution. The locating committee accepted Tehuacana's offer. The name Trinity University was chosen because the synods had founded three Presbyterian colleges. Trinity University remained in Tehuacana from 1869 to 1902. In 1902, the university moved to Waxahachie. It moved to San Antonio in 1942.[54]

University of Central Texas

The institution was established in 1973 as private university called the American Technological University. The university offered both undergraduate and graduate degrees that focused on career education and technology. It name was changed to University of Central Texas. In 1995 Governor George W. Bush encouraged the Central Texas University Task Force to review higher education in Texas. As a result of this study the University of Central Texas was dissolved and it turned its assets over to the State of Texas. In 1999 Tarleton State University-Central Texas opened. In 2009 the legislature changed its name to Texas A&M University-Central Texas.[55]

University of Dallas

The University of Dallas opened its campus in Irving on 1,000 acres of land in 1956. This Catholic institution is managed by a group of laymen; the first chancellor was Bishop Thomas K. Gorman, bishop of Dallas. The faculty is made up of Cistercian Fathers, Sisters from St. Mary of Namur, and the Dominican Fathers along with lay faculty. The Graduate School of Management was established in 1966 and by 2001 was the largest MBA-granting program in the Southwest. In 1989 the university purchased a site for its Rome, Italy, program, where it maintains classrooms, a student center with a library, a chapel, and housing.[56]

University of Houston

The university is a state research university and the flagship institution of the University of Houston System. Founded in 1927, it is the third-largest university in Texas. The University of Houston started out as a junior college in 1927 and did not become a senior college until 1934. The Board of Education of the Houston Independent School District governed the university until a separate board of regents was established in Houston in 1945.[57]

University of Houston-Clear Lake

The University of Houston-Clear Lake is an upper division and graduate branch of the University of Houston System that serves the Texas Gulf Coast. It was established in 1971 and opened in 1974.[58]

University of Houston-Downtown College

The University of Houston-Downtown College is an open admission undergraduate university serving the needs of greater Houston, particularly career-entry students. The school began in 1942 as a downtown business school. The university itself was founded after it acquired the assets of the South Texas Junior College. The university became a four-year unit of the University of Houston System in 1975.[59]

University of Houston-Victoria

The University of Houston-Victoria is an upper-level and graduate branch of the University of Houston System. The branch was established in 1973 and became a separate degree-granting institution in 1983.[60]

University of Mary Hardin-Baylor

The University of Mary Hardin-Baylor was formerly Baylor Female College in Independence and moved to Belton in 1886. It has the distinction of being the oldest college for women west of the Mississippi. In 1971 it became coeducational. It never merged with another college and still operates under its original Republic of Texas charter of 1845.[61]

University of the Incarnate Word
The University of the Incarnate Word, which is in San Antonio, was chartered in 1881 as a Catholic college for women and was operated by the Sisters of Charity of the Incarnate Word. The school was first known as the Academy of the Incarnate Word. In 1909 it changed its name to College and Academy of the Incarnate Word, and in 1912 became affiliated with the Catholic University of America in Washington, DC. In 1971 the school became coeducational, and in 1996 became the University of the Incarnate Word.[62]

University of Texas at Arlington
The University of Texas at Arlington began at a site that had been occupied by a series of private institutions since 1895. In 1917 local citizens obtained approval for funds from the legislature to purchase the property and form a branch of Texas A&M under the name of Grubbs Vocational College, a junior college with a high school department. In 1923 the school changed its name to North Texas Junior Agricultural College, and in 1949 to Arlington State College. In 1965 the legislature moved the college into the University of Texas System.[63]

University of Texas at Austin
The idea of the University of Texas at Austin dates to 1839 when the Congress of the Republic of Texas called for its establishment, but because of political events the university was not organized until 1881 when the first board of regents was appointed and Ashbel Smith was elected president of the board. The school opened September 15, 1883. The legislature made several major gifts of land to the Permanent University Fund that, particularly since the discovery of oil on that land, made major financial contributions to the university. The university has grown into one of the most outstanding research universities in the country.[64]

University of Texas at Dallas

In 1959–1960 the founders of Texas Instruments established the Graduate Research Center of the Southwest in Dallas. Chartered February 14, 1961, and located at Southern Methodist University, it concentrated on education and research in science and technology. Later, land was purchased in Richardson for the college and it moved in 1967, changing its name to Southwest Center for Advanced Study. Legislation was passed to make the Center part of the University of Texas and the first students entered in September 1969. In the beginning the school served juniors, seniors, and graduate students. It has since become a four-year institution with strong graduate programs.[65]

University of Texas at Brownsville

The University of Texas at Brownsville began as Pan American University-Brownsville in 1973. In 1977 the school became a separate entity governed by the Pan American University regents. In 1989 it became part of the University of Texas System.[66]

University of Texas at El Paso

The University of Texas at El Paso began in 1914 as the Texas School of Mines and Metallurgy under the supervision of the University of Texas Board of Regents. In 1919 it became a branch of the university. As course offerings grew the name changed first in 1949 to Texas Western College and then in 1967 to the University of Texas at El Paso.[67]

University of Texas–Pan American

The University of Texas-Pan American began in 1927 as Edinburg College, a junior college. In 1951 the legislature allowed Hidalgo County to hold a referendum for a four-year university. As a result of a successful election the school became Pan Regional College. The next year the name was changed to Pan American College. In 1971 when the school obtained university status the name was changed to Pan American University. In 1973 a second campus was added at

Brownsville. The university became part of the University of Texas System in 1988 and the name was changed to University of Texas-Pan American.[68]

University of Texas at the Permian Basin
The University of Texas at the Permian Basin in Odessa was authorized by the legislature in 1969 to accept junior, senior, and graduate students as part of an experiment in upper-level education. The institution was restructured in 1991 to accept freshman and sophomore students.[69]

University of Texas at San Antonio
The University of Texas at San Antonio was established June 5, 1969, as a coeducational university, and has grown to be one of the largest public institutions in Texas.[70]

University of Texas at Tyler
Tyler State College was established in 1971 and in 1973 opened with upper-level classes in an unused junior high school. In 1975 it became Texas Eastern University and moved to permanent quarters on 200 acres of land. In 1979 it became part of the University of Texas System.[71]

University of St. Thomas
In 1945, Reverend Christopher E. Byrne, Bishop of Galveston, announced the opening of the University of St. Thomas in Houston under the direction of the Basilian Fathers. Pope Pius XII bestowed Pontifical Blessing on the school in 1946.[72]

Wayland Baptist College
The school began in 1908 in Plainview, as Wayland Technological and Literary Institute. The name was changed to Wayland Baptist College, named for J. H. Wayland who donated land and money in 1908. In 1981 it became Wayland Baptist University.[73]

West Texas A&M University

The college was opened in Canyon in 1910 and was called West Texas State Normal College. In 1923 it became West Texas State Teachers College. In 1963 the legislature changed its name to West Texas State University. On September 1, 1990, the university joined the Texas A&M System and its name was changed to West Texas A&M University.[74]

Wiley College

Wiley College is the oldest black college west of the Mississippi River. It was established in Marshall by the Freedman's Aid Society of the Methodist Episcopal Church in 1873. The college offered regular college courses, some vocational training, and courses below college level until 1922 when it began only offering college courses. In 1907 it received the first Carnegie college library west of the Mississippi.[75]

* * * * *

INSTITUTIONS FROM THE PAST

Add-Ran College

Add-Ran College was started in Thorp Springs in 1873 as Add-Ran Christian College, and was the predecessor to Texas Christian University (see entry below).[76]

Add-Ran Jarvis College

Add-Ran Jarvis College began as Jarvis College in 1897, which was established by Randolph Clark at Thorp Spring. Jarvis College became Add-Ran Jarvis College in 1904. The college closed in 1909. The Church of Christ bought the property to establish Thorp Spring Christian College.[77]

Alma Male and Female Institute

Alma Male and Female Institute was a standard four-year college that was authorized to grant degrees and diplomas. It was established at Hallettsville in 1852 and began as a private institution. It came under the control of the Colorado Baptist Convention when the Southern Baptist Convention sent John V. E. Covey to be its president in 1858. It is unclear if it became a Baptist school, but it did receive support from members of the Baptist church. The college was successful until the Civil War when most of its students left, and the school closed about 1861.[78]

Alta Vista Agricultural College
Founded in March 1878 with eight students, Alta Vista Agricultural College was the forerunner of Prairie View A&M University.[79]

Amarillo College
The college opened in 1896 with four teachers. The leaders in establishing the school were W.C. Twichell and James D. Hardin. The college was not affiliated with any religion. Because it was located in what was at the time a remote and sparsely settled area in a small village, the college struggled to survive and closed in 1910.[80]

Ambassador College
The college was located in Big Sandy and was established by the Worldwide Church of God. It opened in 1964, and because of financial difficulties it closed in 1977.[81]

Andrew Female College
The Methodist Church established Andrew Female College at Huntsville in 1852. The college closed in 1879 after the establishment of Sam Houston Normal Institute at Huntsville made it unnecessary.[82]

Andrew Normal
Founded in 1876, Andrew Normal was the predecessor of Samuel Huston College.[83]

Aranama College
Aranama College was a Presbyterian senior college located at Goliad started in 1854. The town's gift of the old Aranama Mission and

twenty-one acres made the college a possibility. The college was damaged during the Civil War and destroyed by storm in 1886.[84]

Austin Female Academy
The school was opened in 1850 at Austin by G. C. Baggerly. In the beginning it operated as a preparatory school, but in 1851 Baggerly added what he called a "thorough collegiate course." However, there is no record of any degree being awarded and the school closed in 1853.[85]

Austin Female Collegiate Institute
Although it was a private school, it received strong support from the Presbyterian Church. It began in 1852 in Austin and made several unsuccessful efforts to gain legislative funding. Even without that support, the school continued until 1872.[86]

Baylor Female College
The 1845 charter for Baylor University provided for a female department. The female department became Baylor Female College at Independence, at that time the oldest college for women west of the Mississippi River. In 1886, Baylor Female College moved to Belton. In 1934, Baylor Female College became Mary Hardin-Baylor College, after Mary Hardin, a benefactor of the college.[87]

Bay Ridge Christian College
Bay Ridge Christian College was started in Mississippi in 1960; in 1961 it moved to Texas and was located in Kendleton. The school was affiliated with the Church of God whose headquarters is in Anderson, Indiana.[88]

Bay View College
Thomas M. Clark, of the Clark family that founded Add-Ran College, bought property in Portland overlooking Corpus Christi Bay, to establish a private school for girls in 1894. Bay View College was destroyed by a storm and closed in 1917.[89]

Belle Plain College

Belle Plain College was started in 1881 at Belle Plain and had a short life. The town of Belle Plain died when it was bypassed by the Texas and Pacific Railroad. Additionally, severe droughts in 1885–1887 had hurt local cattlemen. Belle Plain College could not survive these conditions and closed in 1888.[90]

Bishop College

Bishop College was founded in 1881 as South-Western Baptist College, a school for black Baptists in Marshall. In 1925, the State Board of Education gave the college senior ranking. In its early years, the school had financial difficulties but, despite setbacks, its religious program drew the attention of prominent religious leaders such as the Rev. Martin Luther King, Jr. and the Rev. Jesse Jackson. In 1957, multiple donations of land and funds prompted the school to make plans to move to Dallas. In 1961, construction of the new campus was completed and the college changed locations. Additional construction continued throughout the 1960s. Beginning in the 1970s, the school faced several problems. A series of financial difficulties caused it to file for bankruptcy in 1987, and it closed in 1988. Its properties passed to Paul Quinn College.[91]

Bosque College and Seminary

Bosque College and Seminary was a non-sectarian school in Bosque (later Bosqueville), about five miles north of Waco. It succeeded Bosque Academy and also Waco Female Seminary, which held their last terms in 1856–1857. The same faculty and nearly the same board members who had been with Waco Female Seminary were involved in establishing the school. It received its charter from the state on February 16, 1858. It was the first coeducational college in McLennan County, even though the male and female departments were a mile apart. The school prospered, and in 1861 it had 400 students. The advent of the Civil War reduced its enrollment, and the school closed in 1865.[92]

Burnetta College

Located in Venus, Burnetta College, which was named for Burnetta Barnes, operated from 1896 until it closed in 1906. It was under the control of the Disciples of Christ. The college built a four-story frame building with $500 from the citizens of Venus and $5,000 from the college's first president, A. D. Leach. The school opened with an enrollment of 250 students in 1896 and ultimately reached an enrollment of 350 students. The school building burned (on an unknown date) and, although it was rebuilt, the school closed in 1906 and the property was given to the Venus public schools.[93]

Buffalo Gap College

Buffalo Gap College, which began in 1881, was founded as a result of the efforts of Rev. A. J. Haynes and Rev. Alpha Young to establish a coeducational higher education institution. The Buffalo Gap and San Saba Presbyteries of the Cumberland Presbyterian Church controlled the college. The college awarded both Bachelor of Arts and Bachelor of Science degrees. The college graduated twelve students in 1898. It was later turned into Buffalo Gap Public School and closed in 1902.[94]

Burleson College

Burleson College, a Baptist institution, opened in Greenville in 1895, with S. J. Anderson as president. It became a junior college in 1899. In 1919, the college had a faculty of twenty-one teachers and a student body of 447. Burleson closed in December 1930.[95]

Butler College

Butler College was founded in 1905 as Texas Baptist Academy in Tyler. It began as a coeducational junior college for blacks. In 1932, the school began receiving aid from the Texas Baptist Convention. Following World War II, the college slowly expanded its course offerings, and by 1951 had become a senior college. It was unable to achieve full four-year accreditation. Enrollment began to decrease in the 1960s, and the college closed in 1972.[96]

Calhoun College
The college began in 1880 in Kinston but did not receive its charter until 1887. It was a private nondenominational college owned by J. L. Clemmons and J. C. Todd. It offered a Bachelor of Arts degree. The exact date of its closing is not clear but appears to have been around 1900.[97]

Carlton College
Charles Carlton, a graduate of Bethany College in West Virginia, founded Carlton College at Kentuckytown in 1865. It was the first college in Texas recognized as a church school of the Christian Church but not financed or controlled by the church. Carlton moved the college to Bonham in 1867. After his death in 1913, the college declined and merged with Carr-Burdette College in Sherman. [98]

Carr-Burdette College
Mrs. O. A. Carr founded Carr-Burdette College in 1894. It was a "typical seminary" and closed because of financial difficulties in 1929.[99]

Centenary College
Centenary College was located at Lampasas. It was founded in 1883 by the Methodist Church. Marchal McIlhaney served as the college's first president. According to the 1888–1889 catalogue, the college had five faculty members and 180 students. It closed in 1897.[100]

Centennial College
Founded in Marshall as an elementary school for blacks, Centennial College failed in 1881. It was a predecessor to Bishop College.[101]

Central College
Central College, chartered in 1883, operated under the control of the Methodist Episcopal Church, South. In 1884, it was purchased by H. P. Eastman, who changed the name to Eastman College

and Conservatory of Music and Art. A fire destroyed the school in 1900.[102]

Central Nazarene College

Central Nazarene College opened in 1911 in Hamlin. The college had various primary, academy, and collegiate departments. Additionally, the school's catalogue refers to a "strong theological course" that required training to read the Bible in the original language. In 1922–23, the college enrolled 122 students and graduated eight. In 1931, it merged with Bethany Peniel College in Bethany, Oklahoma.[103]

Central Plains College and Conservatory of Music

The Holiness Church established this college in 1907. It offered instruction from elementary grades to a bachelor's degree. It was a coeducational institution and emphasized military training for both boys and girls. Its campus was sold to the Methodist Church in 1910 when the school did not develop as had been anticipated. The Methodist Church established a new school named Seth Ward College.[104]

Central Texas College

Founded in 1902 by black Baptists, Central Texas College began as an educational facility offering instruction from first grade through college. In 1907 it became a full-time college, but remained small, with a mostly part-time faculty. By 1931, the school's financial difficulties caused it to close. [105]

Chapel Hill College

Chapel Hill College opened in 1852 in Daingerfield, with land donated to the Cumberland Presbyterian Church. It offered free education for Presbyterian ministers in order to increase enrollment. New buildings were constructed in 1858. Fears of a Union Army invasion in 1860 prompted the school to cease college-level education. Even though the college was financially solvent, it closed in 1869.[106]

Chappell Hill Female College

Chappell Hill Female College in Chappell Hill was originally part of the Chappell Hill Male and Female Institute, founded in 1852. By August 29, 1856, the Methodist Texas Conference decided to split the college between the male and female departments, and Chappell Hill Female College was chartered as a separate school. The college began construction on new buildings in 1872 and was debt free by 1873. Expansion continued through the 1880s, with 112 students enrolled in 1885. During the 1890s, enrollment dropped sharply, and in 1912 the college closed due to low enrollment and financial difficulties.[107]

Childers Classic Institute

Childers Classic Institute began in 1906 and was the predecessor of Abilene Christian University.[108]

Christian College of the Southwest

Originally called Garland Christian College, the school opened in 1952. It changed its name to Christian College of the Southwest in 1963, and by 1970 had become a four-year degree-granting school. In 1971, despite an increase in enrollment, the school closed, and Abilene Christian College acquired its properties.[109]

Clarendon College

The Methodist Texas Conference sponsored Clarendon College in 1898. In 1915 it received an influx of students when Seth Ward College closed. It reached its highest enrollment of 340 students in 1927, the same year a special commission of the Methodist Texas Conference closed the college. Afterwards, Clarendon residents voted to purchase the college plant for a municipal junior college.[110]

Clebarro College

In 1909, the Church of Christ in Cleburne established Clebarro College, named for its founders Allen Bokker Barret and Charles H. Robertson. The school offered college courses in addition to elementary and secondary education. By 1911, the course work expanded to include sociology, political science, and philosophy. The school closed in 1919.[111]

Clifton College

Clifton College was organized on May 6, 1896, as the Lutheran College of Clifton. Its charter was approved on May 26, 1896, and the first building was dedicated October 14 that same year. The school was financially supported by the Norwegian Lutheran Churches of America and opened as Clifton High School on October 28, 1897. The Missouri Synod of German Lutherans helped to support the college from 1902 to 1914. In 1922, the school began offering courses at the junior college level, and in 1954, it merged with Texas Lutheran College in Seguin.[112]

Cold Springs Female Institute

The Institute, also known as Cold Springs Female Academy, was located at Cold Springs in Polk County (now San Jacinto County), and was incorporated on February 7, 1853. It opened under the leadership of Daniel Webster Steele in 1854. The act of incorporation provided the school would be nonsectarian, but by 1858 the Tyron Baptist Association was providing support for the school, which closed because of a lack of students in 1861.[113]

Colegio Jacinto Treviño

Founded in 1969 in Mercedes by the Mexican American Youth Organization, Colegio Jacinto Treviño was established to offer higher education to Hispanics. Poor administration and conflicts over enrollment caused the school to close by mid-1979.[114]

Colorado College

Colorado College, established in 1857, is reputedly the first Lutheran college established in Texas. It was established in Columbus under the control of a board of twenty-five trustees, with a majority of trustees required to be members of the Evangelical Lutheran Church. Enrollment reached a high of 300 students. The college was last reported as operating in 1886.[115]

Columbia College
The town of Van Alstyne established Columbia College in 1889, and it grew to include 578 students by 1894. A fire destroyed the main building in the late 1890s and the school never recovered.[116]

Concrete College
J. V. E. Covey founded Concrete College in 1865 at Concrete in DeWitt County. The college was a coeducational institution where students were classified by ability and merit. It failed because the railroad was built several miles away from Concrete in 1880. In 1881, Covey founded McMullen College in Tilden, but it failed shortly thereafter due to competition from public institutions.[117]

Coronal Institute
Coronal Institute was founded by O. N. Hollingsworth and was a "pioneer" private institution in Southwest Texas. Its first catalogue, published in 1869, shows the school offered preparatory and college courses. Coronal Institute aspired to confer bachelor of arts, bachelor of laws, and master of arts degrees. However in 1871, Hollingsworth sold the school to R. H. Belvin, who in turn sold it to the Methodist Church in 1876. Under the control of the Methodist Church, the Institute awarded 450 degrees. In 1913, it had its largest graduating class of twenty-six. When the Institute closed in 1918 its grounds and buildings were sold to the city schools of San Marcos.[118]

Cumberland College
The Texas Synod of the Cumberland Presbyterian Church established Cumberland College at Leonard, in Fannin County, in 1911. The college opened with sixty-three students. However, the synod

could not afford to maintain the college and its property was sold to settle the synod's debt in 1918.[119]

Daniel Baker College

Daniel Baker College was founded in Brownwood under the Presbyterian Church in 1889 and became part of a merger with Southwestern University in 1946. In 1950, the college became an Episcopal college in the Episcopal Diocese of Dallas and merged with Howard Payne College in Brownwood in 1953.[120]

Decatur Baptist College

Northwest Texas Baptist College at Decatur opened in 1892 and closed shortly thereafter. The college was auctioned and sold to the Baptist General Convention of Texas in 1897. The Convention renamed the college Decatur Baptist College and opened it in 1898. In 1965, the college moved to Dallas and was re-named Dallas Baptist College.[121]

Dominican College

The college was founded in Houston by the Catholic Congregation of the Sacred Heart as an extension of its religious training program. Originally built as a junior college, the school became a senior college in 1948. Despite having an internationally recognized nursing program, the college closed in 1975.[122]

East Texas Normal College

East Texas Normal College was founded by W. L. Mayo in 1889 in the town of Cooper. The college was moved to Commerce in 1894. Under Mayo's leadership, the school developed into "one of the largest private colleges in the South." It enrolled 88 students in 1894–1895, 324 students in 1900–1901, and 2,400 in 1916–1917. The 1916–1917 school year was the college's last year as a private institute. The state took over the college in 1917 and changed its name to East Texas State Normal College.[123]

East Texas State University

In 1917 when the state took over East Texas Normal College it renamed it East Texas State Normal College and in 1923 "Normal" was replaced with "Teachers." In 1957 the school became East Texas State College to reflect its broader offerings and in 1962 it became a university as it began offering its first doctoral program. In 1996 the school became Texas A&M at Commerce.[124]

Eastern Texas Female College

Originally, Eastern Texas Female College was the female department of Tyler University. The college, founded in 1853, was a Baptist female seminary serving Smith County residents. Financial struggles and a fire in 1862 caused the board of regents to lease the remaining property to J. T. Hand, the school's president, who renamed the school Charnwood Institute.[125]

Emerson College

Established at Campbell in 1903, Emerson College was a coeducational, four-year college. A severe drought in 1904 and 1905 decreased the revenue from tuition and fees. Unable to pay its debts and facing competition from the public college nearby, East Texas Normal College, Emerson closed its doors in 1906.[126]

Evangelical Lutheran College (Rutersville)

This was the first of two colleges by the same name. It was founded in 1870 at Rutersville, in Fayette County. The college met with small success, and in 1878 it closed.[127]

Evangelical Lutheran College (Brenham)

The second Evangelical Lutheran College was established in Brenham in 1891, and was the predecessor to Texas Lutheran College.[128]

Fairfield Female College

In 1859, the town leaders of Fairfield established Fairfield Female College to offer education to local women. In 1861, the school's president, Henry L. Graves, bought the property and continued operating the school until it closed in 1889.[129]

Fort Worth University
Fort Worth University started as Texas Wesleyan College in 1881. An amended charter in 1889 changed it to Fort Worth University, controlled by the Northern Methodist Church. In 1897, Fort Worth University enrolled 860 students and employed 50 faculty members. From 1887 to 1900, 120 students graduated from the university. Fort Worth University was forced to close in 1911 after it attempted to establish schools of law and medicine and graduate courses, which was not within its financial ability. In 1911 it became part of the Methodist Episcopal University at Oklahoma City.[130]

Galveston University
This college was one of the few established by the Republic of Texas. Although its charter stated that it was to be a nondenominational school, it clearly was under the control of the Presbyterian Church. The school's charter was granted on January 20, 1841, although it had begun operation in 1840. It closed in 1844 due to lack of support.[131]

Goliad College
Goliad College received its charter on February 16, 1852, and was authorized to grant diplomas and degrees. It was unique in that it granted both Bachelor of Arts and mistress of arts degrees. It appears to have closed around 1884.[132]

Gonzales College
Gonzales College was chartered on February 16, 1852, as a private nondenominational college. The enrollment was 80 percent preparatory and 20 percent college level. In 1874 the college closed and the property was sold to the city of Gonzales.[133]

Goodnight College
Goodnight College was founded by Charles and Mary Dyer Goodnight and the school's president, Marshall McIlhaney; it opened in 1898. The Goodnights envisioned a coeducational industrial institute where students could work to pay part of their expenses. They offered to give the school to the Methodists, who declined, but the Baptists accepted. The school prospered and by 1906 had 175 students. A summer school and a summer Normal school were started, which were the first of their kind in the Panhandle area. The competition from West Texas Normal School and from Clarendon College, coupled with a lack of financial support, caused the college to close in 1917.[134]

Granbury College
Granbury College was opened by the Methodist Episcopal Church, South. It offered courses from elementary to college level. Only a small number of degrees were awarded even though the enrollment reached 300 students. Competition from other colleges caused the school to close in 1889. The property was sold to Weatherford College, which is considered by some to be a continuation of Granbury College.[135]

Grayson College
Grayson College opened in Whitewright in 1886 under the direction of H. L. Piner and James F. Anderson. The college's main building was destroyed by fire in 1904. According to its catalogues, the college conferred 224 degrees, three of which were master's degrees. The college was also affiliated with the University of Texas. In 1888, the college enrolled 368 students. Enrollment grew to 694 in 1904 but dropped to 274 in 1907. Though the college received state school funds to defray maintenance costs for its free primary and elementary departments, the college closed. The facility grounds and equipment were sold to Whitewright for Whitewright High School in 1918.[136]

Guadalupe College

Founded in 1884 and chartered in 1888, Guadalupe College focused on training teachers and ministers and fostering academic awareness among black Texans. Financial support for the college came from local black community members, in particular Baptists. Beginning in 1901, the school grew under president David Abner, Jr., but in 1906, when Abner resigned, the school began to face difficulties. Financial difficulties and tensions between the administration and George W. Brackenridge, the school's chief financial backer, caused the school's reputation to decline. By the 1920s, however, the school had regained some of its former status, and in 1929 it was officially designated a senior college. The Great Depression hit the school hard, and in 1931 its senior college status was downgraded to a junior college. A fire destroyed the main building in 1936, and efforts to revive the school failed.[137]

Gulf-Coast Bible College

The college was established as South Texas Bible Institute in 1953. It was renamed Gulf-Coast Bible College in 1955. It was located in the Heights area of Houston. In 1984 the college moved to Oklahoma and changed its name to Mid-America Bible College.[138]

Hearne Academy

Founded in 1881 as a school for blacks, Hearne Academy was located just outside the town of Hearne. In 1909, it was transferred to Fort Worth and renamed Fort Worth Industrial and Mechanical College. The school continued to offer important vocational courses to black Texans until it closed due to financial difficulties in 1929.[139]

Henry College

Henry T. Bridges and Henry Easton established Henry College in Campbell in 1892. A rivalry between Bridges and William L. Mayo, president of East Texas Normal College, led to a public condemnation of Bridges by Mayo. This in turn led to both of their arrests in

1896 after a fight broke out between them when Bridges tried to force Mayo to issue an apology. A fire in 1871 burned down the administration building, and the school never recovered financially. It closed in 1901, and in 1904 Emerson College took its place.[140]

Hereford Christian College
Hereford Christian College was established in 1902 with an initial enrollment of 250 students. However, by 1904 control of the school was transferred to the Disciples of Christ, for financial reasons. The following year, it was renamed Panhandle Christian College, but changed it back in 1909. The college struggled with finances, and in 1912 it closed.[141]

Hermann's University
Hermann's University was chartered as a stock company in 1844 with Lutheran trustees, and a European "scheme of organization" that offered four faculties of theology, law, medicine, and philosophy. Despite stock in the university being reduced from $50 to $15 and the granting of a league of land in Gillespie County by the Congress of the Republic of Texas, the university never opened.[142]

Holding Institute
The Methodist Church founded Holding Institute at Laredo in 1880 for the purpose of educating Mexican children. Of the 11,000 students who attended the school, more than 35 percent were from Mexico. It closed because of financial difficulties in May of 1983.[143]

Houston College for Negroes
Houston College for Negroes was established in 1934 as an upper-division branch of the Houston Colored Junior College, which had been opened in 1927 as a municipal college. Although they were part of the same institution they continued to operate as separate entities until both closed in 1947. At that time, it was taken over by the state to use as the newly authorized Texas State University for Negroes.

For a time the upper level operated as a branch of the University of Houston.[144]

Houston International College

Founded as Hispanic International University in 1970, the school sought to provide education for the city's Hispanic community. In 1974, the school gained the authority to grant bachelor of arts and bachelor of science degrees. It changed its name to Houston International University in 1983 and began to change its focus from Hispanics to working-class adults, to encourage higher enrollment and graduation rates. It closed in 1990 due to financial difficulties.[145]

Juarez-Lincoln University

One of several Hispanic-oriented colleges founded in the early 1970s, Juarez-Lincoln was established in 1971 following a split with Jacinto Treviño College over political differences within the administration. In 1972, the school moved to Austin, and in 1975 it began conferring Bachelor of Arts degrees. The school closed in 1979 after one of its sponsors, Antioch University of Ohio, withdrew its support.[146]

Kidd-Key College

Kidd-Key College was opened in 1878 and was a fine arts college that grew out of North Texas Female College and Kidd-Key Conservatory of Music. When the Methodist Church withdrew support for the college in 1933, Kidd-Key was forced to close two years later.[147]

Larissa College

Larissa College was founded by Cumberland Presbyterians in 1848. Financial difficulties caused a decline in enrollment and a temporary suspension of the female department in 1857. By 1860, the school had recovered, but the outbreak of the Civil War caused it to close. In 1886, the school reopened, but the Brazos Synod withdrew its support in favor of Trinity University. Shortly thereafter, Larissa College closed permanently in 1867.[148]

Liberty Normal and Business College

The residents of Liberty Hill established Liberty Normal and Business College in 1885. The school grew during the 1890s, but at the turn of the century it began to decline. In 1910, the school was closed and its building was passed to the public school system.[149]

Lockney Christian College

J. D. Burleson founded Lockney Christian College at Lockney, under the control of the Church of Christ in 1894. The school offered only elementary and high school courses for its first ten years. When Professor James L. German assumed the presidency in 1906, he raised funds for the construction of a college building and the establishment of four-year college courses. The college's enrollment peaked at 200 students before it began to decline. Lockney Christian College permanently closed in 1918 at the end of World War I.[150]

Mansfield Male and Female College

Mansfield was founded in 1870 by John C. Collier. Despite widespread recognition and a well-regarded faculty, the college closed in 1887.[151]

Marvin College

Marvin College was established in Waxahachie in 1868 by the Northwest Texas Conference of the Methodist Episcopal Church. The school quickly experienced financial troubles and was closed in 1878.[152]

Mary Allen College

Mary Allen College, a junior college in Crockett, began in 1871 as Crockett Presbyterian Church Colored Sabbath School. From 1875 to 1885, the school was known as Moffatt Parochial School and from 1885 to 1933 as Mary Allen Seminary. It closed in 1972.[153]

Mary Nash College

Jesse G. and Mary Louise Nash, with sponsorship from the Baptist Church, founded Mary Nash College in Sherman in 1877. Officially known as Sherman Female Institute, the college was well known for its music program. The school closed in 1901 and the property was sold to Kidd-Key College.[154]

McKenzie College

McKenzie College was founded in 1841 near Clarksville by John Witherspoon Pettigrew McKenzie, an itinerant Methodist preacher and a graduate of the University of Georgia. The college offered a standard four-year college course and had a female department. Enrollment reached 300 by 1854. Before the Civil War, McKenzie had sixty graduates, the highest number of graduates of any higher education institution in Texas. In 1860, McKenzie College awarded both bachelor's and master's degrees. The college did not survive long after the Civil War and closed in 1868.[155]

Meridian Junior College

Located in Meridian in Bosque County, the school originated as Meridian Training School and began in 1907 under the leadership of a Methodist pastor who envisioned a school to train ministers and their children. In 1920 the school achieved Class A Junior College Status and its name was changed to Meridian Junior College. It closed in 1917.[156]

Methodist Female College

Methodist Female College was founded in Waco in 1857. It is unclear if the college ever operated.[157]

Midland Christian College

Midland Christian College was established in 1909 to meet the need for a college in Midland. R. L. Marquis served as the college's first president and later as president at North Texas State College at

Denton. Midland Christian College closed in 1921 due to a combination of insufficient enrollment and high operating expenses.[158]

Mineral Wells College
Mineral Wells College was established in 1891 by John W. McCracken.
It was a coeducational institution granting four-year degrees, and it
closed in 1900.[159]

Montgomery Institute
R. W. Elliott, bishop of the Episcopal Diocese of West Texas, opened
the Montgomery Institute in Seguin in 1878. The curriculum was
strong and even offered Master of Arts degrees. Programs were
offered in Bible and Dictionary and each student was required to
learn a page from each every day. In 1892 the school was forced
to close because of financial difficulties. Upon closing it was recommended to students that they attend St. Mary's Hall in San Antonio,
so it appears that Montgomery Institute was a female college.[160]

Mound Prairie Institute
J. R. Malone founded Mound Prairie Institute, which was chartered
in 1854 and opened in 1855. It was eight and one-half miles east of
Palestine. The institute admitted women in 1857 and reached a peak
enrollment of 100 in 1859. It closed in 1860.[161]

Nacogdoches University
One of the first nonsectarian schools in Texas, Nacogdoches
University was founded in 1845. The school served as a hospital
and soldiers' quarters during the Civil War. After its first charter
expired, it came under the control of the Catholic Church. During
the 1870s and 1880s, the school changed hands several more
times—to Milam Lodge No. 2 in 1873 and Kaechi College in 1887.
In 1895 the second charter expired and, due to financial troubles,
the property came under the control of the Nacogdoches Independent School District.[162]

Nazarene Central Plains College

Nazarene Central Plains College was located in Hamlin; it opened in 1911. Its catalogue mentions a "strong theological course" which required sufficient academic training to read the Bible in the original language. The college was closed when it was merged with Bethany Peniel College in Bethany, Oklahoma, in 1931.[163]

North Texas Baptist College

When it opened in 1891, North Texas Baptist College offered courses at the elementary, secondary, and college levels. It closed in 1897 due to competition from other North Texas schools.[164]

Our Lady of Victory College

Our Lady of Victory College opened in Fort Worth in 1910, and was chartered by the state of Texas and authorized to confer degrees in 1911. The college was dedicated to training young women who had already completed high school. It was merged with the University of Dallas in 1958.[165]

Paine Female Institute

Paine Female Institute, which opened its doors in 1856, was founded by the citizens of Goliad with the aid of the Methodist Church. By 1874 the school had an enrollment of 130 students. Conflicts between the Methodist Church and the school's administration led to the selling of the school to Goliad High School in 1885.[166]

Pan-Handle Christian College

Pan-Handle Christian College began as Hereford College and Industrial School at Hereford in 1902, with Randolph Clark serving as the school's first president. In 1905, the school was known as Pan-Handle Christian College. From 1909 to 1911, the college was again known as Hereford College. It closed in 1911, and its property went to the Hereford public schools.[167]

Parker Institute

Parker Institute began as a private school in 1881 and was operated by a Professor Bales and his wife. It was located at the town of Whitt in Parker County. In 1884 the Institute was chartered by the Whitt Methodist Church. In spite of its small size the school had some distinguished graduates, including Jefferson Davis Sandefer, who later was president of Hardin-Simmons University, and Charles S. Potts, who later was dean of the law school at Southern Methodist University. It closed because of the increased number of colleges in close proximity, in 1893.[168]

Peniel College

Peniel College opened in 1899 as Texas Holiness University. Its sponsor was the local Nazarene Church, and in 1911 the college received the endorsement of the Pentecostal Church of the Nazarene national office. In 1917 the name was changed to Peniel College. The school put a strong emphasis on religion and enforced strict rules governing social conduct. It was successful and reached an enrollment of 351 in 1915. The high cost of tuition finally caused the school to close in 1920 and it was consolidated with Oklahoma Holiness College.[169]

Pennington College

Pennington College opened in 1866 at Pennington with a state charter and operated as a private college for several years. It began with fifty students. It was sold to the Neches River Baptist Association in 1874. Enrollment increased to more than one hundred by 1873 but then decreased until, in 1882, the school property was transferred to the public schools by the association.[170]

Randolph College (Lancaster)

Randolph College was established by Randolph Clark (see also Pan-Handle Christian College) and his son-in-law in Lancaster in 1899. They lacked the students and money to maintain the college, and it closed in 1902.[171]

Randolph College (Cisco)

The oil boom in Cisco spurred the local Christian Church to open Cisco Christian College in 1922. The name of the college was changed to Randolph College in 1924. It closed in 1937.[172]

Rusk Baptist College

Rusk Baptist College was known by several names after it opened in 1895. After a series of disputes with Baylor University and the Baptist Convention, the college was allowed to become a member of the Baptist General Convention of Texas. Financial difficulties and declining enrollment caused the school to close in 1928.[173]

Rutersville College

Rutersville College, which was active from 1840 to 1856, was once located in Rutersville, northeast of La Grange in Fayette County. It had been the dream of Martin Ruter, a linguist and author nicknamed the "Apostle of Methodism in Texas," who was the first person to initiate the founding of a denominational college in Texas. In 1837 he wrote a charter for a school he intended to call Bastrop College, but he died the following year. Soon after, a group of ten other Methodists took up the push for a charter and in 1840 it was approved by the legislature. The Methodist Church appointed a president and renamed the school Rutersville College. The town of Rutersville donated land and the college opened in 1840 with sixty-three students. Over its history, Rutersville College enrolled more than 800 students, and it was the first Texas college to publish a catalogue. In 1856, Rutersville College became a private school known as Texas Monumental and Military Institute.[174]

Sabinal Christian College

Sabinal Christian College enrolled 139 students in 1907—its first year of operation. It had five presidents during its ten-year existence, and it closed in 1917.[175]

Sabine Baptist College

Sabine Baptist College was founded in Milam in 1858 with aid from the Central Baptist Association. The college closed during the Civil War, but reopened in 1868 with the help of the Bethlehem, Mount Zion, New Hope, and Sabine Baptist Associations. The school closed permanently in 1870 due to financial difficulties.[176]

Sabine Valley University

Sabine Valley University opened in 1875 in Hemphill after the Baptists in the Mount Zion Association wanted a college to teach Christian principles and conducted a study that recommended a college in the area. The school was located in Hemphill because the city offered to donate the facilities of a private school operating there. Over the years, other Baptist associations offered support, which suggested the school would have a bright future. However, the competition from public colleges caused the school to close in 1881.[177]

Salado College

Salado College enrolled sixty students in its opening year of 1860, 180 students in 1862, 126 students in 1864, and 289 students in 1866. A delegation of Salado citizens failed to secure Salado as the location for a state college in 1874, and Salado declined to be the location when the Santa Fe and MK&T Railroad was built north and east of the town. In 1919, stockholders of Salado College donated the former grounds to the free Texas public school system.[178]

Samuel Huston College

The predecessor of Samuel Huston College was Andrew Normal College, which opened in Dallas in 1876. Failing to gain support there, Methodist leaders moved it to Austin. In 1900 the Methodist Episcopal conference established Samuel Huston College, a coeducational facility serving blacks in Austin. The school, named after one of the school's donors, opened with an enrollment of eighty students. The school continued to grow and by 1906 had an enrollment of 517. The college offered a wide range of subjects and by 1927 the state recognized it as a Class A senior college. In 1952 it merged with Tillotson College to become Huston-Tillotson College.[179]

San Antonio Female College

J. E. Harrison, backed by the West Texas Conference of the Methodist Episcopal Church, established the San Antonio Female College on September 6, 1894. By 1898 the school received its charter. In 1912 the college began to offer Bachelor of Arts degrees in literature and music. The University of Texas recognized the school as a junior college in 1916. In 1918 the college changed its name to Westmoreland College and in 1937 changed it again to the University of San Antonio. In 1942 the University of San Antonio and Trinity University merged.[180]

San Saba Masonic College

San Saba Masonic College was established in 1863. By 1879 the Methodist Episcopal Church took control of the school and in 1885 renamed it San Saba College. In 1886 the college closed only to reopen briefly in the 1890s.[181]

Savoy Male and Female College

R. R. Halsell organized Savoy Male and Female College when he came to Texas from Missouri, in 1876. A charter for the college was granted in 1879. In 1887–1888, the college enrolled 301 students. From 1885–1886, the Commissioner of Indian Affairs in the Indian Territory subsidized boarding and schooling of Indian students at Savoy Male and Female College, forty-four of whom attended at one time. The institution claimed to be the "first collegiate institute chartered in Texas in which young men and women shared academic privileges without discrimination." The college closed when its plant burned in 1890.[182]

School of Mines and Metallurgy

This school was started in 1913 as a "school of miners and metallurgy" for the state of Texas. It opened in 1914 under the supervision of the University of Texas Board of Regents. In 1919 the legislature made the school a branch of the University of Texas and changed its name to Texas School of Mines. In 1967 it was moved into the University of Texas at El Paso.[183]

Seth Ward College
The Methodist Church opened Seth Ward College in 1910 near Plainview when it purchased buildings occupied by Central Plains College and Conservatory of Music (see above). The school was named Seth Ward College in honor of a bishop of the church. It began operation as a junior college. Sometime after 1915 the buildings burned; school records were transferred to Clarendon College (see entry) and Seth Ward College closed in 1916. It was, however, a predecessor to McMurry College (see entry), and eventually the alumni of Seth Ward College were considered alumni of McMurry College in Abilene.[184]

Seven Points College
Opening in 1888, Seven Points College was established in Westminster with help from local citizens. In 1895 the school changed its name to Westminster College and received a charter as a four-year college. The college moved to Tehuacana in 1902, but the property remained in use as a preparatory school until 1916, when it closed.[185]

Simmons College
Simmons College was started in Abilene and was chartered in 1891. It later became Hardin-Simmons University.[186]

Soule University
After Rutersville College failed in 1840, a convention of delegates from the Texas Conference of the Methodist Church established Soule University in 1855 in Chappell Hill. It received its charter in 1856 and began offering college courses. University president H. S. Thrall was quoted as saying: "at the breaking of the Civil War, Soule University was the best endowed, best manned, and most liberally patronized

institution of higher grade in Texas." The Civil War caused the school to close in 1861, but by 1867 it had reopened. However, enrollment was curtailed by an outbreak of yellow fever. Despite being debt free by 1873, the school struggled with its finances. The area never recovered from the war and the yellow fever outbreak; enrollment continued to drop and the school closed in 1888.[187]

South Texas Baptist College
Founded in Waller in 1898 by the South Texas Baptist Educational Conference, South Texas Baptist College was intended to provide Baptist education to local residents after Baylor moved to Waco. In 1900 the Galveston hurricane damaged the school's one building, which prompted the school to close.[188]

Southern Bible College
Worden McDonald opened Southern Bible College in 1958 in Houston. It was established at the suggestion of the East Texas District of the Pentecostal Church of God of America because the denomination needed a bible college. The school was owned and operated by the Pentecostal Church to provide programs in minister training and theology. By 1968 the college was a recognized member of the Accrediting Association of Bible Colleges, but it closed in the early 1980s because of financial difficulties.[189]

Southland University
Southland University was founded in 1901 in Denton because of concerns that the newly established North Texas State Normal College would only attract students interested in teaching. Originally called John B. Denton College, the school saw enrollment decline during its first three years of operation. In 1904 the Church of Christ took control of the school and renamed it Southwestern Christian College, until 1908 when it was re-chartered as a university. The school closed its doors in 1909 because of conflicts between the administration and the faculty.[190]

Southwestern Christian College

Southwestern Christian College was established in 1904 on the former property of John B. Denton College at Denton. During A. G. Freed's presidency, the college grew rapidly and reached a peak enrollment of 300 students. After Freed resigned, A. B. Barrett and C. H. Robertson initiated an expansion program to convert the college into Southland College under their leadership. The program failed and the college closed in 1909. The city of Denton bought the college's property.[191]

Stamford College

Stamford College, originally called Stamford Collegiate Institute and located in Stamford, was opened in September 1907 with an enrollment of 236 students and a faculty of 13. Growth continued and the school was renamed Stamford College. It suffered from high debt and had to be supported by the Northwest Texas Methodist Conference. Enrollment stayed between two hundred and three hundred students until 1917. World War I and a drought caused enrollment to decline, and in 1918 after a fire the school closed. Its properties passed to Clarendon College.[192]

St. Basil's College

St. Basil's College was founded in 1899 by the Basilian Fathers in Waco. The opening enrollment was sixty students. The main purpose of the school was college preparation, to which were added business courses, Romance languages, and a small amount of music. The library contained 3,000 volumes. By 1915 the enrollment had declined and the institution was taken over by the Sisters of St. Mary of Namur and soon closed.[193]

St. Mary's Hall

St. Mary's Hall was "the pioneer Protestant College in San Antonio" when it was founded in 1860. It closed in 1866 and reopened in 1879 as a secondary school.[194]

St. Mary's College

Bishop Alexander Charles Garrett of the Protestant Episcopal Church of Dallas promoted the establishment of St. Mary's College, a women's senior college. St. Mary's College opened in 1889 with twenty-six students. By 1903, the college had a faculty of twenty-seven but was forced to close because of financial troubles in 1929.[195]

St. Mary's Institute

Founded in 1852 in San Antonio, it later merged with St. Mary's University.[196]

St. Philip's College

St. Philip's College was started by the Episcopal Church in San Antonio in 1898 and was one of only four black colleges begun by the church. It later was under the control of the American Church Institute for Negroes. It was unique because it was not a liberal arts college but emphasized vocational courses. Today it operates as a junior college.[197]

Texas Baptist College

Texas Baptist College was established by the Baptist Missionary Association of Texas in 1904. It was located in Dallas and offered a bachelor's degree alongside a college preparatory course. Increased debt caused the school to close in 1912.[198]

Texas College

Texas College was established in 1894 by the Colored Methodist Episcopal Church in Tyler. It received junior college status in 1924, and four-year accreditation in 1932. Texas College focused its attention on low-income families, offering degrees in liberal arts, home economics, and a variety of sciences.[199]

Texas Holiness University

Texas Holiness University was established in Greenville in 1899 and enrolled seventy students the first year. The university offered a four-year preparatory course, a four-year collegiate course, and courses in music, art, and voice. In 1911, it was adopted as a church university by the Pentecostal Church of the Nazarene, and the Church called it Peniel University. In 1917, the name was changed to Peniel College. Peniel College reached its highest enrollment in 1915–1916 with 351 students. Peniel College consolidated with the Oklahoma Holiness University in 1920.[200]

Texas Lutheran College

Texas Lutheran College began as Evangelical Lutheran College in 1891 in Brenham, but it did not offer college work. It later moved to Seguin when the residents of that community made a generous financial offer to get the school to move. The school opened there as an academy in 1912. It operated as an academy and a pre-theological institute from 1912–1928. It became a junior college in 1928, and a senior college in 1948. The American Lutheran Church then decided to make Texas Lutheran College its senior college in the Southwest. The Augustana Lutheran Church, Evangelical Lutheran Church, and the United Lutheran Church in America all cooperated with the American Lutheran Church to maintain and govern Texas Lutheran College. In 1929, Texas Lutheran merged with Trinity College, a junior college established at Round Rock by the Augustana Synod in 1905. In 1948 Texas Lutheran added two upper levels and became a four-year college.[201]

Texas Presbyterian College

In 1901, a board of trustees appointed by the Presbyterian Synod of Texas accepted ten acres of land and $25,000 from the town of Milford for the establishment of a college for girls. In 1902, the college opened under the presidency of Henry C. Evans with an enrollment of fifty-five students. It experienced its highest enrollment in 1914–1915 with 226 students. In 1929, the Commission on Consolidation closed the college, returned endowments, and transferred the college's equipment and the Henry C. Evans Memorial Library to Austin College at Sherman.[202]

Texas Presbyterian University

Texas Presbyterian University was chartered in 1896 but failed to open in spite of a donation of one hundred acres of land in Highland Park given by J. S. Armstrong in 1907.[203]

Texas Western College

The Texas legislature created the State School of Mines and Metallurgy in 1913 and placed it under the control of the University of Texas Board of Regents. The school was located on the reservation of the El Paso Military Institute and opened in 1914. In 1919, the legislature made the school a branch of the University of Texas. The school's program was expanded to include liberal arts courses in 1927. The college did not confer a Bachelor of Arts degree until 1931. In 1949, the Texas legislature changed the school's name to Texas Western College of the University of Texas. In 1931–1932, the school had an enrollment of 753 students and in 1945–1946 it was 1,329.[204]

Thorp Spring Christian College

Thorp Spring Christian College went through several iterations in the late nineteenth and early twentieth centuries. It began as Thorp College in 1871 but by 1873 became Add-Ran Male and Female College. When the college moved to Waco in 1895, Randolph Clark and R. F. Holloway did not move with it. In 1897 Randolph Clark opened Jarvis Institute (Jarvis College) in Thorp Springs. In 1909 the college closed and its property was sold to the Church of Christ to establish Thorp Spring Christian College.

The school enrollment peaked in 1916 with 300 students. Between 1917 and 1921 competition from the larger colleges sparked interest in moving the college to a larger city. These initial attempts to move the college were stopped, but in 1928 Thorp Spring Christian College moved to Terrell and became Texas Christian College. In 1931 the college closed to build better facilities. Construction was never finished, and in 1937 the property was transferred to the city of Terrell.[205]

Tyler University
G. G. Baggerly, a pastor in Tyler, led the movement to establish Tyler University. The school was chartered in 1854. It experienced a decline in enrollment after the male department's main building was destroyed by a fire in 1857. Even though the female department remained intact and continued to operate as Eastern Texas Female College, it did not survive the beginning of the Civil War and closed in 1861.[206]

University of Corpus Christi
The Baptist Church in South Texas had been dissatisfied with the lack of colleges in their region since Baylor University relocated to Waco in 1882 and Baylor Female College to Belton in 1886. The city of Corpus Christi invited the Baptist General Convention of Texas to locate the Arts and Technological College in Corpus Christi in 1947, the same year the board of trustees changed the name to the University of Corpus Christi. The university was sold to Texas A&M University and became part of the Texas A&M University System in 1973.[207]

University of Eastern Texas
Founded by the unification of the University of San Augustine and Wesleyan College, the University of Eastern Texas was founded in 1847 in San Augustine by Oran M. Roberts. The school closed in 1851.[208]

University of Plano
The University of Plano was founded in 1964 and originally featured an academy offering education to students with learning disabilities. The school expanded in the 1960s, but by 1976 financial difficulties—partially due to using school funds to participate in land speculation, but also because of low enrollment numbers and competition from public colleges—caused the school to close.[209]

University of San Augustine

The Congress of the Republic of Texas granted its first charter to the University of San Augustine in 1837. Fallout from intense sectarian rivalry between the University of San Augustine and Wesleyan College forced both colleges to close early. In 1847 there was an effort to save both schools by merging them with a new entity called University of Eastern Texas. By that time it was too late to save the colleges and the University of Eastern Texas closed in 1851.[210]

University of San Antonio

In 1888 George W. Brackenridge successfully secured a charter for the University of San Antonio, under the control of the Methodist Church, but no action was taken at that time. Instead, J. E. Harrison opened San Antonio Female College (see above) in 1894 on land the West End Town Company donated to the Methodist Church for a women's college. In 1918, San Antonio Female College's name was changed to Westmoreland College, and then to the University of San Antonio so as to conform to the original 1888 charter. The University of San Antonio was transferred to the Trinity University Board of Trustees in 1942.[211]

Waco Classical School

Waco Classical School began in 1856, and later became Waco University.[212]

Waco Female College

Waco Female College was a combination of Waco Female Seminary and Waco Female Academy. The college was chartered in 1860 and was under the supervision of the Methodist Church even though it was nonsectarian. The college closed in 1895 and its properties were purchased by Add-Ran Christian University.[213]

Waco University

Waco University, originally named Trinity River High School, was founded in 1856 by the Trinity River Baptist Association. The Waco

Baptist Association changed the school's name to Waco Classical School in 1860 when they purchased the property. Its growth was slowed by the Civil War. In 1866 it began admitting women. The university was transferred to the Baptist General Association in 1881 and merged with Baylor University in 1886.[214]

Wayland Technological and Literary Institute
Wayland Technological and Literary Institute began in 1908, and was the predecessor of Wayland Baptist College.[215]

Wesley College
Wesley College was founded in Terrell in 1905 as North Texas University School. It became Wesley College in 1909, and in 1912 it was moved to Greenville. Lacking support, Wesley College was forced to close in 1938. All of the college's records and student credits were turned over to Southern Methodist University.[216]

Wesleyan College
Methodist interest in locating a college in San Augustine led to the establishment of Wesleyan College there in 1842. Patronage of Wesleyan College declined after sectarian rivalry between it and the University of San Augustine led to the assassination of James Russell, who was president of the University of San Augustine. Russell's killer never came to trial. The college's board of trustees consolidated it with the University of San Augustine, and that consolidated institution became the University of Eastern Texas, which closed in 1851.[217]

Westminster College
Reverend J. M. Harding, with the help of Seven Points, started the Seven Points College, later renamed Westminster College in 1888. The school was sold to I. P. Rosser in 1893 who sold it to the Methodist Protestant Church, which renamed it. In 1895 the school was chartered as a Methodist school for training ministers.

By 1902 it moved to Tehuacana where it became associated with the Southwestern University. In 1950 the school closed and its property was purchased by the Congregational Methodist Church.[218]

William Carey College

William Carey College was established in 1886 in Independence after Baylor moved to Waco. In 1889 the school's president, R. E. Binford, changed its name to Binford University, but later he was forced to sell the main building to pay off debts.[219]

NOTES

1. Donald W. Whisenhunt, *The Encyclopedia of Texas Colleges and Universities* (Austin TX: Eakin Press, 1986), 50.

2. Whisenhunt, *The Encyclopedia of Texas Colleges and Universities*, 6.

3. Sangeeta Singg, "ANGELO STATE UNIVERSITY," *Handbook of Texas Online* (http://tshaonline. org/handbook/online/articles/kca07) published by the Texas State Historical Association.

4. Brian Hart, "ARLINGTON BAPTIST COLLEGE," *Handbook of Texas Online*, (http:// tshaonline.org/handbook/online/articles/kbach), accessed September 30, 2014. Published by the Texas State Historical Association.

5. Whisenhunt, *The Encyclopedia of Texas Colleges and Universities*, 115.

6. C. E. Evans, *The Story of Texas Schools* (Austin, TX: The Steck Co., 1955), 310–13.

7. Whisenhunt, *The Encyclopedia of Texas Colleges and Universities*, 79.

8. Ibid., 93.

9. Whisenhunt, *The Encyclopedia of Texas Colleges and Universities*, 43; Nancy Beck Young, "EAST TEXAS BAPTIST UNIVERSITY," *Handbook of Texas Online* (http://www.tshaonline.org/ handbook/online/articles/kbe01), accessed January 16, 2016. Uploaded on June 12, 2010. Published by the Texas State Historical Association.

10. Hugh E. Cosby and John R. Hutto, *History of Hardin-Simmons University* (Abilene, TX: Hugh E. Cosby Co., 1954), 4–14.

11. Whisenhunt, *The Encyclopedia of Texas Colleges and Universities*, 62.

12. Ibid., 64.

13. Evans, *The Story of Texas Schools*, 216–217.

14. Whisenhunt, *The Encyclopedia of Texas Colleges and Universities*, 63.

15. Ibid., 66.

16. Ibid., 67.

17. Clifford H. Taylor, "Jarvis Christian College: Its History and Present Standing" (research paper submitted to the Faculty of the Brite College of the Bible of Texas Christian University in lieu of a thesis for the Degree of Bachelor of Divinity, 1948), 7–10.

18. Evans, *The Story of Texas Schools*, 279.

19. Whisenhunt, *The Encyclopedia of Texas Colleges and Universities*, 75–76.

20. Ibid., 78–79.

21. Ibid., 30.

22. Ibid., 57.

23. Ibid., 92.

24. Evans, *The Story of Texas Schools*, 359.

25. Heintze, *Private Black Colleges in Texas 1865–1954*, 21–23.

26. Evans, *The Story of Texas Schools*, 304.

27. Whisenhunt, *The Encyclopedia of Texas Colleges and Universities*, 105; John B. Boles, "RICE UNIVERSITY," *Handbook of Texas Online* (http://www.tshaonline.org/handbook/online/articles/kbr05), accessed January 23, 2016. Uploaded on June 15, 2010. Published by the Texas State Historical Association.

28. Evans, *The Story of Texas Schools*, 290.

29. Whisenhunt, *The Encyclopedia of Texas Colleges and Universities*, 120.

30. Ibid., 99.

31. Ibid., 69.

32. Ibid., 130.

33. Ibid., 18.

34. Ibid., 132.

35. Ibid., 135–36.

36. Evans, *The Story of Texas Schools*, 360.

37. Evans, *The Story of Texas Schools*, 358.

38. Whisenhunt, *The Encyclopedia of Texas Colleges and Universities*, 136–38.

39. Earl H. Elam, "SUL ROSS STATE UNIVERSITY," *Handbook of Texas Online*, (http://tshaonline.org/handbook/online/articles/kcs21), accessed on October 1, 2014, Published by the Texas State Historical Association.

40. Whisenhunt, *The Encyclopedia of Texas Colleges and Universities*, 138.

41. Ibid., 2.

42. Ibid., 37.

43. Nancy Beck Young, "TEXAS A&M UNIVERSITY-COMMERCE," *Handbook of Texas Online*, (http://tshaonline.org/handbook/online/articles/kct50), accessed October 1, 2014, Published by the Texas State Historical Association.

44. Whisenhunt, *The Encyclopedia of Texas Colleges and Universities*, 34.

45. Jimmie R. Picquet, "TEXAS A&M UNIVERSITY-KINGSVILLE," *Handbook of Texas Online*, (http://tshaonline.org/handbook/online/articles/kct10), accessed on October 1, 2014, Published by the Texas State Historical Association.

46. Whisenhunt, *The Encyclopedia of Texas Colleges and Universities*, 182.

47. Ibid., 145.

48. Evans, *The Story of Texas Schools*, 348–51.

49. Whisenhunt, *The Encyclopedia of Texas Colleges and Universities*, 152–53.

50. Evans, *The Story of Texas Schools*, 292.

51. Evans, *The Story of Texas Schools*, 275–76. Lawrence L. Graves, "TEXAS TECH UNIVERSITY," *Handbook of Texas Online* (http://tshaonline.org/handbook/online/articles/kct32), accessed February 02, 2016. Uploaded on June 15, 2010. Published by the Texas State Historical Association.

52. Minor, David, "TEXAS WESLEYAN UNIVERSITY," (http:www.tshaonline.org/hkandbook/online/articles/kbt24) accessed September 10, 2017, Published by the Texas State Historical Association.

53. Whisenhunt, *The Encyclopedia of Texas Colleges and Universities*, 156.

54. Ibid., 189.

55. Ibid., 6.

56. Sister Lois Bannon, O.S.U., "UNIVERSITY OF DALLAS," *Handbook of Texas Online*, (http://tshaonline.org/handbook/online/articles/kbu02), accessed October 1, 2014. Uploaded on June 15, 2010. Published by the Texas State Historical Association.

57. Evans, *The Story of Texas Schools*, 300–301.

58. Whisenhunt, *The Encyclopedia of Texas Colleges and Universities*, 164–66.

59. Ibid., 163.

60. Ibid., 165–67.

61. Ibid., 167–68.

62. Nancy Beck Young, "UNIVERSITY OF THE INCARNATE WORD," *Handbook of Texas Online*, (http:// tshaonline.org/handbook/online/articles/kbu07), accessed October 1, 2014, Published by the Texas State Historical Association.

63. Whisenhunt, *The Encyclopedia of Texas Colleges and Universities*, 171.

64. Ibid., 170–72.

65. Ibid., 172.

66. Alicia A. Garza, "UNIVERSITY OF TEXAS AT BROWNSVILLE," *Handbook of Texas Online*, (http://tshaonline.org/handbook/online/articles/kcusu), accessed October 1, 2014, Published by the Texas State Historical Association.

67. Whisenhunt, *The Encyclopedia of Texas Colleges and Universities*, 172–73.

68. Rex Field, "UNIVERSITY OF TEXAS-PAN AMERICAN," *Handbook of Texas Online*, (http://tshaonline.org/handbook/online/articles/kcunf), accessed October 1, 2014, Published by the Texas State Historical Association.

69. Whisenhunt, *The Encyclopedia of Texas Colleges and Universities*, 179.

70. Ibid., 174.

71. Ibid., 174.

72. Evans, *The Story of Texas Schools*, 360–61.

73. Whisenhunt, *The Encyclopedia of Texas Colleges and Universities*, 184–85.

74. Ibid., 188.

75. Heintze, *Private Black Colleges in Texas 1865–1954*, 23–26.

76. Evans, *The Story of Texas Schools*, 349.

77. Evans, *The Story of Texas Schools*, 353.

78. Whisenhunt, *The Encyclopedia of Texas Colleges and Universities*, 3.

79. Ibid., 102.

80. Ibid., 405.

81. Ibid., 5.

82. Ibid., 6.

83. Ibid., 116.

84. Ibid., 8–9.

85. Ibid., 11.

86. Ibid., 11.

87. Ibid., 192.

88. Ibid., 12.

89. Ibid., 12–13.

90. Ibid., 335.

91. Ibid., 17.

92. Ibid., 19.

93. Ibid., 22.

94. Ibid., 21.

95. Ibid., 56.

96. Ibid., 144.

97. Ibid., 22.

98. Ibid., 23.

99. Ibid., 23.

100. Evans, *The Story of Texas Schools*, 332–38.

101. Michael R. Heintze, *Private Black Colleges in Texas 1865–1954* (College Station: Texas A&M University Press, 1985), 30.

102. Whisenhunt, *The Encyclopedia of Texas Colleges and Universities*, 46.

103. Ibid., 24.

104. Ibid., 121.

105. Ibid., 25.

106. Ibid., 26.

107. Ibid., 26.

108. Ibid., 50.

109. Ibid., 53.

110. Ibid., 121.

111. Ibid., 130.

112. Ibid., 149.

113. Ibid., 34.

114. Aurelio M. Montemayor, "COLEGIO JACINTO TREVINO," *Handbook of Texas Online*, (http://tshaonline.org/handbook/online/articles/kbc51) accessed September 30, 2014, Published by the Texas State Historical Association.

115. Whisenhunt, *The Encyclopedia of Texas Colleges and Universities*, 35.

116. Ibid., 35.

117. Whisenhunt, *The Encyclopedia of Texas Colleges and Universities*, 84; Evans, *The Story of Texas Schools*, 322.

118. Whisenhunt, *The Encyclopedia of Texas Colleges and Universities*, 337.

119. Evans, *The Story of Texas Schools*, 338.

120. Evans, *The Story of Texas Schools*, 364.

121. Whisenhunt, *The Encyclopedia of Texas Colleges and Universities*, 38–42.

122. Ibid., 110.

123. Ibid., 44.

124. Ibid., 44.

125. Ibid., 163.

126. Ibid., 59.

127. Ibid., 48.

128. Ibid., 48.

129. Ibid., 49.

130. Ibid., 155.

131. Ibid., 53.

132. Ibid., 54.

133. Ibid., 54.

134. Ibid., 54.

135. Ibid., 186.

136. Ibid., 55.

137. Heintze, *Private Black Colleges in Texas 1865–1954*, 31.

138. Whisenhunt, *The Encyclopedia of Texas Colleges and Universities*, 125.

139. William E. Montgomery, "HEARNE ACADEMY," *Handbook of Texas Online*, (http://tshaonline.org/handbook/online/articles/kbh16) accessed September 30, 2014. Published by the Texas State Historical Association.

140. Whisenhunt, *The Encyclopedia of Texas Colleges and Universities*, 59.

141. Whisenhunt, *The Encyclopedia of Texas Colleges and Universities*, 39.

142. Evans, *The Story of Texas Schools*, 367.

143. Whisenhunt, *The Encyclopedia of Texas Colleges and Universities*, 33.

144. Whisenhunt, *The Encyclopedia of Texas Colleges and Universities*, 152.

145. Teresa Palomo Acosta, "HOUSTON INTERNATIONAL UNIVERSITY." *Handbook of Texas Online*, (http://tshaonline.org/handbook/online/articleskch18) accessed September 30, 2014.

146. Maria-Cristina Garcia, "JUAREZ-LINCOLN UNIVERSITY," *Handbook of Texas Online*, (http://tshaonline.org/handbook/online/articles/kcj03), accessed September 30, 2014. Published by the Texas State Historical Association.

147. Evans, *The Story of Texas Schools*, 339.

148. Whisenhunt, *The Encyclopedia of Texas Colleges and Universities*, 74–75.

149. Ibid., 76.

150. Ibid., 76–77.

151. Ralph H. Walker, "MANSFIELD MALE AND FEMALE COLLEGE," *Handbook of Texas Online*, (http://tshaonline.org/handbook/online/articles/kbm39), accessed October 1, 2014. Published by the Texas State Historical Association.

152. Whisenhunt, *The Encyclopedia of Texas Colleges and Universities*, 80–81.

153. Ibid., 81.

154. Ibid., 69.

155. Ibid., 82–83.

156. H. Allen Anderson, "MERIDIAN JUNIOR COLLEGE," *Handbook of Texas Online*, accessed May 4, 2017, tshanonline.org/handbook/online/articles/kbm20.

157. Mary M. Standifer, "WACO FEMALE COLLEGE," *Handbook of Texas Online*, (http://tshaonline.org/handbook/online/articles/kbw02), accessed on October 1, 2014, Published by the Texas State Historical Association.

158. Evans, *The Story of Texas Schools*, 161.

159. Donald W. Whisenhunt, "MINERAL WELLS COLLEGE," *Handbook of Texas Online*, (http://tshaonline.org/handbook/online/articles/kbm28), accessed October 1, 2014. Published by the Texas State Historical Association.

160. Whisenhunt, *The Encyclopedia of Texas Colleges and Universities*, 88.

161. Evans, *The Story of Texas Schools*, 323–24.

162. Whisenhunt, *The Encyclopedia of Texas Colleges and Universities*, 69.

163. Evans, *The Story of Texas Schools*, 368.

164. Sherrie S. McLeRoy, "NORTH TEXAS BAPTIST COLLEGE AND SEMINARY," *Handbook of Texas Online*, (http://tshaonline.org/handbook/online/articles/ibnla), accessed October 1, 2014), Published by the Texas State Historical Association.

165. Evans, *The Story of Texas Schools*, 362.

166. Whisenhunt, *The Encyclopedia of Texas Colleges and Universities*, 96.

167. Ibid., 59.

168. Ibid., 99.

169. Ibid., 149.

170. Evans, *The Story of Texas Schools*, 324.

171. Evans, *The Story of Texas Schools*, 353.

172. Whisenhunt, *The Encyclopedia of Texas Colleges and Universities*, 20.

173. Evans, *The Story of Texas Schools*, 324.

174. Evans, *The Story of Texas Schools*, 329; Judson S. Custer, "RUTERSVILLE COLLEGE," *Handbook of Texas Online* (http://www.tshaonline.org/handbook/online/articles/kbr17), accessed January 23, 2016. Uploaded on June 15, 2010. Published by the Texas State Historical Association.

175. Evans, *The Story of Texas Schools*, 356.

176. Whisenhunt, *The Encyclopedia of Texas Colleges and Universities*, 109.

177. Whisenhunt, *The Encyclopedia of Texas Colleges and Universities*, 110.

178. Whisenhunt, *The Encyclopedia of Texas Colleges and Universities*, 109.

179. Heintze, *Private Black Colleges in Texas 1865–1954*, 38; Whisenhunt, *The Encyclopedia of Texas Colleges and Universities*, 6.

180. Whisenhunt, *The Encyclopedia of Texas Colleges and Universities*, 118–19.

181. Ibid., 120.

182. Ibid., 120.

183. Ibid., 172.

184. Ibid., 25–30.

185. Ibid., 121.

186. Ibid., 38.

187. Ibid., 26.

188. Ibid., 124.

189. Ibid., 125.

190. Ibid., 32.

191. Ibid., 32.

192. Ibid., 83.

193. R. E. Lamb, C.S.B., "ST BASIL'S COLLEGE," *Handbook of Texas Online*, (http://tshaonline.org/handbook/online/articles/kbs65), accessed on October 1, 2014, Published by the Texas State Historical Association.

194. Evans, *The Story of Texas Schools*, 363.

195. Evans, *The Story of Texas Schools*, 354.

196. Evans, *The Story of Texas Schools*, 358.

197. Heintze, *Private Black Colleges in Texas 1865–1954*, 36.

198. Whisenhunt, *The Encyclopedia of Texas Colleges and Universities*, 144.

199. Heintze, *Private Black Colleges in Texas 1865–1954*, 34.

200. Evans, *The Story of Texas Schools*, 368.

201. Evans, *The Story of Texas Schools*, 365–66.

202. Evans, *The Story of Texas Schools*, 345.

203. Whisenhunt, *The Encyclopedia of Texas Colleges and Universities*, 152.

204. Evans, *The Story of Texas Schools*, 368–69.

205. Whisenhunt, *The Encyclopedia of Texas Colleges and Universities*, 157.

206. Whisenhunt, *The Encyclopedia of Texas Colleges and Universities*, 162.

207. Sister Lois Bannon, O.S.U., "UNIVERSITY OF DALLAS," *Handbook of Texas Online*, (http://tshaonline.org/handbook/online/articles/kbu02), accessed October 1, 2014. Uploaded on June 15, 2010. Published by the Texas State Historical Association.

208. Whisenhunt, *The Encyclopedia of Texas Colleges and Universities*, 187.

209. Whisenhunt, *The Encyclopedia of Texas Colleges and Universities*, 168.

210. Evans, *The Story of Texas Schools*, 346.

211. Whisenhunt, *The Encyclopedia of Texas Colleges and Universities*, 190.

212. Ibid., 184.

213. Whisenhunt, *The Encyclopedia of Texas Colleges and Universities*, 184. Mary M. Standifer, "WACO FEMALE COLLEGE," *Handbook of Texas Online* (tshaonline.org.handbook/online.articles/kbw02), accessed February 02, 2016. Uploaded on June 15, 2010, Published by the Texas State Historical Association.

214. John Robert Guemple, "A History of Waco University" (master's thesis, Baylor University, Waco, Texas, 1964), 4.

215. Whisenhunt, *The Encyclopedia of Texas Colleges and Universities*, 185–86.

216. Ibid., 186.

217. Ibid., 187.

218. Ibid., 189.

219. Ibid., 192.

BIBLIOGRAPHY

Acosta, Teresa Palomo. "HOUSTON INTERNATIONAL UNIVERSITY." *Handbook of Texas Online*, (http://tshaonline.org/handbook/online/articleskch18) accessed September 30, 2014. Published by the Texas State Historical Association.

Anderson, H. Allen. "Meridian Junior College," *Handbook of Texas Online*,tshaonline.org/handbook/online/articles/kbm20.

Bannon, Sister Lois, O.S.U., "UNIVERSITY OF DALLAS," *Handbook of Texas Online*, (http://tshaonline.org/handbook/online/articles/kbu02), accessed October 1, 2014. Uploaded on June 15, 2010. Published by the Texas State Historical Association.

Berry, Margaret Catherine. *UT History 101: Highlights in the History of the University of Texas at Austin.* Austin, TX: Eakin Press, 1997.

Block, Viola. *History of Johnson County and Surrounding Counties.* Waco, TX: Texian Press, 1970.

Boles, John B. "RICE UNIVERSITY," *Handbook of Texas Online* (http://www.tshaonline.org/handbook/online/articles/kbr05), accessed January 23, 2016. Uploaded on June 15, 2010. Published by the Texas State Historical Association.

Castaneda, Carlos E. *The Church in Texas Since Independence.* Austin, TX: Von Boeckmann-Jones Co., 1958.

Cosby, Hugh E., and John R. Hutto. *History of Hardin-Simmons University.* Abilene, TX: Hugh E. Cosby Co., 1954.

Cross, Linda Brown, and Robert W. Glover. *History of Tyler Junior College, 1926–1986.* Tyler, TX: Tyler Junior College, 1985.

Custer, Judson S., "RUTERSVILLE COLLEGE," *Handbook of Texas Online* (http://www.tshaonline.org/handbook/online/articles/kbr17), accessed January 23, 2016. Uploaded on June 15, 2010. Published by the Texas State Historical Association.

Dolph Briscoe Center for American History, Vertical Files, University of Texas at Austin.

Downs, Fane, Nita Keene, Paul D. Lack, Gary W. Shanafelt, Robert W. Sledge, Joe W. Specht, Martha Sibley Spence, Vernon Gladden, Sharon Strawn, and Donald W. Whisenhunt. *Pride of our Western Prairies: McMurry College, 1913–1988.* Abilene, TX: McMurry College, 1989.

Dietrich, W. O. *The Blazing Story of Washington County.* Brenham, TX: Banner Press, 1950.

Eckstein, Stephen Daniel. *History of the Churches of Christ in Texas 1824–1950.* Austin, TX: Firm Foundation, 1963.

Eby, Frederick. *The Development of Education in Texas.* New York: Macmillan Co., 1915.

Elam, Earl H., "SUL ROSS STATE UNIVERSITY, "Handbook *of Texas Online,* (http://tshaonline.org/handbook/online/articles/kcs21), accessed on October 1, 2014, Published by the Texas State Historical Association.

Evans, C. E. "Establishment and Appropriations 1943 Southwest Texas State Teachers College," San Marcos, TX, 1943.

———. *The Story of Texas Schools.* Austin, TX: Steck Co., 1955.

Field, Rex, "UNIVERSITY OF TEXAS-PAN AMERICAN," *Handbook of Texas Online,* (http://tshaonline.org/handbook/online/articles/kcunf), accessed October 1, 2014, published by the Texas State Historical Association.

Garza, Alicia A. "UNIVERSITY OF TEXAS AT BROWNSVILLE," *Handbook of Texas Online,* (http://tshaonline.org/handbook/online/articles/kcusu), accessed October 1, 2014, published by the Texas State Historical Association.

Garcia, Maria-Cristina, "JUAREZ-LINCOLN UNIVERSITY," *Handbook of Texas Online,* (http://tshaonline.org/handbook/online/articles/kcj03), accessed September 30, 2014. Published by the Texas State Historical Association.

Graves, Lawrence L. "TEXAS TECH UNIVERSITY," *Handbook of Texas Online* (tshaonline.org/handbook/online/articles/kct32), accessed February 02, 2016. Uploaded on June 15, 2010. Published by the Texas State Historical Association.

Guemple, John Robert. "A History of Waco University," master's thesis, Baylor University, Waco, Texas, 1964.

Hall, Colby D. *Texas Disciples.* Fort Worth: Texas Christian University Press, 1953.

Hart, Brian, "ARLINGTON BAPTIST COLLEGE, "Handbook *of Texas Online,* (http://tshaonline.org/handbook/online/articles/kbach), accessed September 30, 2014, published by the Texas State Historical Association.

Heintze, Michael R. *Private Black Colleges in Texas 1865–1954.* College Station: Texas A&M University Press, 1985.

Hoopes, Roy. *State Universities and Colleges.* Washington, DC: Luce Publishing, n.d.

Independent Colleges and Universities of Texas (ICUT). Member Institutions. http://icut.org/pages/institutions/list-of-institutions

James, Eleanor. *The First 100 Years in Belton, University of Mary Hardin-Baylor.* Belton, TX: University of Mary Hardin-Baylor Press, 1986.

Kelly, Dayton, ed. *The Handbook of Waco and McLennan County, Texas.* Waco, TX: Texian Press, 1972.

Lamb, R.E., C.S.B., "ST BASIL'S COLLEGE," *Handbook of Texas Online,* (http://tshaonline.org/handbook/online/articles/kbs65), accessed on October 1, 2014, Published by the Texas State Historical Association.

McLeRoy, Sherrie S., "NORTH TEXAS BAPTIST COLLEGE AND SEMINARY," *Handbook of Texas Online,* (http://tshaonline.org/handbook/online/articles/ibnla), accessed October 1, 2014), Published by the Texas State Historical Association.

Meiners, Frederika. *A History of Rice University 1907–1963.* Houston, TX: Rice University Studies, 1982.

Montemayor, Aurelio M. "COLEGIO JACINTO TREVINO," *Handbook of Texas Online,* (http://tshaonline.org/handbook/online/articles/kbc51) accessed September 30, 2014, Published by the Texas State Historical Association.

Montgomery, William E., "HEARNE ACADEMY," *Handbook of Texas Online,* (http://tshaonline.org/handbook/online/articles/kbh16) accessed September 30, 2014. Published by the Texas State Historical Association.

Murr, Erika, "TEXAS A&M INTERNATIONAL UNIVERSITY," *Handbook of Texas Online,* (http://tshaonline.org/handbook/online/articles/kctnj), accessed on September 30, 2014, Published by the Texas State Historical Association.

Nicholson, Patrick J. *University of Houston.* Printed in the United States of America: NP, 1977.

Picquet, Jimmie R., "TEXAS A&M UNIVERSITY-KINGSVILLE," *Handbook of Texas Online,* (http://tshaonline.org/handbook/online/articles/kct10), accessed on October 1, 2014, Published by the Texas State Historical Association.

St. Basil's College. *Catalogue.* St. Basil's College, Waco, TX, 1912–1913.

Singg, Sangeeta, "ANGELO STATE UNIVERSITY," *Handbook of Texas Online* (http://tshaonline.org/handbook/online/articles/kca07) published by the Texas State Historical Association.

Standifer, Mary M., "WACO FEMALE COLLEGE," *Handbook of Texas Online,* (http://tshaonline.org/handbook/online/articles/kbw02), accessed on October 1, 2014, Published by the Texas State Historical Association.

Taylor, Clifford H. "Jarvis Christian College: Its History and Present Standing." Research Paper submitted to the Faculty of the Brite College of the Bible of Texas Christian University in lieu of a thesis for the Degree of Bachelor of Divinity, 1948.

"TILLOTSON COLLEGE," *Handbook of Texas Online* (http://tshaonline.org/handbook/online/articles/kbt27), accessed February 02, 2016. Uploaded on June 15, 2010. Modified on June 5, 2013. Published by the Texas State Historical Association.

Wilson, Carl Bassett. "History of Baptist Educational Efforts in Texas 1829–1900." PhD diss., University of Texas, 1934.

Walker, Ralph H., "MANSFIELD MALE AND FEMALE COLLEGE," *Handbook of Texas Online,* (http://tshaonline.org/handbook/online/articles/kbm39), accessed October 1, 2014. Published by the Texas State Historical Association.

Whisenhunt, Donald W. *The Encyclopedia of Texas Colleges and Universities.* Austin, TX: Eakin Press, 1986.

———. "MINERAL WELLS COLLEGE," *Handbook of Texas Online,* (http://tshaonline.org/handbook/online/articles/kbm28), accessed October 1, 2014, published by the Texas Historical Association.

Williams, Michael E. *To God Be the Glory: The Centennial History of Dallas Baptist University 1898–1998.* Arlington, TX: Summit Publishing Group.

Young, Nancy Beck, "EAST TEXAS BAPTIST UNIVERSITY," *Handbook of Texas Online* (http://www.tshaonline.org/handbook/online/articles/kbe01), accessed January 16, 2016. Uploaded on June 12, 2010. Published by the State Texas State Historical Association.

———. "TEXAS A&M UNIVERSITY-COMMERCE," *Handbook of Texas Online,* (http://tshaonline.org/handbook/online/articles/kct50), accessed October 1, 2014, Published by the Texas State Historical Association.

———. "TEXAS A&M UNIVERSITY-TEXARKANA," *Handbook of Texas Online,* (http://tshaonline.org/handbook/online/articles/kct51), accessed October 1, 2014, Published by the Texas State Historical Association.

———. "UNIVERSITY OF THE INCARNATE WORD," *Handbook of Texas Online,* (http://tshaonline.org/handbook/online/articles/kbu07), accessed October 1, 2014, published by the Texas State Historical Association.

CONCLUSION

Our review of the history of higher education in Texas has been about complex historical events and the importance of the context of those events.

It is difficult to truly understand Texas without looking at its vast land holdings and the diverse people and policies that have governed them. While a large amount of land was given away to encourage settlement, some of this land was used to fund public institutions devoted to higher education. These land policies began with Spain in the seventeenth century and continued after Mexican independence in 1821.

After the Texas Revolution, the Republic of Texas, a government short of cash but rich in an almost unimaginable amount of unoccupied land, began an aggressive effort to attract settlers, in large part from residents of the southern United States. These efforts were successful in luring thousands of new families to Texas and these policies continued when Texas was admitted into the Union in 1845.

Early leaders of the state led by Mirabeau B. Lamar began to look at the availability of land as a cheap way to provide for public education. In his speech to the Congress of the Republic in 1838 he proposed that two colleges of "the first class" to be funded by a large gift of public land. The Congress agreed and its support led to the development of the Permanent University Fund, which continues to play a major role in higher education in Texas.

Because the government of Texas was slow in actually opening public colleges, religious communities provided the first colleges. The Methodists were the first to establish a college, denominational or otherwise, with Rutersville College in La Grange in 1837. It was quickly followed by the work of other religious leaders and their congregations to establish many institutions. Denominational communities provided important leadership for higher education and produced some of Texas's first college graduates.

By 1876, with assistance from the federal government and the newly passed Morrill Act, Texas opened Texas A&M College—the first public college in Texas. This was followed by the legislature's creation of Sam Houston Normal Institute in 1879. It was organized to begin training the teachers so badly needed by the public schools. The long delayed opening of the University of Texas occurred in 1883.

The control and distribution of income from the Permanent University Fund (PUF) consumed much of the early efforts of the Texas Legislature in its first fifty years. While discussions about the distribution of funds were taking place, oil was discovered at the now-famous Santa Rita oil well on university lands. It was then that the value of the farsighted vision of the Texas Legislature in passing mineral rights laws and continuing the policy of donating land to the PUF became evident to the entire country. The wealth generated by these lands has added many billions of dollars for the benefit of the universities that share in the income.

Texas, like most places, struggled with the effort to provide equal access to higher educational opportunities to women. The movement started slowly but the educational success of early women students proved they had equal talent and abilities. Many of the earliest efforts to educate women occurred in the religious colleges and those successes encouraged public colleges to open their doors to women as well.

Abraham Lincoln's *Emancipation Proclamation* opened new doors for African Americans in Texas, who quickly demonstrated a passion for learning though the educational opportunities provided in local churches. Ultimately the state legislature established Prairie View College, as the first public college in Texas dedicated to the education of black citizens. The true integration of African Americans into all higher education venues took many years of hard work and legal action.

The last of the minority groups in Texas to gain full access to higher education was the Hispanic community. Because the Constitution of 1876 considered Hispanics to be "white" it was actually more difficult in the early years for them to achieve their rightful legal status and access to many things, including higher education institutions. When that finally occurred, Hispanics responded by enrolling in the colleges and universities of the state in ever increasing numbers.

The role of the junior/community colleges in the state provided what was a missing piece of the puzzle for potential students of all ages, genders, and ethnic backgrounds. These institutions have provided opportunities for students to grow and learn while remaining in their local communities. The wide range of courses taught in these colleges has helped students up and down the societal and economic ladder. They facilitate entry into four-year schools, acquisition of vocational skills, and lifelong learning opportunities.

As public higher education institutions grew and matured, so did the organizational structures that oversaw their management and success. Much of this leadership was provided by Governor John Connally who saw the need for new state oversight of public higher education and pushed for legislation that resulted in what is known today as the Texas Higher Education Coordinating Board. Working with the legislature, this organization has continued to provide oversight and inspiration for higher education.

THOUGHTS ON ADDITIONAL RESEARCH

The writing of this book began with the point that it is really impossible to write the complete history of higher education in Texas. Each college or university in most cases has had someone write at least one book on the history of that particular school. The effort behind this book was to pick subjects that the author felt had a broad appeal to anyone who was interested in understanding the history of higher education in Texas. This method of research clearly has left out other areas of the research; some examples are below.

It would be of interest to understand what impact the race into space that began with President Kennedy had upon the increased enrollment in the STEM programs in our colleges.

Further research is needed to understand some of the drivers that caused increased enrollment of minority students in the colleges. For example, what role did college sports play in college admission policies?

The Civil Rights Movement had an impact on enrollment of minorities in Texas colleges but there is more that we need to understand. How were policies put into place to make the transition easier for communities of color to participate? Enrollment, student services, increased openings in college campus participation, and scholarship opportunities are just a few of the areas where it would be helpful to have a clear understanding of the impact of not only the Civil Rights Act of 1965 but the entire civil rights movement.

The treatment of minorities is an area that is ripe for research. For example, when working on gathering information on the treatment of Hispanics I had many people tell me that in their communities there was an ease of assimilation that clearly did not exist in other parts of Texas. How and why this occurred would be valuable information.

Lastly, the Texas Legislature has played and continues to play a major role in the success of public higher education. A major research effort should take place to understand how each session of the legislature, beginning in 1845, had an impact on higher education. The research in this book will provide some insight but the full story can only be understood if each legislative session is examined individually.

PHOTO GALLERY

Historical Photographs

The following photographs are of historical buildings at higher education institutions in Texas. Most of these building no longer exist; many
were lost to fire. Some of the institutions are no longer in operation.
These pictures are included to provide the reader with a feeling of the
architecture and construction of these building. At the time they were
built they must have been a source of great pride in these institutions
and provided hope for the possibilities of the future.

1. University of Texas, Austin

Main Building, University of Texas at Austin. In a special election held September 6, 1881, that was called to locate the University, the contest was between Tyler and Austin, the city of Austin won and in 1883 the University was opened and this building was built. (Texas Collection, Baylor University, Waco, Texas.)

2. Salado College

The above picture, dated about 1875, is believed to be one of the oldest existing photographs of old Salado College. The picture is from the collection of Dr. Chas. W. Ramsdell, professor of Southern History, University of Texas. The college was opened in 1860 with 20 students. By 1865 enrollment had increased to 307. In 1885 the property and grounds were turned over to trustees of the local public school and operated as a free school until 1890. Between 1890 and 1913 it was known as the Thomas Arnold High School. Remains of the old building may still be seen on a hill overlooking the village of Salado, where many former citizens and students will meet Saturday for their annual reunion.

Belton Journal—July 18, 1957

The college was opened on February 20, 1860; it had sixty students its first year. After the town was unable to secure a railroad to run through the town the town began to decline and the college closed. This picture was published in the *Belton Journal* in 1957, long after the college was gone. (Texas Collection, Baylor University, Waco, Texas.)

3. Southwest Texas Normal, San Marcos, TX

SAN MARCOS,
TEXAS.

this is where
I go to school
I often get
home sick
to see you.
You was
always so
kind to me.
I will never
for get you
be sure

and write my address is Box 376

SOUTHWEST TEXAS NORMAL.

Southwest Texas State Normal College, now Texas State University, established 1899 in San Marcos. This was the first permanent building built and is still in use. The school was built on a plot of land that contained about eleven acres and was known as Chautauqua Hill. The legislature on March 28, 1901, appropriated $35,000 to build this building; because the amount was insufficient, later in the year the legislature appropriated an additional $20,000. It was the desire of the State Board of Education that the building be a duplicate of the building built at Sam Houston Normal Institute. (Texas Collection, Baylor University, Waco, Texas.)

4. St. Basil's College

St. Basil's College in Waco was founded by the Basilian Fathers who came from France at the invitation of the Bishop of Galveston in 1899. The main purpose of the school was college preparation, to which was added business courses, Romance languages, and music. It had a large library for the time of 3,000 volumes. By 1915 the college closed. (Texas Collection, Baylor University, Waco, Texas.)

Women's dormitory at Baylor University at Independence. Later the women's department split off from Baylor and moved to Belton and became Mary Hardin Baylor College. This picture was probably taken in the late 1840s or early 1850s. (Texas Collection, Baylor University, Waco, Texas.)

6. Texas Christian University

This picture was of the campus of Texas Christian University prior to 1910 when it was located in Waco. In 1910 a fire destroyed the main building. The city of Ft. Worth aggressively courted the college to move to their city and it was relocated to its present location. (Texas Collection, Baylor University, Waco, Texas.)

7. Trinity University

In 1866, the Brazos, Colorado, and Texas Synods of the Presbyterian Church started to accept bids for a location for a centrally located Presbyterian institution. The town of Tehuacana offered to donate 130 acres in the Tehuacana Hills and 1500 acres in the prairie below the hills for the institution. Trinity University remained in Tehuacana from 1869 to 1902. This picture is of the original building. (Texas Collection, Baylor University, Waco, Texas.)

8. Waco University

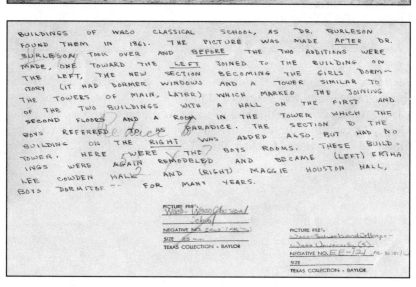

BUILDINGS OF WACO CLASSICAL SCHOOL, AS DR. BURLESON FOUND THEM IN 1861. THE PICTURE WAS MADE AFTER DR. BURLESON TOOK OVER AND BEFORE THE TWO ADDITIONS WERE MADE, ONE TOWARD THE LEFT JOINED TO THE BUILDING ON THE LEFT, THE NEW SECTION BECOMING THE GIRLS DORM-ITORY (IT HAD DORMER WINDOWS AND A TOWER SIMILAR TO THE TOWERS OF MAIN, LATER) WHICH MARKED THE JOINING OF THE TWO BUILDINGS WITH A HALL ON THE FIRST AND SECOND FLOORS AND A ROOM IN THE TOWER WHICH THE BOYS REFERRED TO AS PARADICE. THE SECTION TO THE BUILDING ON THE RIGHT WAS ADDED ALSO, BUT HAD NO TOWER. HERE WERE THE BOYS ROOMS. THESE BUILD-INGS WERE AGAIN REMODELED AND BECAME (LEFT) ERTHA LEE COWDEN HALL AND (RIGHT) MAGGIE HOUSTON HALL, BOYS DORMITOR - FOR MANY YEARS.

PICTURE FILE:
Waco - Waco Classical School

NEGATIVE NO. I463 (PR. '96)
SIZE 8.5 mm
TEXAS COLLECTION - BAYLOR

PICTURE FILE:
Waco - Schools and Colleges - Waco University (S)
NEGATIVE NO. EE-124 PR. 86.151/14
SIZE
TEXAS COLLECTION - BAYLOR

Waco University was originally named Trinity River High School, and was founded in 1856 by the Trinity River Baptist Association. The Waco Baptist Association changed the school's name to Waco Classical School in 1860 when they purchased the property. The university was transferred to the Baptist General Association in 1881 and merged with Baylor University in 1886. (Texas Collection, Baylor University, Waco, Texas.)

9. Meridian Junior College

Meridian Junior College in Meridian in Bosque County, originated as Meridian Training School and was incorporated in 1907. In 1920, the college achieved Class A Junior College status and its name was changed to Meridian Junior College. It closed in 1927. (The Bosque County Collection; Bosque County Historical Commission; Meridian, Texas, USA.)

10. Clifton College

This building was the "Boys' Dorm" and was built in 1897 but was called by various names such as Clifton College, Old Main, and lastly Boys' Dorm. For the first eleven years of the college this building was the only building and it provided classrooms, offices, housing facilities, dining facilities, and a large auditorium. It was the first of three buildings. A girl's dorm was built in 1908 and the Administration Building was built in 1923. Only the Administration Building remains. (The Bosque County Collection; Bosque County Historical Commission; Meridian, Texas, USA.)

11. North Texas State Normal College

This is a photograph of the campus of North Texas State Normal College during World War 1. The picture was taken along an unpaved street beside the campus. The college's power plant, with smokestack, is visible in the right foreground. In the right background, behind the power plant, is the college's original library building (later known as the Historical Building, and then Curry Hall). In the left background is the Main Building. (University of North Texas Libraries, The Portal to Texas History, texashisstory.unt.edu.crediting UNT Libraries Special Collections.)

12. Lutheran Concordia College

Photograph showing Kilian Hall and science building at Lutheran Concordia College at a distance, with lawn in the foreground, Inscribed "L.C.C. Austin, Texas 1929–1930." (This photograph was taken by Theodore Schmidt. University of North Texas Libraries, The Portal to Texas History, texashistory.unt.edu; crediting Concordia University Texas.)

13. Abilene Christian College

This photograph is from Abilene Christian College; it is the front of the building with people standing in the doorway and in the windows. Taken March 20, 1905. (University of North Texas Libraries, The Portal to Texas History, texashistory. unt.edu; crediting Abilene Christian University Library.)

14. Panhandle Christian College

Panhandle Cristian College. Hereford Tex. 3-24-06.

Picture taken March 24, 1906, of the Panhandle Christian College Building in Hereford. The three-story brick and frame building includes a pitched roof with gables on the third floor, a portico over the main entrance, and a central tower over the front façade. Two men stand in the tower windows, one leans from a third story window, and one stands on the front step. A windmill is visible at the rear of the building. (University of North Texas Libraries, The Portal to Texas History, texashistory.unt.edu; crediting Panhandle-Plains Historical Museum.)

Administration building at Clarendon College. The three-story brick building is seen from the front. (University of North Texas Libraries, The Portal to Texas History, texashistory.unt.edu; crediting Deaf Smith County Library.)

16. McMurry College

This photograph is of the President Dormitory at McMurry College in Abilene and was taken in 1916. The picture shows a three-story building with a bare lawn. This building is the second oldest building on the campus and is still in use today. (University of North Texas Libraries, The Portal to Texas History, texashistory.unt.edu; crediting McMurry University Library.)

17. Simmons College

Photograph of the College Home, also known as Val Halla or Toly Hall, at Simmons College in Abilene. The two-story building with white wood siding has multiple porches and chimneys. Picture taken about 1907. (University of North Texas Libraries, The Portal to Texas History, texashistory.unt.edu, crediting the Abilene Photograph Collection at Hardin-Simmons University.)

18. Weatherford College

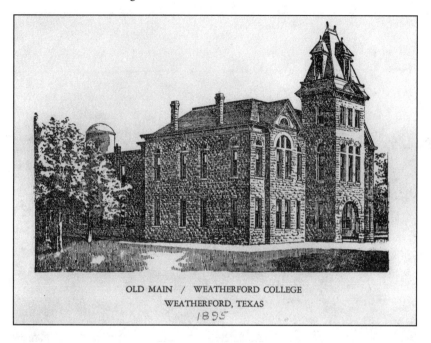

OLD MAIN / WEATHERFORD COLLEGE
WEATHERFORD, TEXAS
1895

Drawing of the Old Main Building at Weatherford College, 1895; Weatherford, Texas. (University of North Texas Libraries, The Portal to Texas History, texas-history.unt.edu; crediting Weatherford College.)

19. West Texas State Teachers College

Photograph of the construction of the education building on the West Texas State Teachers College campus. The structure had reached its full height, and several men are working on the roof. Building materials and construction debris are scattered around the site. Houses and other structures of the town of Canyon are visible in the background. (University of North Texas Libraries, The Portal to Texas History, texashistory.unt.edu; crediting Panhandle-Plains Historical Museum.)

20. Goodnight College

This photograph was taken in 1906 and is of the girl's dormitory. Most of the students are women, and many of them are wearing mortarboards. The dormitory is a four-story wood frame building with dormer windows on the third floor and gables on the fourth. (University of North Texas Libraries, The Portal of Texas History, texashistory.unt.edu; crediting Panhandle Plains Historical Museum.)

INDEX